SQUADRON BADGES OF THE SAAF

The devices illustrated were correct at the time of publication, but all will eventually be redrawn to ensure they are heraldically correct, and some designs – like that of No. 87 Advanced Flying School – are scheduled to be totally changed.

2 Squadron

Upward and onward

3 Squadron

Always fighting

4 Squadron

Death to the enemy

We shall confront all difficulties

7 Squadron

Lords of the skies

8 Squadron

Until death

12 Squadron

First into battle

15 Squadron

The eagle seeks the heights

17 Squadron

As the occasion arises

19 Squadron

Fame from deeds

21 Squadron

Unbeatable

22 Squadron

That the sea may be free

AIRCRAFT
OF THE SOUTH AFRICAN
AIR FORCE

Pictures: Herman Potgieter
Text: Willem Steenkamp
Research: Dave Becker
Additional Research: Louis Vosloo

AIRCRAFT
OF THE SOUTH AFRICAN
AIR FORCE

JANES PUBLISHING COMPANY
London · New York · Sydney

Published in Great Britain in 1981 by
Jane's Publishing Company Ltd,
238 City Road, London ECIV 2PU

ISBN 07106 0117 4

Design & typography by C. Struik Publishers
Dustjacket design by Janice Ashby Design Studio, Cape Town
Photoset by McManus Bros (Pty) Ltd, Cape Town
Lithographic reproduction by Hirt & Carter (Pty) Ltd, Cape Town
Printed and bound by Tien Wah Press (Pte) Ltd, Singapore

Gathering of Eagles, by James Ambrose Brown, quoted on p. 18 with kind
permission of Purnell & Sons (SA) (Pty) Ltd, Johannesburg

First published in 1980 by C. Struik (Pty) Ltd, Struik House, Oswald Pirow Street,
Foreshore, Cape Town

CONTENTS

ACKNOWLEDGEMENTS 8

FOREWORD 9

NOTES ON AERIAL PHOTOGRAPHY 13

HISTORY OF THE SAAF 16

THE DASSAULT MIRAGE F1 Knock-out punch of the SAAF 36

THE DASSAULT MIRAGE III Fighter of many faces 44

THE HAWKER-SIDDELEY BUCCANEER The warbird that nearly wasn't 52

THE CANADAIR CL-I3B SABRE 6 Beautiful Canadian 58

THE ENGLISH ELECTRIC CANBERRA Friday 13's child 64

THE MB-326 IMPALA Gazelle in camouflage 70

THE DOUGLAS DAKOTA Methuselah with wings 80

THE DOUGLAS DC-4 SKYMASTER Old fiddle, new tune 86

THE LOCKHEED C-13OB HERCULES Aircraft for all seasons 90

THE C-160Z TRANSALL South Africa's pocket Hercules 96

THE AVRO SHACKLETON MR. 3 St Bernard of the sky 102

THE PIAGGIO P-166S ALBATROSS Unseen but not unheard 108

THE WESTLAND WASP Below them the waves 112

THE AEROSPATIALE ALOUETTE III From shipwrecks to drugs 118

THE AEROSPATIALE PUMA Samaritan with teeth 124

THE SUD AVIATION SA-321L SUPER FRELON Landbound flying-boat 132

THE NORTH AMERICAN HARVARD Schoolmaster of the sky 138

THE AM-3CM BOSBOK and THE ATLAS C-4M KUDU Children of a Mexican dream 144

THE CESSNA 185 Odd-job man of the SAAF 150

NO. 21 SQUADRON Quart in a pint pot 152

THE DE HAVILLAND VAMPIRE S.A.'s jet pioneer 156

A SPITFIRE CALLED EVELYN 158

THE FIESELER STORCH Rommel's runabout 164

THE SAAF MUSEUM 165

FURTHER SQUADRON HISTORIES AND UNIT NOTES 166

AIRCRAFT SPECIFICATIONS AND IDENTIFICATION 168

INDEX 179

ACKNOWLEDGEMENTS

My grateful thanks and appreciation to the following SAAF personnel who have assisted me in making this book possible:

Lt.-Gen. Bob Rogers, Chief of the Air Force (CAF) (retired)
Lt.-Gen. Mike Muller (present CAF)

Col. Robert Blake	Maj. Derek Kirkland
Col. Mickey Brand	Maj. Alan Lurie
Col. 'Cassie' Carstens	Maj. Neil Malan
Col. Dan Zeeman	Maj. Johan Nieuwoudt
Cmdt. Jack Grundlingh	Maj. 'Pez' Parsonson
Cmdt. Gert Havenga	Maj. Graham Rochat
Cmdt. Willem Hechter	Maj. George Snyman
Cmdt. Dick Lord	Maj. Gert Theron
Cmdt. Jan Marais	Maj. Steyn Venter
Cmdt. Bob Masson	Maj. Denzil White
Cmdt. 'Kallie' Minnaar	Maj. 'Monster' Wilkins
Cmdt. Koos Smit	Maj. Des Wise
Maj. Malcolm Browning	Capt. Ray Houghton
Maj. 'Sej' Dunning	Capt. Robert Swann
Maj. Ted Hawker	Capt. Jannie van der Merwe

My grateful appreciation also goes to Dave Aronowitz of Messrs. Frank & Hirsch, distributors of Nikon cameras and lenses; Werner Sachs of Fotosax; Dave Mullany, editor of *Scope;* Willem Hyman, Leon Bennett and Carl Steyn of Republican Press; and Bob Reid of Castrol, for their assistance.

There are many others to whom I owe a great debt of gratitude, far too many to mention by name: the pilots who cheerfully and skilfully flew me around the skies to obtain the photographs I needed; the ground crew and administrative personnel who made it their business to ensure that all my needs were met; and the squadrons, especially No. 5 Squadron and No. 19 Squadron's B. Flight, who accepted me into their ranks as one of their own.

HERMAN POTGIETER

I record with gratitude the invaluable assistance of Mike Schoeman, who spent many long hours researching the squadron histories, and acknowledge, with thanks, the help of Anthony Badger and Ronnie Belling.

WILLEM STEENKAMP

I acknowledge with gratitude the assistance given to me in the course of my research by Ken F. Smy, the Aviation Society of Africa, my fellow staff members of the SAAF Museum and the Central Documentation Services, SADF.

DAVE BECKER

FOREWORD

BY JOHN W. R. TAYLOR
EDITOR JANE'S ALL THE WORLD'S AIRCRAFT

To sit in a comfortable chair, amid the familiar sights and sounds of an English home, and study a book like this is a humbling experience. It is all too easy to imagine the onset of vertigo as the Alouette helicopter in picture 91 settles gingerly on the minute, jagged summit of the awe-inspiring Devil's Tooth in the Drakensberg mountain range, or acute disorientation as the pilot of another Alouette cuts power and plummets steeply past the sheer face of the Amphitheatre in those same Mountains of the Dragons.

Herman Potgieter tells on page 13 how he took such photographs, listing the types of camera, motor drive and lenses that were used, and his preferred combinations of speed, aperture and film. But who among his readers could add to such equipment Mr Potgieter's immense talent, or the stamina and courage needed to produce perfect pictures during aerobatic manoeuvres, or in very close formation, in cramped cockpits never intended for air photography? Leonardo da Vinci might as well have listed the brushes and paints used to produce the *Mona Lisa* and expected others to turn out equivalent masterpieces. The South African Air Force is fortunate to have had the services of such a man to photograph its aircraft in action.

Every aspect of the book reflects the comparable professionalism of the Air Force itself in the sixty years since the first recruit was sworn in, in June 1920. There was an earlier South African Aviation Corps during the 1914-18 War. Its story is not overlooked, but the operational history of the SAAF began with the receipt of Britain's Imperial Gift of 100 surplus D.H.9 reconnaissance-bombers, S.E.5a scouts and Avro 504K trainers, worth £2 000 000. Willem Steenkamp, who wrote the text accompanying Mr Potgieter's photographs, expresses doubt that any other air force sprang into being overnight with so many aircraft and all required infrastructure, from complete workshops, spare engines and motor vehicles to thousands of gallons of special oils and dope, varnish and paint.

Certainly, no air force has made better use of its equipment from the start. Scrutiny of the photographs will reveal few stray spots of oil, or missing flecks of paint, on the immaculate aircraft; yet this should not suggest sparing or gentle usage. In both World Wars, the Berlin Airlift and the Korean War, the SAAF was among the first to answer the call for assistance to its allies. Under the Joint Air Training Scheme of World War II, South Africa trained 33 347 aircrew, including 7 764 pilots, divided almost equally between the RAF and SAAF. During that war, members of the SAAF were awarded one Victoria Cross, one CB, eight CBEs, 32 DSOs, 26 OBEs, 63 MBEs, five MCs, 413 DFCs, 88 AFCs, two George Medals, five King's Medals, two MMs, 24 DFMs, 14 AFMs, 36 British Empire Medals and 660 Mentioned-in-Despatches. In the Korean War, members of No. 2 Squadron gained many American decorations,

including three Legions of Merit, two Silver Stars, 50 DFCs, one Soldier's Medal, 40 Bronze Stars, 176 Air Medals and 152 Clusters to the Air Medal.

This book contains the stories of men who received some of the awards, of the aeroplanes they flew, the squadrons with which they served, and the men and aeroplanes that have followed them in the South African Air Force of the 'seventies and 'eighties. They tell of battles against enemies of many kinds, in war and in what passes today as peacetime, including oil-spills from doomed tankers which might have polluted and killed wildlife over vast areas, and the snows and floods of natural disasters which would have claimed more victims but for the intervention of SAAF helicopters.

There stands in Parliament Square, London, a statue of General Jan Christiaan Smuts, once a bitter enemy of Britain, later a firm friend, and remembered in this book as the father of the SAAF. He knew and valued those qualities of the human spirit that transcend war and politics, and which inspired the Air Force's motto *Per Aspera ad Astra*. Jan Smuts would have been well pleased with what is recorded in this book.

AERIAL PHOTOGRAPHY

My first air-to-air photography of military aircraft was on a par with being pushed in at the deep end. Until that first flight I had had no previous experience of this type of photography, and to boot, the aircraft into which I was strapped – suited and 'bone-domed' – was a Mirage III DZ whose pilot was known for his lack of consideration for novice 'bang-seat' passengers.

Afterwards anyone looking into the cockpit could readily see what I had had for lunch, but the flight was exhilarating; probably more important, I had chosen the correct camera equipment to carry with me into that cramped cockpit.

Here then is some 'gen' (as the SAAF fliers say) on military aircraft photography: What format? I have always favoured 35 mm, simply because a bigger format becomes unwieldy and is bulky. Mass too, is a problem – particularly when the aircraft is pulling anything up to 5 Gs or more and your 2kg camera suddenly weighs 10kg. A 35-mm system also offers a host of lenses, bodies and other accessories to ease one's task.

What about quality? I hear the 4 x 5 enthusiast ask. Today's 35-mm films (especially for transparencies) are so good that here, wherever possible, I used Kodachrome 64 – a film fast enough, with excellent colour rendition and extremely fine grain.

What about cameras and lenses? Important, although not imperative, is a motor winder or drive. I have used mostly a Nikon F2 with an MD2 motor drive for all the photographs in this book. So many things are happening during a photographic sortie – you are issuing instructions to the pilot of the camera aircraft, left hand on on/off switches for the intercom . . . removing your oxygen mask so that the camera can fit to your face . . . focusing . . . and a 'bone-dome' that prevents one's thumb winding on film – that a motor drive is a necessity. Certain photographs in this book would not have been possible without a motor drive. The photograph on page 48/49 is an example of this.

I have also used a Nikon FM and motor drive, and lately a Nikon F3 with its MD4 motor drive. The F2 and FM do not fit flush to one's face while wearing an oxygen mask, but the MD4 motor slopes away to the front, thus introducing a previously unknown luxury to high-speed aerial photography – no further groping for on/off mike switches, oxygen mask removal straps and lugs, or even emergency oxygen.

When an oxygen mask is removed when flying in a high-speed aircraft, such as a Mirage or Impala, there is a lot of noise from the air conditioning and from the motor drive – so one has to switch off the intercom. To speak to the pilot the mask must be held to the face and the intercom switched on, wasting time that could be used for photography. The new F3 has changed all that.

Now lenses: I took 105 mm and 28 mm lenses with me on my first flight. The 105 mm lens proved an excellent choice and about 60% of the photographs in this book have been taken with it. The 28 mm lens seemed neither here nor there and, subsequently, I have resorted to a 35 mm or 20 mm lens, depending on the subject aircraft and nature of the flight.

The above comments relate to an ejection seat aircraft being the camera aircraft. Transport and spotter aircraft and helicopters allow one to handle two cameras because of extra space and their slower speeds. Here my indispensable companion is the 80-200 mm zoom on the F2 with, once again, the 35 mm or 20 mm on the FM. Another lens that is useful is the 300 mm for shots from the ground to air.

Now for the best speed/aperture/film combination. In high-speed aircraft I use a speed of at least 1/500th because of the high frequency vibration coming through the airframe from the jet turbine. On a fine day 1/500th of a second with Kodachrome 64 will easily give an aperture of f8 to f11 in the air, showing less haze and giving more reflections of clouds. This allows for a depth of field that will correct any slight focusing errors caused by high-speed manoeuvring and imperfections in the canopy glazing.

Why no zoom in high-speed aircraft? Zooms normally have a lot of elements in them, and the canopy of, say, an Impala is not optically corrected, so that the use of a zoom creates difficulty in focusing, and the average zoom f-stop (of about f4) drastically decreases one's depth of field. However, with fresh air from an open doorway, and nothing to obscure the light reaching the zoom, the 80-200 mm has no equal, and all the flying shots of helicopters in this book have been taken with the zoom.

I have known photographers to load their cameras with 400 ASA film and, with a combination of 1/500th at f22, produce pictures that are grainy and with such incredible depth of field that in the picture area every dust speck and squashed fly on the canopy appears in the photograph.

My main objective in taking photographs of SAAF aircraft is to depict the atmosphere of flying at its most exciting and exhilarating best.

HERMAN POTGIETER

Previous pages:
1. Banking sharply, an Impala Mk II surveys the effect of 450-kg bombs on a ground target. Golden light from the rising sun tinges the smoke from the bombs.
2. A line astern formation by Impala Mk Is from No. 5 Squadron shows clearly just how close to each other the aircraft fly.
3. A self portrait taken from the back seat of a Mirage III DZ epitomizes the feeling of freedom from earthly bonds. A Mirage FIAZ keeps close company.

Overleaf:
4. Armourers replenish the ammunition in the gun pack of a Mirage III.
5. A pilot of No. 5 Squadron peers up anxiously as he is winched from his dinghy into a Puma, during air-sea rescue exercises.
6. A ground crew member screws down the engine cowling of a Harvard.
7. A pilot's gloved hand and arm rest on the nose of an Impala Mk I while he waits for his aircraft to be refuelled.
8. The four different helicopter types in SAAF service stand on a taxiway during a spring morning at Ysterplaat Air Base. They are (from left to right): an Alouette III, a Puma, a Wasp and a Super Frelon.
9. A colourful Dakota, used for target pulling, and known as the 'Dazzle Dak' is flown by, and on strength with, No. 25 Squadron.
10. The face of a fighter pilot – with a Mirage III DZ taking off in the background.
11. A pilot raises his hands in the air to indicate a snag with his aircraft, and a ground-crew member hurries towards him.
12. The powerful foam fire-tender's ability and tremendous reach is shown during this SAAF fire-fighting exercise.
13. The radar screen glows eerily while a controller vectors an aircraft onto its adversary during an exercise. Unsung, but very important, the men of the SAAF radar units do vital work checking every square metre of South Africa's airspace for the possible approach of enemy aircraft.

4

5

6

7

8

9 10

11

12 13

HISTORY OF THE SAAF

Part 1: Early Days

With extended wing-tips as rebuilt by its pupil pilots, the Paterson No. 2 Biplane rests on the 'air-strip' at Kimberley a few days before its last and fatal crash. (Photo McGregor Museum.)

Officially the South African Air Force dates back only to 1920; but its roots can be found a good eight years deeper, where they were planted by a far-seeing former Boer general who looked past the flimsy frailty of the aircraft that sputtered timidly through the lower reaches of the air – and realized they were the natural successors to the hardy scouting ponies on which he had fought the British in the Anglo-Boer War.

His name was Brigadier-General Christiaan Beyers, and in 1912 he was Commandant-General of the new-born Union of South Africa's tiny defence force.

Only ten years had passed since the end of the second and greatest of the South African Wars, and the new Union Defence Force was still deeply rooted in the attitudes and practices of that and previous conflicts. The South African soldier marched or (preferably) rode into battle. In good times he looked after his horse, and in bad times ate it. South Africans were, after all, *par excellence* a nation of horsemen. What other way of fighting was there?

But the day of the horse as the ultimate scouting and fighting machine was beginning to wane. More and more motor vehicles were beginning to be used; and in 1911 the air age had arrived in the form of a London-based company called the African Aviation Syndicate Ltd, the purpose of which was to 'promote the science and practice of aviation in South Africa'.

The company arrived in South Africa that year, headed by Guy Livingstone, and included two intrepid airmen – a pioneering British pilot, Cecil Compton Paterson, and a Pietermaritzburg man, Evelyn Driver.

They arrived in Cape Town with a French Bleriot and a biplane of Paterson's own design, and gave demonstration flights at a cycle track and two race courses, to the intense interest of admiring crowds.

It is said a number of UDF officers were among the spectators, and were as impressed as any; if so, that might be where the seed of today's South African Air Force was sown.

What is a fact is that the Prime Minister, General Jan Smuts, gave Christiaan Beyers certain specific instructions the following year, when the latter sailed for Europe to observe military manoeuvres in Switzerland, France, Germany and England.

Beyers was to visit the British Army's new aviation school on Salisbury Plain, Smuts ordered, and 'obtain as many details as possible for a guide in establishing a military aviation school in South Africa on a small and economical scale'.

Beyers carried out his orders, and more. In France he watched the military aviators perform; in Germany he went up for a flight in a Rumpler-Taube monoplane; in England he watched the field forces change course after their commanders had read messages dropped to them by aircraft which had sought out the 'enemy'.

Beyers returned to Pretoria an enthusiastic advocate of air power. He had no foreboding of the aerial battles that were only a few years away, and did not possess the poetic vision which had seized Tennyson many years earlier, so that he 'Heard the heavens fill with shouting, and there rain'd a ghastly dew/from the nations' airy navies grappling in the central blue . . .'

Beyers was a practical soldier who had learnt his craft as a fast-moving mounted guerrilla, and he realized he stood before the ultimate scouting device; aeroplanes, he said, should be 'a great saving in horses and men'.

There was no doubt in his mind, he reported to Smuts, that flying would play 'a very important part in military operations in the future'. It was an accurate prophesy, but Beyers did not live to see it come true. When World War I broke out Beyers went into rebellion, and drowned while attempting to escape from the soldiers he had formerly commanded.

But Beyers's tragedy and the larger one of the Great War still lay two years in the future. In the meantime it was decided that the South African army must have its own aviation section; and so in a *Government Gazette* published in May 1913, there appeared an advertisement inviting young men to apply for training as 'officer-aviators'.

From the hundreds that applied, an initial ten were selected and sent to the diamond town of Kimberley, where Paterson had set up the Paterson Aviation Syndicate Ltd in conjunction with De Beers after the premature demise of the African Aviation Syndicate.

Paterson's contract with the Union Government specified that he would give the ten their initial flying training; for each one who was not 'washed out' (figuratively or literally) along the way and received his F.A.I. certificate, Paterson would be paid £150.

£150 was a lot of money in those days, but both Paterson and his pupils earned it. The aviation school's educational material consisted of Paterson's home-designed aircraft, which he grandly called the 'Paterson No. 2 Bi-Plane,' and only the sublime inexperience of his pupils prevented them from realizing what they had let themselves in for. One of them, K. R. van der Spuy (later a Major-General and one of South Africa's most famous airmen) wrote many years later: 'I look back with pleasant memories on those early days of flying at Kimberley when, secure in ignorance, a cheery party of souls happily convinced themselves that flying was in truth the Sport of Kings, and that the medium of their sport, namely the Paterson Bi-Plane, was the last word in modern aircraft! Given the opportunity, I wonder whether any airman today would have the courage to take the atmosphere in this doughty old machine; I think not . . . '

Paterson's pupils soon discovered the perils inherent in their new profession. The Paterson Bi-Plane lasted just long enough for them to learn to rig and fly it; then one morning it went into an uncontrollable side-slip and dashed itself to fragments, although the pilot (Paterson) and pupil (Van der Spuy) were unharmed.

The airmen of those days were a tough and inventive lot, however.

Part 2: 1914 – 1919

The five pilots – Van der Spuy, Wallace, Creed, Turner and Emmett – did not spend much time in the RFC. As early as August 1914 Generals Botha and Smuts had laid plans to invade neighbouring German South West Africa at the request of London, which wanted to neutralize the ports of Walvis Bay and Swakopmund and various wireless stations. As a result, it was decided in November to recall the South African airmen and order them to raise, train and equip a self-supporting South African Aviation Corps which would chase and capture the wily German commander in South West Africa, Colonel Francke, and his 2 000 men.

For the five comparatively inexperienced young officers it was a monumental task in every way. They had to recruit all sorts of specialist technicians (fortunately, South Africa's gold mines proved a rich recruiting-ground, as was again the case in 1939), and somehow lay their hands on aircraft suitable for operating in South West Africa's harsh climate . . . All this, moreover, at a time when aircraft and spares of any kind were at a premium.

However, they managed it, and on May 6, 1915 the South African Aviation Corps (consisting of several of the new steel-framed Henri Farman F27s and two BE. 2Cs, the latter flown by their own Royal Naval Air Service pilots) was operational under command of Wallace, who was now a major.

The SAAC's main task was to fly reconnaissance missions, and now the long-dead General Beyers's prophesy of 1912 came true. 'For weeks I haven't known the whereabouts of Francke,' an exultant General Botha (who was in personal command of the expedition) told Van der Spuy. 'Now I can see for hundreds of miles.'

On July 9 Francke surrendered at Otavifontein, deep in the hinterland. The campaign was ended – and with it died the South African Aviation Corps. All of its personnel who volunteered for further service were sent to England, formed into No. 26 (South African) Squadron, RFC, and sent to German East Africa for operations in the Kilimanjaro area, where British and South African troops were facing an opponent even more wily than Francke – a formidable Prussian, Colonel von Lettow-Vorbeck.

No. 26 Squadron arrived at Mombasa in January 1916 and began flying scouting (and later, bombing) sorties for the Imperial forces.

It was a trying campaign for the airmen of No. 26 Squadron. Tortured by a climate which more often than not was hostile, they had to contend with everything from hungry lions and malarial mosquitoes to faulty equipment and landing-strips that were no more than clearings in the endless bush.

In the air it was better, and for hours at a time the sturdy Henri Farmans droned to and fro, scouting for information about roads, railways and rivers or bombing troops and bridges . . . Although at each pilot's shoulder hovered the knowledge that a forced landing would mean disaster in this wild land of huge swamps, jagged mountain-ranges and tangled tropical forests.

Paterson simply inspanned his students, and with their help constructed another machine from the bits and pieces of its predecessor. Surprisingly, the aircraft flew quite well, but before long it, too, succumbed to a side-slip and crashed. The instructor was injured and later died though the pupil escaped with his life. From one of his civilian pupils by the name of Carpenter, Paterson acquired another biplane, which was fortunately almost ready to fly, and was thus able to complete his contract.

After the ten pupils completed the course, six, as originally intended, were selected to go to England for advanced training (such as it was in those days). These were Lieutenants K. R. van der Spuy, G. P. Wallace, G. S. Creed, E. C. Emmett, B. H. Turner and M. S. Williams.

The six started their RFC training on April 25, 1914. But their training was to last considerably less than a year. Just over three months after they went on RFC strength, World War I broke out and suddenly there was an urgent need for pilots. By October 31 five of the six were adjudged trained pilots and drafted to France. They were to be the first of many South Africans to serve in Britain's aerial fighting forces in two world wars.

A Henri Farman F27, similar to those used by the SAAC in South West Africa, in service in German East Africa with the Corps's successor No. 26 Squadron (RFC). (Photo Maj. Genl. K. R. van der Spuy)

And the worst of it was that the airmen – so effective in South West Africa – achieved little of real importance for their pains. It was one thing to spot a town or a bridge, but Von Lettow shrewdly kept his troops in thick bush which effectively screened them from the prying eyes in the sky and neutralized the effect of the small aerial bombs.

True, one of the few clear-cut successes of the campaign – the destruction by British naval monitors of the German cruiser *Konigsberg* as it lay in hiding far up the Rufiji River – was largely because the ship was spotted by a South African airman H. D. Cutler. But Cutler was not a member of No. 26 Squadron, he belonged to the Royal Naval Air Service, both he and his Curtiss seaplane having been commandeered by the Admiralty at Simon's Town at the outbreak of war.

And so, in June 1918, No. 26 Squadron returned to England, leaving the weather-beaten Imperial forces to deal with Von Lettow in the traditional way. (They failed, and he laid down his arms undefeated at the end of the war.)

In Europe it was another story. The war had proved that South Africans had a peculiar affinity for air fighting, and almost from the start they flocked to the RFC. By the beginning of 1916 nearly 2 000 of them were flying or learning to fly, and about 3 000 served in the RFC during the war.

Many reached the RFC through the efforts of Swaziland-born

Major Allister Miller, who toured the Union in 1916 and recruited 450 men, all of whom later obtained their wings, and then returned in 1917 and recruited another 2 000.

In the ranks of 'Miller's Boys', as they came to be known, were young men who were destined for undying fame. One was Captain Andrew Weatherby Beauchamp-Proctor, who shot down 41 German aircraft and became the Empire's most decorated airman of World War I – in the space of a few months he was awarded the Victoria Cross, the Military Cross, the Distinguished Flying Cross and admitted to the Distinguished Service Order.

Others were C. J. 'Boetie' Venter, who scored 22 victories and ended up as a major-general in World War II and Captain S. M. Kinkead, who scored 30 victories. Yet another South African 'ace' was Hugh Saunders, who came out of World War I with 19 victories, was later knighted and became Air Chief Marshal of the RAF.

But not all of the South African aces were from the ranks of 'Miller's Boys'. One of the South Africans who got into the RFC under his own steam was Lieutenant-Colonel Helperus Andrias (Pierre) van Ryneveld, a young Orange Free State Afrikaner who had just obtained an engineering degree in London when the war broke out. Commissioned into the infantry, he transferred to the RFC in July 1915 and went on to make a name as an 'airman's airman' in theatres of war as far apart as Europe and the Middle East.

Van Ryneveld cut his teeth on night-flying Zeppelins over England, fought at Gallipoli and went from there to the Western Desert to help suppress the short-lived Senussi rising. In Egypt and Palestine he flew against the Turks and in Salonika against the Bulgarians before being recalled to England in 1916 to take over No 78 Home Defence Squadron, a night-flying unit formed to deal with the raids on England by the Germans' heavy Gotha bombers. By the age of 25 he had been severely wounded, awarded the DSO and MC and was in command of the 11th Army Wing of the 2nd Army.

James Ambrose Brown, in his book *A Gathering of Eagles,* paints a compelling portrait of Van Ryneveld at that time: 'A tall, commanding young man of typical Boer features . . . A born leader, cold, ambitious, decisive, authoritarian, a man who took criticism ill but was capable of inspiring; and a wit when he chose. Above all, he understood the mind of the airman.' This was the man who was to found the South African Air Force.

Van Ryneveld, a 27-year-old full colonel when hostilities ended, was not very high up on the list of top-scoring fighter pilots (he was credited with only five 'kills') but he was quite obviously that rare thing, a leader of leaders, and when the Union's new Prime Minister, General Smuts, decided in 1919 that the country's own air force had to be established, the tall Free Stater was the obvious man for the job.

Van Ryneveld carried out one valedictory feat when he and another South African pilot, Major Quintin Brand, made an epic flight from England to South Africa, for which both were subsequently knighted. The flight began at Brooklands on February 4, 1920 in a Vickers Vimy, 'Silver Queen'. After a crash at Korosko, a second Vimy, 'Silver Queen II' took them as far as Bulawayo where they again crashed and a D.H.9 H5648 'Voortrekker' was used to complete the flight to Cape Town where they arrived on March 20. The total cost was £8 336.

In early 1920 Van Ryneveld settled down to form the South African Air Force. Officially his first title was Director of Air Services, and he was intended to form an air arm which would be part of the Army. Van Ryneveld fought this suggestion of subordinate status tooth and nail, and won; consequently the SAAF has been independent from the day the first recruit was sworn in, in June 1920. (Curiously, however, there is no known statutory authority dated earlier than February 1, 1923, when it was listed under the provisions of the South Africa Defence Act Amendment act.)

The Vickers Vimy 'Silver Queen II' stands on a rough bush landing field during the epic flight down Africa by Van Ryneveld and Brand. (Photo SAAF Museum.)

Part 3: 1920 – 1939

The South African Air Force got off to a far better start than might have been expected in those penny-pinching post-war years when South Africa pared its defence force to the bone.

This was the result of what became known as the 'Imperial Gift' – the donation by the British government of 100 surplus military aircraft, complete with spares and maintenance equipment.

Van Ryneveld lost no time in working out what he needed and then laying hands on it. By 1921 the whole of the astonishing windfall had arrived in South Africa and been unloaded at the Aircraft and Artillery Depot at Roberts Heights, Pretoria. He had asked for, and obtained, 48 De Havilland D.H.9s, 30 Avro 504Ks and 22 S.E.5a Scouts – a magnificent basis for the new-born air arm of a poor nation still recovering from the most terrible war in history.

But there was more to the Imperial Gift than planes. Along with the aircraft came spare engines, complete workshops, motor vehicles, tool-sets, photographic equipment and thousands of gallons of special oils and dope, varnish and paint. To make the acquisition even sweeter, the Overseas Club of London donated ten D.H.4 aircraft and the City of Birmingham one D.H.9. There were also two BE2e aircraft left behind by Major Miller after his final wartime recruiting drive.

It was a fantastic haul, worth £2 000 000. Surely no other air force in history has ever sprung into being overnight with no less than 113 aircraft and their infrastructure on charge. It gave the SAAF a flying start.

The year 1921 saw the SAAF get down to business. Three kilometres east of Roberts Heights a 23,5-morgen field was bought for the SAAF's first airfield and named Zwartkop, and a number of officers were taken on strength – amongst whom was K. R. van der Spuy, of Kimberley crash fame, who had done great things during the war and now became Staff Officer Aeronautics in the rank of major. Applications flowed in, and the SAAF could take its pick of the best and most experienced officers and men.

Van Ryneveld knew exactly what he wanted – a small, elite body of men trained in all aspects of aerial warfare, especially under conditions likely to be encountered locally; a force, moreover, which would be autonomous and not part of any other service (Van Ryneveld felt so strongly about this last aspect that he warded off one suggestion to the contrary by threatening to resign.)

Drawing on his own experience of warfare, he laid down a strict set of age-limits for pilots and carefully organized the SAAF so that it could rapidly expand to several times its normal size in time of war.

Restricted by a tight-fisted treasury, in Van Ryneveld's scheme of things there could be no place for such RAF-style luxuries as separate squadrons devoted to specific tasks. A squadron would consist of four flights, three operational and one a headquarters unit. Each flight would be trained and equipped for a different purpose – interception and ground attack, bombing and long-range reconnaissance, artillery observation and so on. In the event of war any given flight could be used as the nucleus for a squadron, with the administrative flight expanded into a wing headquarters.

At the same time the formation of a reserve of part-time flying officers was put in hand, since a war situation would demand two pilots to each operational aircraft – a requirement which would halve the SAAF's projected two-squadron flying strength.

All in all, Van Ryneveld was acting in the spirit of the man who was ultimately responsible for the formation of the SAAF, General Smuts. With his uncanny knack of looking into the future, Smuts had told the British House of Commons after the war: 'There is absolutely no limit to the scale of its future independent war use. And the day may not be far off when aerial operations with their devastation of enemy lands and destruction of industries and populous centres on a vast scale may become one of the principal operations of war, to which the older forms of military and naval operations may become secondary and subservient.'

He was very largely right, of course, although many of the old guard thought otherwise. But both Smuts and Van Ryneveld would live to see the day of 1 000-bomber raids over Europe – and a South African Air Force larger than they could have imagined when the SAAF came into being.

Almost immediately, however, Van Ryneveld's painstaking plans ran aground on the intransigence of the Treasury, which hacked away at his budget with such vigour that the radio section had to be abolished and the photographic and armaments sections reduced to mere nuclei. Worst of all, the one full squadron with which he had started out in 1921 had to be pruned by a third.

The Treasury's financial curtailments did not mean a slackening off in SAAF activities, however. Each of the aircraft supplied through the Imperial Gift had to be taken apart and overhauled – a lengthy process – and 1922 also saw the SAAF twice called out on active duty.

A dispute among white miners on the Witwatersrand blossomed into open rebellion which eventually claimed 200 lives in fighting between strikers and government forces. On March 10 martial law was declared and the SAAF was called out to reconnoitre the Rand towns of Benoni and Brakpan, where the rebels had gathered. Led by Van Ryneveld himself, a flight of D.H.9s took off from Zwartkop and headed over the affected areas.

Among the rebels there were many old trench-fighters of the Great War, and they loosed fusillades of small-arms fire on the approaching aircraft. Van Ryneveld's machine was so badly damaged he had to make a forced landing, while another aviator, Captain W. W. Carey Thomas, was fatally wounded.

Next day Van Ryneveld was given permission to arm his aircraft, and for the next four days he and his men bombed and strafed the rebels. By March 15 it was over. The SAAF had flown 172 operational hours and lost two killed, two wounded and two aircraft irreparably damaged.

Wearing its RAF PC 10 brown colours and the SAAF roundel of red, green, lemon-yellow and blue, used throughout most of the 'Twenties', a D.H.9 flies over Cape Town. (Photo Maj. M. J. Mitchell.)

One of the two D.H. 9Js built in South Africa from D.H.4 airframes, No. 151 incorporated an enlarged D.H.50 fuel tank, clearly visible in the centre section of the top mainplane. Its over-all silver finish bore the later orange, white and blue roundels. (Photo SAAF.)

No. 159, seen in flight, was the third of the Mantis aircraft to be built.

Top: One of the seven Hawker Furies which the SAAF bought during the 1930s to succeed the earlier SE5a's as the nucleus of its fighter squadron. (Photo SAAF.) Bottom: This spectacular collision between two Avro Avian IVMs occurred at Zwartkop Air Station in the early 1930s. No. 521 has the early high pressure tyres, while 519 has the newer balloon-type tyre. (Photo SAAF.)

Less than three months later the Bondelswart Hottentot clan in South West Africa rose in rebellion, the result of a dispute which started with general lawlessness and a refusal to pay dog-tax.

The Bondelswart affair escalated into armed confrontation when one of their heroes – Hendrik Morris, who had fled after leading a rising in 1904 and had never been allowed to return – came back to his old stamping-grounds. When a small party of policemen were sent to bring him to court they ran up against a large group of armed

Hottentots who not only turned them back but later refused to lay down their arms.

A combined military and police field-force was hastily organized and sent to the troubled area. Flying in support of the ground forces, SAAF aircraft bombed and strafed the insurgents, who – being backvelders – were thoroughly demoralized by this taste of 20th century warfare. Within a few days the rising was over, the SAAF having flown a total of 105 operational hours and lost one aircraft.

For years afterwards Smuts's decision to send the Air Force after the Bondelswarts was criticized as both ludicrous and an over-reaction. Yet it made a great deal of sense from the military point of view.

The Bondelswarts had proved formidable fighters during the 1904 rising against the Germans – good shots and adept at veld-craft. Whatever the political rights or wrongs of the matter, there can be little doubt that but for the shock value of the air attacks the whole affair might well have been much more costly in terms of time, lives and money than it was. (SAAF aircraft were used to suppress two more minor disturbances in South West Africa between the wars – at Rehoboth in 1925 and Ovamboland in 1932.)

Rebellions apart, the 1920s were busy years for the SAAF. In 1925 and 1926 its pilots helped to gather hydrographic information in the great Kalahari semi-desert and dusted eucalyptus planta-tions using D.H.9s. In the years that followed they manned an experimental airmail service, flew diamonds from the State Dig-gings at Alexander Bay to Cape Town, made meteorological flights, carried out flood-relief operations and mercy flights, sprayed locust swarms and took part in civil air displays.

Three categories of SAAF activity during this period can be regarded as investments against a troubled but still distant future: Firstly, it took part in periodic liaison flights to Khartoum and Cairo in conjunction with the RAF, leading to the establishment of a chain of airfields which were to prove vitally important during the early cam-paigns of World War II; secondly, the Aircraft and Artillery Depot at Roberts Heights started building Westland Wapiti aircraft under licence, engines and instruments being imported and everything else built locally from imported materials (later 65 Hawker Hart-bees 8 (a local variant of the Hind) were similarly constructed, as well as Avro Tutors – 42 of the latter being built by the beginning of World War II); and thirdly, great efforts were made to build up a reservoir of personnel in case of emergencies.

The SAAF's first Central Flying School was established at Zwartkop in 1932, and no doubt the Air Force's rigorously high standards of flying training – it is not unusual for a class of pupil pilots to be reduced by half before the climactic wings parade – dates from those hard-driving days when Sir Pierre van Ryneveld was at the helm.

In spite of Van Ryneveld's determination that pilots should not be popularly considered mad-cap flying fools, there is little doubt that there was plenty of individualism, not to say eccentricity, in the ranks of the SAAF during its formative years.

Many stories have been lost, but some ripe ones survive, like that of the well-known pilot who wagered that chickens had a 300-yard ceiling, and to prove it took two of his best roosters up to 1 000 feet in the rear cockpit of an Avro Tutor and then tossed them overboard. The roosters, apparently spun spectacularly . . . There was another pilot, it is said, who landed at Zwartkop after flying from Cape Town, complaining bitterly of a sore arm, which he claimed resulted from the fact that he had had to fly with one wing down all the way, to counteract the drift from a strong cross-wind. Then there was a pilot who so lacked faith in his own navigational ability, that when he had to fly over the rather featureless veld north of Pretoria he was in the habit of releasing a homing pigeon from his D.H.9 and following it.

Training – and the wherewithal to carry it out – hotted up from the mid-1930s as the world situation grew increasingly perilous. In 1934 a five-year plan for the expansion of the SAAF was approved by Parliament, while in 1936 the government approved the Air Force Development Programme, which provided for substantial growth and the building of a SAAF reserve of 1 000 pilots and 1 700 artisans over the next six years.

Out-stations were established at Bloemfontein, Cape Town and Durban, and *ab initio* training was entrusted to civil flying clubs.

Part 4: 1939 – 1941

The outbreak of World War II found South Africa as unready for active service as it was possible for a nation to be. This applied to the SAAF as well. The rearmament and expansion programmes of the late 1930s had not yet begun to bite, and the house that Van Ryneveld had built showed all too obvious signs of the years of penny-pinching between the wars.

The SAAF's total full-time strength stood at 160 officers, 35 officer-cadets and 1 400 other ranks. The 104 aircraft at their disposal were almost all outdated; the only operational types were six Hurricane Mk Is, a Fairey Battle and a Blenheim, and even these were verging on obsolescence.

But things were not quite as bad as they seemed. For one thing, the whole of South African Airways – consisting of 11 Junkers Ju-52/3ms, 18 Ju-86s (the latter capable of being converted to bombers of a sort), 100 aircrew and 200 maintenance personnel –

More – if not necessarily much newer – aircraft were taken on strength as the world began to slide towards World War II. Tutors, Wapitis and Hartbees, three ex-Imperial Airways D.H.66 Hercules transports, a Gloster A.S. 31 survey aircraft, and 200 worn, but still serviceable, Harts were supplied by the British government at a nominal price from 1938 onwards. After the Harts came a number of ex-RAF Hawker Hinds and Audaxes. There were few illusions left, now, about the likelihood of war. . .

Top: With coloured fuselage bands and indentity letters on their noses, a flight of Hawker Hartbees lined up at their base shortly before the outbreak of World War II. (Photo Dave Becker collection). Below: A locally-built Wapiti III in flight during the early 1930s. The 'P' in front of its serial number indicates that it is powered by an Armstrong Siddeley Panther engine. The Wapiti 1bs had Jupiter IXF engines and their serials were prefixed by 'J'.

could be militarized at short notice. Then there was the SAAF expansion programme of 1936 which provided for subsidized civil light aircraft clubs to train a total of 1 000 pilots, 600 observers and 3 000 mechanics to man 12 new squadrons by 1942. There was also the Peace Expansion Scheme approved by Van Ryneveld on October 23, 1939, which called for the expansion of the SAAF to 720 aircraft, 336 being fighters.

All this was fine on paper, but the fact of the matter was that the building of a war-effective SAAF could not wait until 1942, and in the meantime there was a serious lack of suitable light aircraft with which the civil flying clubs were supposed to train pilots.

Nevertheless, all existing resources were harnessed to the task. A motley assortment of light aircraft – Tiger Moths, Moth Majors, Jungmanns, Magisters, Ryan STs and others – were inspanned at training schools at Pretoria, Germiston, Bloemfontein and Barag-

wanath. In addition the SAAF's Central Flying School moved from Swartkop to Kimberley.

At the same time efforts were made to reduce the acute shortage of artisans. The maintenance system was reorganized to make good a projected shortage of more than 9 000, and by March 1940 an energetic recruiting campaign was pulling in a steady flow of men suitable for moulding into both air and ground crews. This was followed by the establishment of Training Command SAAF under Colonel W. T. B. Tasker.

A turning-point came in August 1940 with the launching of the brilliantly successful Joint Air Training Scheme, in which SAAF, RAF and other air and ground crews were trained at South African-based air schools, of which there were eventually 38 as well as two operational training units.

Soon the SAAF was growing by leaps and bounds. The end of 1941 saw SAAF strength at 31 204, 4 321 of them members of the Women's Auxiliary Air Force. By now the SAAF had 956 pilots, 715 observers and air-gunners and 2 943 basic trainees.

The growth in aircraft strength was even more remarkable. In September 1940 there had been 219 operational and training air-craft of all types in the Union; a year later the number had swelled to 1 709. Tiger Moths were used for primary training, Ansons and Oxfords for twin-engined conversion, gunnery and navigation train-ing, and pupils in advanced training were flying Harvards, gradually introduced from 1942 onwards, instead of the earlier Hart variants and Masters.

During all this time the SAAF had not been idle operationally. At the outbreak of war the immediate problem had been to provide protection for Allied shipping off the Union's immensely long coast-line (which included that of South West Africa). The solution was the formation of so-called Coastal Reconnaissance Flights, equipped

Top: One of the Junkers Ju 86Z-1 airliners taken over from South African Airways at the beginning of the war and used for coastal patrol duties. It still wears much of its airline colour scheme and carries its civilian identification. (Photo Maj. M. J. Mitchell.) Above: Former S.A.A. Junkers Ju52/3ms, such as 662 'B', formed the backbone of the SAAF's transport fleet in the early days of the war. (Photo Dave Becker collection.) Below: Ventura 6054'Y' drones above the Cape Flats as it sets out on a coastal reconnaissance flight. (Photo Maj. M. J. Mitchell.)

with converted ex-SAA Ju-86s and stationed at Durban, Port Elizabeth, Cape Town and Walvis Bay (one of these airliners in warpaint struck the SAAF's first blow – albeit a small one – against the enemy in December 1939 when it intercepted the German liner *Watussi,* whose crew later scuttled it).

SAAF coastal patrols operated throughout the war, gradually

increasing in effectiveness as more and better equipment came
their way. In 1940 the Ju-86s were replaced by Ansons, and in the
same year these workhorses were supplemented by a number of
Marylands and, in 1941, Beauforts. All these aircraft were later
replaced by Venturas and RAF and RNethAF Catalinas.

For some time a Japanese invasion on the east coast was
regarded as a serious possibility, and in due course the guardians
of the coasts were reinforced by two mobile fighter squadrons,
No. 6 and No. 10, flying Mohawks (the island of Madagascar was
seized early in 1942 to pre-empt any Japanese attempt to use it as a
staging-post, and Beauforts of No. 36 and No. 37 Flights were sent
there in May 1942 to assist the operation, but they were not a
success, and more were lost through engine failure than enemy
action).

Nearly 250 000 tonnes of Allied shipping was sunk off the South
African coasts during World War II, but without the SAAF's extensive
patrols – a total of 26 submarines were attacked from the air – the
losses would have been much higher. Coastal patrol aircraft also
helped intercept 17 Axis blockade-runners and rescue 437 survivors of sinkings. The coastal reconnaissance squadrons carried
out more than 15 000 sorties between September 1939 and the end
of the war in Europe.

Top left: One of seven Miles M.14a Magisters taken over by the SAAF from
civilian owners in 1940. Top right: A Miles M2H Hawk No. 1576, formerly
ZS-AFM, was among the civilian aircraft impressed into SAAF service at the
outbreak of the war. Centre: This Gloster AS31, bought from the Aircraft
Operating Co. in March 1933, was still in service with the SAAF's Photo Flight
when pictured at Zwartkop Air Station in 1941. (Photo SAAF.) Above: Two of
the Curtiss Mohawk IVs flown by the SAAF were subscribed for by people in
the Union and named after their communities. 'Die Waterberg' was the first
Mohawk delivered to the SAAF. (Photo SAAF Museum.)

The Hawker Hurricane Mk I was the most modern fighter available to the SAAF during the East African campaign. No. 289 'A' of No. 3 Squadron bore a 'Fighting Wasp' insignia on its nose. (Photo via K. F. Smy.)

Over the land, as over the sea, it was the SAAF which drew first blood in World War II. In Sub-Saharan Africa the immediate threat to the Allies was posed by the 200 000 soldiers and 383 aircraft Benito Mussolini had stationed in Italian East Africa – a huge stretch of territory comprising Abyssinia (now Ethiopia), Somaliland and Eritrea.

Facing this mighty force was a much smaller British presence consisting largely of ground troops. But the Italians were cautious; Mussolini did not declare war for nine months, and this dilatory entry into hostilities provided the Union with some valuable breathing-space during the chaotic first few months.

While an expeditionary force was being whipped into shape in the Union, a first instalment of airmen from the expanding SAAF was sent 'Up North' in May 1940, even though Italy had not yet declared war.

This consisted of No. 1 Squadron, flying Hurricanes and Furies (augmented after their arrival by some Gladiators collected from Egypt); and two bomber units, No. 11 and No. 12 Squadrons, equipped respectively with Hartbees and Ju-86s. One flight of No. 1 Squadron was stationed in the Sudan, while the other flight (later to become No. 2 Squadron) and the two bomber squadrons were based in Kenya.

No. 12 Squadron had the honour of opening the activities when Mussolini finally declared war on June 11. Led by Major Danie du Toit, four Ju-86s took off from Nairobi's Eastleigh Aerodrome and proceeded to bomb and strafe an Italian camp at Moyale, much to its inhabitants' surprise.

Now the war was on with a vengeance, and the South African airmen went over to continuous operations. With only 40 aircraft on strength overall, they were hopelessly outnumbered by the *Regia*

The semi-desert thorn-scrub of East Africa's Northern Frontier District provides a backdrop for this Gloster Gladiator of No. 1 Squadron. (Photo Lt. Col. O. G. Davies.) Left: At the outbreak of World War II the bulk of the SAAF's serviceable aircraft were locally-built Hawker Hartbees such as these. Though out-dated, they served with distinction in East Africa with Nos. 11, 40 and 41 Squadrons. (Photo SAAF.)

Aeronautica (the Italian Air Force), but before long they were joined by No. 3 Squadron, flying Hurricanes, and two army co-operation squadrons, No. 40 and No. 41, equipped with Hartbees. The Springbok striking-power further improved when No. 11 Squadron was re-equipped with Fairey Battles, which were an improvement on the Ju-86s, while the East African flight of No. 1 Squadron was built up to unit strength and renumbered to become No. 2 Squadron. Still later No. 1 survey flight (later No. 60 Squadron) and the reconnaissance flight of No. 14 Squadron, flying Marylands, also joined in the fray.

The detailed story of how these squadrons fared in East Africa will be found in the squadron histories elsewhere in this book; suffice it to say that the South African airmen carried out their tasks with verve and courage, and not infrequently a touch of inspired zaniness of the kind that creates legends . . . And obscures the fact that these young men were risking their lives daily and living in appalling conditions out in the bush.

Take the story of the 'Sultan of Osmandelas' and the disgruntled Italian (the fighter pilots had fallen into the habit of conferring titles on themselves; in addition to the 'Sultan' there were also such worthies as the 'Sheikh of El Wak', the 'D. C. of Dalaki' and the 'Buna Kid'.) The 'Sultan' was sitting in a tree, wearing only a singlet, when his bushveld base was raided by the Italians. The 'Sultan' leapt into his Gladiator, was soon involved in a dogfight, and shot down a Caproni bomber. Afterwards one of the Caproni's survivors, dirty but still dapper in full uniform, asked to meet the pilot who had shot him down. To his consternation he was confronted by the 'Sultan'. Sadly the Italian shook his head, remarking: 'To think that an ace of the Spanish War should be shot down by boys who fly naked.'

On another occasion the commander of No. 1 Squadron's Sudan flight – which had suddenly been scrambled to try to intercept a high-flying Italian SM-79 – was amazed to observe that the Gladiator with him in the air contained a naked pilot. It transpired that the pilot in question, a man who believed in getting plenty of sleep, had been taking a quick nap when scrambled, and had been so sure it would turn out to be only a 'flap' that he had climbed into his cockpit with nothing but a blanket to clothe his nakedness.

Then there was Lieutenant Charles Kearey, who became so bored with flying a lumbering old Vickers Valentia on communications duties that he bombed an Italian fort with an 'infernal machine' made from a 44-gallon drum stuffed with explosive and assorted articles of scrap iron, which included parts of a sewing-machine.

The climactic moments of the attack were hair-raising. The drum, complete with smoking fuse, stuck in the Valentia's door until persuaded to leave by a hearty shove, after which it fell on to its target and in due course exploded, sowing destruction and despondency. In spite of Kearey's efforts at maintaining secrecy, the story of his completely unauthorized raid leaked out, and he was severely reprimanded . . . but a new legend had been woven into the fabric of the SAAF.

In November 1941 the Italians surrendered. Now the SAAF had been well and truly blooded. In a total of 6 517 sorties it had shot down 71 Italian aircraft (No. 1 Squadron had the biggest 'bag', 46, followed by No. 3 Squadron with 20) and had destroyed many more on the ground, together with vehicles and installations.

But there was no time for the SAAF to rest on its laurels. Already some of its men and aircraft were involved in a much tougher proposition: the war in the Western Desert.

Early photographic operations by No. 60 Squadron were flown in this BA Double Eagle, 1415, which had been owned by the Aircraft Operating Co. (Photo H. Sharman.)

Part 6: The Desert War, 1941 – 1943

The fighting in Italian East Africa was still in the process of winding down when South African forces, both air and ground, began to head northwards. The first to go were two SAAF units – No. 1 Squadron with its Hurricanes and No. 24 Squadron with its Marylands. They arrived in the Western Desert in April 1941, in time to take part in Sir Archibald Wavell's great westward push, the last big Allied victory until the second Battle of Alamein, late in 1942.

Other SAAF units soon began to follow. By September 1941 No. 3 SA Wing had been formed, first with two Maryland units, No. 12 and No. 24 Squadrons. Soon afterwards a third Maryland unit, No. 21

Squadron, also joined the wing, but by this time the other two squadrons had converted to Bostons, and eventually the latecomer also handed over its aircraft, to re-equip with Baltimores.

By the end of 1941 No. 1, No. 2 and No. 4 (fighter) Squadrons, No. 40 (Tactical reconnaissance) and No. 60 (photo-reconnaissance) Squadron had also joined the famous Desert Air Force.

Now there dawned a year of high endeavour, hard fighting and sometimes grievous losses. 1942 was to be a turning-point in the desert war, though this was not to be apparent for a long time, and

Martin 167F Maryland, 1637, of No. 12 Squadron taxies out for take-off from a sandy airfield in the Western Desert. (Photo SAAF.) Below: Hawker Hurricane IIa's of No. 1 Squadron at the time of the 'Stuka Party'. (Photo SAAF Museum.)

the South African airmen played a vital role in what often seemed a losing battle.

Mid-year saw Field-Marshal Erwin Rommel begin his great sweep eastwards, irresistibly driving the British Eighth Army back towards Cairo. Now the Desert Air Force snatched up the gage and saved the Eighth Army from annihilation as it streamed back, packing the narrow coast road with transport that simply begged to be attacked by Rommel's Luftwaffe.

So hot was the pace at times that at one stage, during the battle of the El Adem 'box' (a large fortified area), the DAF's three South African fighter squadrons were told to keep operating from their landing-ground at Gambut until the attacking Allied aircraft's bomb-bursts could be seen on the horizon – at which stage the enemy would be only 19 kilometres away. It was, to use an airman's term, an 'extremely ropey situation', for the airfield was itself helpless, having no adequate ground forces to defend it. However, they did it – and got away with it.

Equally daring was No. 40 Squadron, which continued until the last possible moment with tactical reconnaissance flights for 30 Corps, spotting the location and movement of the enemy tanks and their supporting columns.

No. 2 Squadron came close to being bagged in its entirety by a German-Italian armoured column at Landing Ground 9, south of Fuka. Fortunately a squadron patrol at last light discovered that an 'Allied' force in the vicinity was spearheaded by Axis armour, and LG9 was evacuated one hour before it was overrun by the unfriendly

'friends'. The pilots took off in the dark, and when they finally landed, one pilot found he had actually touched down without any problems on the crest of a hill.

June and July saw the most intensive air operations experienced in the desert war so far. The two Boston squadrons, led by Colonel Harry 'Kalfie' Martin, OC No. 3 Wing – escorted by No. 2, No. 4 and No. 5 Squadrons in Kittyhawks (which also carried bombs, on the understanding that these could be jettisoned if enemy fighters were met) – worked like Trojans on enemy troop concentrations and landing-grounds, damaging Axis supply columns and hindering the advancing armoured forces.

In June alone the Boston squadrons carried out 85% of the record total of 950 light bomber sorties flown, carrying out 126 raids, some of them by moonlight, and dropped 600 tonnes of bombs. In 53 days from May 26 to July 17, No. 24 Squadron flew 1 000 sorties with No. 12 Squadron reaching an equivalent figure on July 27.

The Allied air effort reached its peak on July 3, which has been called the most critical day of the whole battle for Egypt, with 151 light bomber and 524 fighter sorties – 132 of the former and 219 of the latter flown by the DAF's South African squadrons.

No. 1 Squadron also remembers July 3 as the day of the 'Stuka Party'. Led by the commanding officer, Major C. J. le Mesurier, 11 Hurricanes of the squadron 'bounced' a bombing group consisting of 15 Ju-87B Stukas with a Bf-109 escort. The Stukas were sent reeling all over the sky and all but two were shot down, together with one Bf-109.

The following day the Boston units repeated their feat and flew more than 100 sorties, a remarkable achievement which was rewarded by a signal from the Air Officer Commanding Western Desert, Air Vice-Marshal Sir Arthur Coningham, reading: 'The sortie strength and aircraft serviceability of Nos. 12 and 24 Squadrons have made a record that, in the circumstances, will probably never be beaten. The Eighth Army, the Press and the BBC have all wondered at your work, but in due course the best testimony will come from the enemy.'

It was a hard-won record and a great deal of the credit belonged to the 'erks' of the ground crew, who worked day and night on an endless round of servicing, refuelling, bombing up and sometimes rearming; when they ate and slept it was within reach of the increasingly weary and battered machines they served. (As the AOC later pointed out, peacetime standards put the average squadron's peak output at 20 sorties a day for four days while No. 24 Squadron had flown more than that figure every consecutive day for more than seven weeks, in spite of constant moves, the harsh climate and enemy bombing raids.)

All in all, SAAF fighters flew 2 344 sorties during July 1942, with another 720 carried out by the bombers and No. 60 Reconnaissance Squadron; in June-July the fighters scored 75 confirmed victories, with a particularly brilliant performance by the Tomahawks of No. 5 Squadron, commanded by a hero of the Abyssinian campaign Major Jack Frost before he was posted missing.

If any future historians attempt to pin-point the SAAF's 'finest hour', it could be justifiably argued that it was achieved over these two cruelly hard months.

And between August 31 and September 4, when Rommel launched his all-out onslaught on the vital Nile Delta, the Boston Squadrons distinguished themselves once more. Teamed up with two RAF Baltimore squadrons and some USAAF Mitchell bombers, they poured an unceasing rain of bombs on the Axis forces. Of the total of 614 bombing sorties flown in that period, more than half (334) were carried out by the Bostons, their high point being ten raids and 102 sorties on September 2. The statistics speak for themselves: 300 160 lb of bombs were dropped, an average of one every 48 seconds.

At El Alamein the Eighth Army's new commander, General Sir Bernard Montgomery, spent months building up his battered forces and preparing them for the offensive he planned. No. 21 Squadron SAAF, flying Baltimores, joined the two Boston squadrons to make No. 3 Wing the first all-South African wing. With No. 5 Squadron and No. 15 General Reconnaissance Squadron becoming operational, there were now 11 SAAF units ready for battle.

They soon found themselves busy as Montgomery's offensive approached. That month the SAAF airmen flew 3 103 sorties.

The offensive began on October 23 with what is remembered as the second Battle of El Alamein, and the SAAF was fully engaged from the start. On 'D plus 1' (October 24) No. 3 Wing flew 133 of the 174 sorties carried out by Montgomery's light bombers, while on October 26 their share was 90 out of a total of 122.

That day also saw one of the SAAF's most famous exploits of the desert war. A vitally important (and heavily protected) Axis convoy was steaming at full speed for Tobruk harbour with supplies for Rommel; one of the ships in it was the 2 700-ton tanker *Proserpina*.

At all costs she had to be stopped from reaching the fuel-starved Germans, and two flights of Bisleys of No. 15 Squadron SAAF, under Major D. W. Pidsley and carrying 250-lb bombs, were sent to sink her. In a deck-level attack in the face of intense flak, Pidsley hit the *Proserpina* with three of his four bombs, bringing her almost to a stop with flames and smoke pouring out of her; she was then finished off by a RAF torpedo-bomber. Pidsley was awarded an immediate DFC.

The SAAF fighters were equally hotly engaged. Between October 19 and October 31, No. 1 Squadron (Hurricanes), Nos. 2 and 4 Squadrons (Kittyhawks) and No. 5 Squadron (Tomahawks) flew 1 377 fighter and fighter-bomber sorties, an average of 106 a day.

November saw Rommel starting the long, hard-fought retreat which ended in surrender at Cape Bon in Tunisia. The South African ground forces did not take part in the pursuit, but the SAAF squadrons saw the struggle through to its end. Between March 11, 1943, when the Eighth Army hurled itself at Rommel's 'Mareth Line', and the end of the war in Africa, the Bostons and Baltimores flew 1 604 sorties, 158 of them at night, while the SAAF fighters recorded 5 615 take-offs in March-April. But statistics like these do not convey the hellish strain and danger of those hectic last months in Africa.

The Germans did not crumble, as had their Italian allies earlier; they fought hard to the end, and proved then (as they were to do later in Italy as well) that they were past masters at staging a fighting withdrawal. This meant that the Bostons and Baltimores faced flak (anti-aircraft fire) that was often so intense that many times 75% of the bombers would be holed during a single raid. The fighters, too, found themselves up against a Luftwaffe which fought as hard in defeat as in the days of victory – a Luftwaffe, moreover, which for the first time in the African theatre of operations included the superb new Focke-Wulf Fw.190.

The closing days of the campaign saw the SAAF fighters making mincemeat of the clouds of German transports and their fighter escorts off Cape Bon. In one two-day period the SAAF aircraft shot down 23 Me-323s, 14 Ju-52/3m's, a Savoia S.81 and three fighters – a feat which prompted the AOC Desert Air Force to signal the fighter wing commander, Lieutenant-Colonel Douglas Loftus: 'This performance proves that you can shoot as well as bomb straight, and you have every right to be proud.

On May 3 the final onslaught on the Axis forces in Africa began with a push by the Allied ground forces and repeated aerial attacks on enemy landing-grounds, lines of communication and positions. In less than a week Tunis and Bizerta had fallen and the net was closing around Cape Bon.

At this stage the South African light bombers were diverted to a subsidiary task, the neutralizing of the fortess-island of Pantellaria. During May 8 and 9 the Bostons and Baltimores of No. 3 Wing carried out an unbroken series of devastating attacks on Pantellaria's harbour and airfield.

With Pantellaria reduced, the last back door had slammed in the

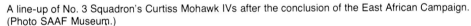
A line-up of No. 3 Squadron's Curtiss Mohawk IVs after the conclusion of the East African Campaign. (Photo SAAF Museum.)

faces of the Axis forces in Africa. Now there could be no evacuation; all that remained was surrender.

On May 12 the Baltimores of No. 21 Squadron took part in the last aerial attack of the campaign, a raid on the remnants of the once-proud 90th Light Division. Soon afterwards an historic and long-awaited message: 'There is no REPEAT no bombline in Africa' was transmitted.

That evening the Germans surrendered. Some Italian troops still resisted, and for a few hours more were pounded by Allied artillery, but at 23h00 the guns fell silent. At 24h30 the following day the last of the Italians surrendered unconditionally.

For some of those involved it was hard to believe that the fighting was over – albeit only temporarily, since Sicily and Italy still lay ahead.

Many of the men who had taken off on the first sortie at El Alamein were dead, others wounded or missing. Yet others had earned renown which had lifted them forever out of the common ruck: Men like Lieutenant Douglas 'Shorty' Rogan, who received the DSO for flying his Tomahawk back to base and landing it though one of his legs had been almost severed by flak (he was fitted with an artificial leg and went back on operations); Major E. C. 'Danny' Saville of No. 2 Squadron, who as a lieutenant found himself confronting an enemy fighter with empty guns – an impasse he solved by ramming and destroying his opponent and then flying his badly damaged aircraft home; and Captain W. L. O 'Bushy' Moon, who was clambering out of his burning Kittyhawk's cockpit when he saw a passing enemy fighter and promptly climbed back in, to give the other aircraft a burst which brought it down.

That the powers-that-be were fully appreciative of the SAAF effort was evident from a signal sent by the Air Officer Commander-in-Chief, Air Chief Marshal Sir Arthur Tedder, which read in part: '. . . Your boys, whether fighter pilots, bomber crews, recce crews or those magnificent ground staff men who got so much of the work and so little of the glory, maintained an effort which, had I been asked before, I should have said was quite beyond the bounds of human endeavour.'

Douglas Boston IIIs of No. 24 Squadron, their 'OZ' unit code letters clearly visible, wing their way above the Western Desert. Below: The Fairey Battles of No. 41 Air School, at East London, were used for gunnery training. (Photo Dave Becker Collection.)

For most of the war, the SAAF's standard twin-engined trainer was the Airspeed AS 10 Oxford, but problems with its mainly-wooden structure led to its gradual replacement by the Avro Anson – a change-over still incomplete at war's end. Here, Oxford IIs from No. 26 Air School, at Pietersburg, practise formation flying. (Photo A. T. Mathew via Dave Becker.) Below: Miles Master II, 2933, operated by No. 25 Air School at Standerton during 1942, was one of the many used at the SAAF's advanced training schools. However they had a high accident rate and were later replaced by Harvards – much to the relief of the flying instructors. (Photo R. F. Roberts.)

With the war in Africa over, Italy was the next step – with the island of Sicily as a stepping-stone. First, however, No. 60 Squadron's photo-reconnaissance Mosquitoes carried out a detailed large-scale photographic survey of parts of Sicily and other Axis-held areas in preparation for the coming 'big push' northwards.

In the next few months the squadron's Tunisian-based Mosquitoes ventured as far north as Genoa, Sardinia, Corsica and the South of France. As time went by the Mosquito pilots reached ever further into the enemy heartland; they were the first to photograph the Ploesti oilfields in Rumania (for which the late Lieutenant A. M. 'Shorty' Miller was decorated with the American DFC), and in November Captain Peter Daphne flew the first long-range P-R mission from North Africa to the Munich-Augsburg area of southern Germany.

The beginning of July saw massive Allied air raids pounding enemy concentrations in Sicily. No. 1 Squadron, now based in Malta, flew escort duties or took part in fighter sweeps over the island, while No. 3 Wing rained tons of bombs on the island in daylight and night-time raids.

It was not a one-sided affair, however, since the German and Italian garrison offered fierce flak and fighter resistance. No. 21 Squadron particularly suffered heavily. (In one raid, on an airfield near Trapani, two Baltimores were downed by anti-aircraft fire and another two by fighters, while two others were so badly damaged they had to crash-land.) But the raids had the desired effect and most of the airfields, radar stations and aircraft on Sicily were battered into uselessness.

The Allied invasion of Sicily started on June 9. A huge fleet of ships bore down on the island's eastern and south-eastern coasts, with the air force supplying maximum cover and support

Among them was No. 40 Squadron, which sent out spotter aircraft as soon as the first Eighth Army troops came ashore, and flew the highest number of sorties it ever carried out in one day during the whole of its operation in the Mediterranean. Soon it and No. 1 Squadron left Malta to base themselves on the island, No. 3 Wing moving from Tunisia to take over their vacated bases.

During the next few weeks the SAAF squadrons scourged the Axis forces with bomb and bullet. The enemy retreated, offering

Top: These Spitfire Mark Vs of No. 40 Squadron flew a tactical reconnaissance role in central Italy in April/May 1944. WR-L has a non-standard six-stub exhaust and Aboukir filter, WR-O is a standard Mk VC, and WR-P has non-standard exhausts with Vokes filter. (Photo Lt. Genl. R. H. Rogers.)
Bottom: Liberator B. Mk VI 'X' of No. 2 (Heavy Bomber) Wing, SAAF, comprising No. 31 and 34 Squadrons famous for their courageous supply operations to the beleaguered Polish partisans in Warsaw. Note how the original USAAF markings have been roughly painted out on the port wing and SAAF roundels overpainted. (Photo Dave Becker Collection.)

bitter resistance all the way, but on August 17, after 38 days, the campaign was over – though the Germans managed to withdraw a large part of their garrison in spite of heavy raids on embarkation and landing points in Sicily and Italy.

The next drive in which the SAAF was involved had a less-satisfactory outcome. The supreme Allied command decided that the islands of Cos and Leros in the Italian Dodecanese, north-east of Crete, must be occupied. A small, and inadequate, British force occupied Cos on September 12 and next day a detachment of Spitfire Mk Vs of No. 7 Squadron, under Major Corrie van Vliet, flew in.

Together with a detachment from No. 74 Squadron RAF, the South Africans constituted the island's only locally-based fighter defence. They failed, but not through want of trying . . .

The Germans in the Axis strongholds of Rhodes and Crete responded to the occupation of Cos with a massive campaign of bombing in preparation for a landing on the island. No. 7 Squadron shot down a dozen of the attackers and damaged others, while losing several of its own pilots.

But that their battle was hopeless became evident on October 3, when Cos was assailed by sea- and airborne attackers who greatly outnumbered the Allied garrison. No. 7 fought on for another two days with a rapidly-diminishing number of serviceable Spitfires; then, with German mortar-bombs dropping on the airfield, they decamped to a nearby beach and fled in waiting boats.

Meanwhile the Italian invasion had started on September 13, the day of No. 7 Squadron's arrival on Cos, with allied landings at Reggio, Catona and Gallico. It had been preceded by intense aerial activity on the part of Allied air forces based in Sicily and elsewhere. The light bomber units were particularly busy, concentrating on railway communications in the south of Italy. No. 40 Squadron flew constant tactical reconnaissance sorties, and spotted for the British battleships *HMS Nelson* and *HMS Rodney* during a bombardment of coastal defences, and No. 1 Squadron flew offensive sweeps which brought its total 'bag' of enemy aircraft to more than 150.

The start of the invasion increased the already hectic tempo of the SAAF squadrons' activities – among other things No. 3 Wing (which was now flying Marauders) shared in the difficult task of supporting the Salerno and Anzio beach-heads.

As 1944 wore on, the SAAF strength in the Italian theatre continued to grow as the result of greatly increased Mediterranean commitments allotted to South Africa at an Air Ministry meeting in London in October 1943. The idea was that this would release a great number of RAF aircrew for the pre-invasion softening up of Europe.

Sir Pierre van Ryneveld's expansion programme designed to meet this new mandate called for the formation of a heavy bomber wing, consisting of No. 31 and No. 34 Squadrons, flying Liberators; another light bomber squadron flying Marauders (No. 30 Squadron); three more fighter or fighter-bomber squadrons, flying Spit-

fires and Kittyhawks; and a second Dakota transport squadron (No. 44) to assist the SAAF's hard-pressed No. 28 Squadron.

In addition, three coastal squadrons would be withdrawn from the Union and sent to the Mediterranean, and the SAAF would take over No. 262 Squadron, an RAF unit flying Catalinas from the Congella base at Durban. (This became No. 35 Squadron SAAF in 1945.)

This gigantic task was carried out on schedule, and in due course the SAAF presence in Italy escalated dramatically. In August 1944 No. 30 Squadron joined No. 3 Wing, and the following month the new No. 8 SA Wing (comprising No. 3 and No. 11 Squadrons flying Spitfires), joined the American 12th Tactical Air Command. Nos. 5 and 15 Squadrons were operating as part of RAF wings, while Nos. 16 and 19 Squadrons, flying Beaufighters, and No. 25 Squadron, flying Marauders, had been drafted to the Balkan Air Force and were engaged extensively over the Adriatic and Yugoslavia.

Top: Beaufighter X 'K' of No. 19 Squadron launches a rocket attack on Zuzemberk during operations in Yugoslavia. (Photo SAAF Museum.) Above: No. 262 Squadron RAF became No. 35 Squadron SAAF in February 1945, operating Catalina flying boats such as FP279'D', which wears a dark slate-grey, extra-dark sea-grey, and sky camouflage scheme. (Photo Maj. M. J. Mitchell.)

The new Liberator force, designated No. 2 SA Wing, began operating from Foggia as part of No. 205 Group RAF in July 1944, and in August and September the wing's two squadrons, No. 31 and No. 34, took part in one of the most tragic and heroic operations in the history of the SAAF – dropping supplies to the Polish underground army fighting in Warsaw.

The Liberator crews' supply operations over Warsaw stand out among the abundant shining deeds in the history of the SAAF.

Top: A rare photograph of one of the Wellingtons operated in West Africa by No. 26 Squadron SAAF. Four radar aerials are mounted on the rear fuselage of HX602 'R'. Above: A development of the Wellington, Vickers Armstrong's Warwick GRV was introduced into SAAF service towards the end of World War II. PN782'G' operated with No. 17 Squadron at Gianaclis. Right: Flown by Lieutenant Oakes, this Marauder III of No. 24 Squadron received a direct hit over Ficardo on April 21, 1945. The last of the squadron's aircraft lost in action, there were no survivors of the crash. (Photo Collin Brown.) Below: Marauder IIIs of No. 30 Squadron lined up on the airstrip at Jesi. (Photo SAAF.)

Night after night the Liberators took off and flew 1 700 miles (2 720 km), through some of the most heavily-defended German night-fighter hot spots, to reach the battered Polish capital. There they would go down to 200 ft, the friendly darkness banished by searchlights and blazing buildings, and batter through a storm of anti-aircraft fire to drop the supplies they carried. And the sadness of it was that the Liberators' heroic efforts accomplished so little, for the Polish rising was already doomed.

SAAF units saw action much further afield as well. During the Battle of the Atlantic No. 26 Squadron, flying Wellingtons from Africa's west coat, watched over the shipping that brought aircraft and other material to Takoradi, a clearing-house of armaments intended for many destinations. To the north, No. 22 Squadron's Venturas, operating out of Gibraltar, flew hundreds of sorties during that long, anxious time when the main supply route to the Middle East and Italian theatres passed through the Pillars of Hercules.

The long, weary months of the Italian campaign dragged on, bringing some of the toughest fighting of the war, and the SAAF was ever in the thick of it SAAF 'Kittybombers' (Kittyhawks fitted with

A Kittyhawk IV of No. 5 Squadron 'bombed-up' and ready for a fighter-bomber mission.

bombs) and light bombers helped to smash strong German counter-attacks when Field-Marshal Kesselring made his stand at the Sangro River; later the same squadrons, joined now by 'Spit-bombers', provided strong support for the British summer offensive of 1944, which took off from the savagely-contested battlefield of Cassino and broke through the German's Gustav and Hitler Lines, sending them reeling. After that they joined in the intense aerial warfare that preceded the capture of Florence; and in August SAAF Marauders, Baltimores and Liberators teamed up with fighter-bombers in the final softening-up before the breaching of the Gothic Line.

Thus it was appropriate that they should be in at the final kill, the so-called 'victory' spring offensive which started on April 9, 1945. The war was almost over now, but April 1945 saw the SAAF fly more sorties than in any other month of the war (the full total is not known, but three SAAF wings flew a total of 6 526 against tactical targets).

On May 2 nearly a million enemy troops surrendered unconditionally. Now the SAAF's weary pilots could stand back for a breather. With the fighting over the SAAF could take stock of what it had accomplished and what its achievements had cost.

Between the end of hostilities in Africa and the surrender in Italy SAAF squadrons flew a total of 82 401 sorties.

The New Arena

In September 1944, when the SAAF was at its peak World War II strength, it consisted of 35 operational squadrons (27 of them active in the Italian theatre) and many other components, with a maximum strength of 45 000 all ranks, serving in eight different theatres on 33 types of aircraft.

In about five years of air fighting the SAAF lost 968 aircrew killed and 320 missing. Another 559 aircrew were killed in flying accidents. Fifty ground crew were killed in action and 66 in flying accidents. These and other casualties added up to 2 402 killed and missing.

By December 31, 1945 the Joint Air Training Scheme trained 33 347 pilots, navigators, observers, bomb-aimers, air-gunners and wireless-operators. Of these 20 000 were RAF, 12 221 were SAAF and 326 were drawn from other Allies. An enormous number of decorations for bravery and many for merit were awarded to SAAF personnel.

One SAAF pilot was awarded the Victoria Cross posthumously. Captain Edwin Swales had been flying a Lancaster as master bomber on a raid on Pforzheim on the night of February 23/24, 1945 when he came under night-fighter attack. In spite of extensive damage he continued to direct the raid, which was very successful. Then he started to limp home to friendly territory. He ran into heavy

cloud, however, and his Lancaster became increasingly difficult to control. Captain Swales then ordered his crew to bail out while he held the aircraft steady. The last man had just exited when the aircraft plunged out of control and crashed, killing its pilot.

Another South African airman who won the VC (although serving in the RAF) was Squadron-Leader J. D. Nettleton, who led a formation of six Lancasters of No. 44 (Rhodesia) Squadron on a raid on Augsberg on April 17, 1942. His Lancaster was the sole survivor of repeated attacks by enemy aircraft and intense anti-aircraft fire, but he succeeded in bombing the target and bringing his badly damaged Lancaster back to base.

Other decorations and medals won by SAAF members included 32 DSOs, eight CBEs, 26 OBEs, 413 DFCs, 88 AFCs, 63 MBEs, two MMs, 24 DFMs, 14 AFMs and four American DFCs.

When the war in Europe ended, no time was wasted in getting every South African serviceman and servicewoman home as soon as possible. The SAAF's justly renowned 'shuttle service', which had operated since 1940, bore the brunt of this mass ferry operation, operating as No. 5 Wing with Dakotas, and before long Ventura light bombers and Sunderland flying-boats, of No. 10 Wing and No. 35 Squadron respectively, were pressed into service.

Nor was time wasted in hacking the SAAF down to peacetime

Top: The F-51D Mustang was the mainstay of No. 2 Squadron's operations in Korea. Piloted by the OC, 306 taxies onto the runway at K-10, Chinhae, before leading a raid. (Photo SAAF.) Above: An F-86F-30-NA Sabre flown by Cmdt. Gerneke, OC No. 2 Squadron with Meteor F8 of No. 77 Squadron Royal Australian Air Force just after the armistice. (Photo Stan Wells.)

size. Many squadrons were disbanded, and the SAAF was reorganized and streamlined, with training on a small budget once more the main preoccupation.

The reorganized SAAF was to have a mobile fighter attack force (No. 1 and No. 2 Squadrons, based at Waterkloof and flying Spitfires); a transport force (No. 28 Squadron, equipped with Dakotas and operating from Swartkop); and a maritime force (No. 35 Squadron, flying Sunderlands from Durban).

No. 60 Squadron (Mosquitoes) and Nos 21 and 24 Squadrons (Venturas) lasted a few years after the war, but then were also disbanded. Part-time squadrons of the Active Citizen Force (now known as the Citizen Force) were formed as a reserve, and the pupil pilot scheme was reintroduced, with training starting at civil flying clubs in the country's main centres.

The SAAF spent 1946 and 1947 on these and other peacetime tasks; it also deployed some Ansons in Tanganyika to combat a red locust plague by aerial spraying of insecticide, and completely eradicated the tsetse fly in Zululand, using its remaining Ju-52s, Ansons and S-51 helicopters (the first use of helicopters by the SAAF) to do so. Various flood-relief work was also carried out.

Then, in September 1948, a new threat appeared – the Russian blockade of Berlin. The South African government contributed 20 crews to the ensuing Berlin Airlift. These underwent intensive training at RAF Bassingbourne and went to the German city of Lübeck on October 18. Operating RAF-supplied Dakotas, the SAAF members flew 1 240 sorties carrying 4 133 tonnes of supplies into Berlin between their arrival and April 15, 1949. Less than a month later, on May 2, 1949, Sir Pierre van Ryneveld retired as Chief of the General Staff.

Within 18 months the SAAF was headed back into battle. The Korean War had broken out; the South African government placed No. 2 Squadron, the 'Flying Cheetahs', at the disposal of the United Nations, and on September 25, 1950, the squadron sailed for Yokohama.

The squadron converted to the F-51D Mustang at Johnson Air Force Base near Tokyo and was then attached to the 18th Fighter-bomber Wing, commencing operations from landing-grounds K-9 and K-24 at Pyongyang.

Hectic days followed as the Chinese Communist forces advanced southward. Operating in near-zero temperatures, daily the South African pilots attacked enemy troops, transport and supply-dumps. On November 30 the squadron fell back to K-13 and then to K-10, near the town of Chinhae, which remained its permanent base for the next two years.

Here the squadron settled down to a long round of armed reconnaissance patrols, interdiction and close support of the ground forces, often operating an uncomfortable 200 miles (320 km) beyond the bombline. No. 2 Squadron flew Mustangs for most of the war, carrying out 10 373 sorties and losing, through enemy action and accidents, 74 of its 95 aircraft: Twelve pilots were killed in action, 30 were listed as missing and four were wounded.

Early in 1953 the squadron converted to F-86F Sabre jets and on March 16 of that year commenced operations from K-55. At first it carried out fighter sweeps along the Yalu and Chong-Chong Rivers, but in April it concentrated on ground-attack operations again.

By the time the armistice was signed on July 27, 1953 the squadron had flown 2 032 Sabre sorties; decorations and medals earned included three Legions of Merit, two Silver Stars, 50 DFCs, 40 Bronze Stars, 176 Air Medals and 152 clusters to the Air Medal (the South Korean government later awarded its order of Military Merit (Taeguk) with Gold Star to all the unknown South African dead of the Korean War).

More important than the medals, perhaps, as a measure of American esteem was the 18th Fighter-Bomber Wing policy order of October 8, 1953, which laid down that 'in memory of our gallant South African comrades . . . at all retreat ceremonies held by this Wing the playing of our national anthem shall be preceded by playing the introductory bars of the South African National Anthem . . . All personnel of the Wing will render the same honours to this anthem as to our own.'

An event unique in SAAF history followed on August 3, 1956 when the United States ambassador to South Africa, Mr Edward T. Wales, presented No. 2 Squadron with a presidential unit citation, awarded for 'extraordinary heroism in action against the armed enemy of the United Nations'.

The rest of the 1950s passed quietly, with the SAAF operating on a relatively low budget (its top fighter aircraft was still the Canadair Sabre Mk 6s it had acquired in 1956).

Then South Africa started rearming. Preparations were made for extension of national service, and the armed forces and their present and future requirements were subjected to a keen scrutiny.

Plans to acquire new aircraft – from Canberra light bombers and Dassault Mirage IIIs to helicopters and Buccaneer low-level strike aircraft – were put in hand. The groundwork for a local aircraft manufacturing industry (the country's first since the pre-war construction of Wapitis, Hartebeestes and Tutors) was laid. By 1970, when the SAAF celebrated its 50th anniversary, it was again fast becoming a force to be reckoned with.

The SAAF's full role in the Angolan campaign remains cloaked in secrecy, and is likely to remain so for some years yet. But without the SAAF's helicopters and air-supply operation, the South African Defence Force (which did not have more than 2 000 men in the field at the most active stage of operations) would have been unable to conduct its extremely fast-moving campaign. (One task force advanced more than 3 000 kilometres in 33 days.)

Since Angola, the SAAF has been fully engaged in the border war, making several pre-emptive strikes into Angola. At least three aircraft are known to have been lost while operating north of the border – a Canberra which crashed, killing its crew, after being hit by ground fire; a locally-built Impala ground-attack fighter, and an Alouette III helicopter, which was hit by a rocket.

Top: Sunderland flying-boats were used for long-range maritime reconnaissance. In a flurry of spray, No. 1703 'H-RB' lands on Lake Umsingazi during the 1950s. (Photo Dave Becker Collection.) Below: This photograph depicts Vampire FB. 5 serial no. 201, the first operational jet aircraft flown by the SAAF. (The Sabres in Korea were on loan from the USAF.) (Photo SAAF Museum.) Bottom: The second of the SAAF's three Sikorsky S-51s, the blue-painted A2, seen during a spraying run in Zululand, was later irreparably damaged in an accident. (Photo Dave Becker Collection.)

A new generation of veterans has grown up, wearing not the Africa Star nor the Italian Star but the simple orange-white-blue ribbon of the modern Pro Patria Medal, denoting border service. A few are also entitled to the class which shows they saw service north of the Cunene River during the Angolan fighting of 1975/76. They have replaced the men of World War I and their successors of World War II.

General Jan Smuts, father of the SAAF, is dead now; so is its midwife, Sir Pierre van Ryneveld; and so is the quiet ace, Boetie Venter. But K. R. van der Spuy, one of the original six members of the South African Aviation Corps, survives as this is written. In his lifetime the SAAF has not changed in its most important aspect, the quality of the men who serve in it.

On the SAAF's monument to its dead near Pretoria is inscribed a quotation from the Book of Samuel: 'They were swifter than eagles, they were stronger than lions.' It is a description as appropriate to the living as to the dead.

THE DASSAULT MIRAGE F1
Knock-out punch of the SAAF

In October 1975 thousands of spectators at an 'open day' at Cape Town's Ysterplaat air base watched with delight while a camouflaged swept-wing fighter simply announced as 'a Mirage-type aircraft' screamed through a few passes high above their heads, then dwindled rapidly into the distance.

Few of them realised that what they had just seen was the hitherto classified Mirage F1, newest and hottest aircraft in the armoury. It was not until 13 months later that the government finally made a public announcement that the F1 was in service with the SAAF.

The swept-wing Mirage F1 has little in common with its ancestor, the Mirage III, but the line of descent is clear, even though the evolution process has blurred most signs of the family relationship.

Its development dates from the mid-1960s, when Dassault designers began to experiment with various improvements on the IIIE, namely the IIIF and IIIG, which were later renamed the Mirage F and Mirage G respectively.

The two aircraft differed considerably. The Mirage F had traditional fixed swept wings, while the Mirage G featured a variable-geometry wing – 'swing-wing' in popular parlance – which was then becoming extremely popular in supersonic aircraft designs.

Ultimately, however, the Mirage G was dropped – though several were built and satisfactorily tested – and Dassault settled on three versions of the Mirage F; the F1, F2 and F3.

The F2 was a two-seater powered by a SNECMA TF306 turbojet engine developed in France under a United States licence, and it flew for the first time on June 12, 1966. It came to a premature end because the French feared, with some justification, that the US would clamp an embargo on its export to unpopular regimes (as had already happened when the SAAF had tried to buy several Mystère 20s a little earlier).

In its place the French settled for the single-seater F1, which first flew on December 23, 1966. The F1 was designed as an all-weather, multi-purpose fighter-interceptor and was driven by the most powerful turbojet then available in France – the SNECMA-Atar 9K-50.

Internally the F1 did not offer improved armament – like the Mirage IIIs it was armed with two 30 mm cannon in its lower front fuselage, but with five stronger attachment points under the wings and belly for other armament and extra fuel tanks, and in other ways, it was a vast improvement on the older Mirages.

As used in the SAAF today the F1CZ variant is little faster than the Mirage III family, capable of Mach 2,2 under combat conditions. Its endurance for patrol or high altitude pursuit is triple that of the earlier aircraft, while it has double the radius of action when employed on close-support missions at low altitude.

It requires 23% less runway for take-off, and the maximum approach speed when landing is 20% lower. (The delta-winged Mirage III's high landing speed of 339 km/h (210 mph) was, in fact, the reason why Dassault had decided on a return to the more conventional swept wing.) The F1's maximum wing-loading is almost double that of its predecessor, while slats on the leading edges of its wings have enhanced its agility in combat.

As its major combat aid the F1 carries in its nose an improved Thomson-CSF Cyrano IV multi-function radar system which provides automatic follow-up and fire control for the pilot.

Financially speaking, Dassault's decision to settle for an all-French product was a wise one, for the F1 was subsequently bought by at least two regimes of which the Americans heartily disapproved – South Africa and Libya.

South Africa was Dassault's first export market for the plane. Long a user of Mirages, she proved the truth of the old business adage that 'a satisfied customer always comes back for more' by placing an order for some F1CZs.

The SAAF also ordered a large number of the F1AZ variant, which is primarily a ground attack fighter. Instead of the sophisticated, ultra-expensive Cyrano IV radar system it features an integrated ground-attack system. It also has two on-board computers which enable the pilot to identify a target 5 km away and then provide him with all the data he needs to home in on it – after which the system automatically releases his bombs at the right moment. However, the range-finding ability of the EMD AIDA 2 radar unit permits the Mirage F1AZ to operate combat and visual interception missiles such as the MATRA R.530.

The remaining space is taken up by an additional fuel tank behind the cockpit and a retractable refuelling probe in the nose.

The first two F1CZs were delivered to No.3 Squadron SAAF on April 4, 1975, after being flown out from France in a Hercules transport aircraft. It was, however, still very much a secret operation at that stage, particularly in South Africa.

At the bi-annual Paris Air Show in June 1975 Dassault displayed a SAAF F1CZ and then the SAAF's first F1AZ – but South Africans had no opportunity of seeing what their money had bought till September that year, when some F1CZs were guardedly displayed at Waterkloof air base near Pretoria . . . where photographs for publication were not exactly welcomed.

The F1AZs started arriving late in 1975 and were allocated to No. 1 Squadron, then still flying Sabre Mk6s out of Air Force Base Pietersburg – which it shared with 85 Advanced Flying School. No. 1 Squadron handed its Sabres over to 85 AFS and moved to Waterkloof, there to operate its F1AZs in such discreet manner that they were not revealed to the general public till another air show was held at Ysterplaat and Waterkloof in February 1980 to celebrate the SAAF's 60th anniversary.

The Waterkloof F1s provide the Republic's northern border with its primary knock-out punch. Two of them are always on standby in a special hangar, umbilical cords keeping their systems gently turning over and their pilots prepared for action in case the early-warning radar network detects suspicious-looking 'blips' heading towards the Pretoria-Johannesburg complex.

If that happens the hangar's door rolls up into its roof and the F1s blast down the runway. In less than a minute they are fast-vanishing dots in the northern sky. It is an awe-inspiring sight.

Historical note on No. 1 Squadron SAAF

South Africa's senior operational flying unit, No. 1 Squadron is almost as old as the SAAF itself. It was formed at Swartkop air force station in February 1920 and equipped with war-surplus De Havilland DH-9s received from Britain as part of the 'Imperial Gift'.

Later the squadron moved to the nearby Waterkloof air base, flying first Hawker Harts and then Hartbees. On August 31, 1939, it was redesignated No. 1 Bomber/Fighter Squadron, but in December that year lost its identity by being renumbered No. 11 (Bomber) Squadron.

No. 1 Squadron was re-formed in February 1940 by renumbering No. 6 Squadron, which had just moved up from Cape Town and been re-equipped with four Hurricane Is and six Hawker Furies – then the most modern fighters in the SAAF.

14. Four Mirage F1CZs of No. 3 Squadron, carrying locally manufactured air-to-air missiles on their wingtips, take off in formation during an air show held at Air Force Base Waterkloof in February 1980 to celebrate the 60th anniversary of the founding of the South African Air Force.

In May 1940, the squadron set off for East Africa. Numerous detachments saw action against the Italians, the squadron flying at various times, the Fury, Hurricane and Gladiator II.

At the end of the East African campaign, it moved to Egypt in April 1941 to join the battles being fought in the Western Desert. Initially the squadron flew the Hurricane I, and later the IIa, IIb and IIc; it then switched to Mk V, Mk VIII and Mk IX Spitfires, flying this type until the end of World War II.

By June 1943 No. 1 Squadron had left the desert and was in Malta. From there it went to Sicily, and September 1943 saw it in Italy, where it remained until the end of hostilities. With 165½ air victories, No. 1 was the SAAF's top-scoring squadron in the war.

The squadron re-formed at Swartkop in 1946, flying Harvards until it moved to Waterkloof to take delivery of new Spitfire IXe's in June 1947. In 1950 these were replaced by Vampires, which were in turn replaced by Canadair Sabre 6s in September 1956.

On January 1, 1951, No. 1 Squadron's Citizen Force element of part-time airmen broke away to be formed into No. 4 Squadron, flying Spitfires and Harvards. Late in 1963 No. 1 Squadron became the SAAF's sole Sabre operator when it received all those formerly flown by No. 2 Squadron, which had been re-equipped with Mirage IIICZs. Early in 1967 No. 1 Squadron moved from Waterkloof to AFB Pietersburg, flying a few Impala Mk Is in addition to its Sabres until the latter part of 1975, when it returned to Waterkloof and was re-equipped with the new Mirage F1AZs early in 1976. On January 14, 1981, it moved to AFB Hoedspruit.

Historical note on No. 3 Squadron SAAF

Boasting a colourful history and today one of the SAAF's first-line Mirage squadrons, No. 3 Squadron was formed at Waterkloof air base in January 1939, equipped with Hawker Hartbees and Hurricane Mk I's.

It moved to Port Elizabeth in September 1939, then was disbanded, only to be re-formed at Waterkloof on September 9, 1940, and equipped with Hurricane Mk Is. From here it went on active service almost immediately, and by October was in East Africa.

On October 28 it flew its first sortie and on November 22 scored its first 'kills' when a pilot, Lieutenant Allen, shot down a Caproni Ca133, another Caproni crashing after the same encounter.

During this time one of No. 3 Squadron's pilots, Captain J. E. Frost, carried out one of the SAAF's most famous wartime exploits by shooting down five Italian aircraft in one dog-fight, for which he was awarded an immediate DFC.

Frost later took part in an even more famous 'stunt' when he was shot down by anti-aircraft fire while strafing Diredawa airfield. Frost landed on a satellite strip, where his friend Lieutenant R. H. C. Kershaw landed and picked him up. Kershaw was awarded an immediate DSO, the SAAF's first in World War II.

Another immediate DFC earned on that raid went to Captain Servaas van Breda Theron, who ended up as a much-decorated brigadier after weathering not only World War II but the Korean War as well.

No. 3 Squadron prided itself on pressing home its strafing attacks

– during an attack on Jimma aerodrome, slightly more than a month after the Diredawa raid, Lieutenant Howitson performed the unlikely feat of sending two enemy aircraft up in flames by strafing them through the open doors of a hangar.

Flying both Hurricanes and Gladiator Mk IIs, and for a short time Curtiss Mohawk IVs, No. 3 Squadron fought all the way through Somaliland and Abyssinia, and by the end of 1941 had destroyed just over 100 Italian aircraft, two dozen in aerial combat and the rest by strafing. Its reward for this fine effort was a move to Asmara, followed by disbandment.

In December 1942 the squadron was re-formed in South Africa and sent to the Middle East. Equipped with the Hurricane IIb and later the Hurricane IIc and Spitfire V, it marked time for a while as fighter defence for the port of Aden, which was no longer in any real danger, and later flew coastal patrols from North Africa.

In August 1944, however, it was re-equipped with Spitfire IXs, sent to Italy and ended up in the new SAAF No. 8 Wing, flying for a while under United States Army Air Force direction.

Most of its operations were strafing sorties and by the end of the shooting in Europe, No. 3 Squadron had racked up 2 300 sorties in Italy for the loss of two pilots killed and three missing – its record being 54 sorties in one day.

Disbanded at the end of the war, No. 3 Squadron was re-formed at the old Baragwanath Airport on September 6, 1952, as a Citizen Force part-time unit flying Harvards, but fell under the axe again some seven years later.

In August 1966 No. 3 Squadron was re-formed at Waterkloof as a 'paper' unit under the control of No. 2 Squadron, its nucleus consisting of some Mirage IIIEZs from No. 2 Squadron. Squadron colours were awarded in February 1970 and the squadron was reactivated as an autonomous squadron in February 1975. No. 3 Squadron received its first Mirage F1CZs on April 4, 1975, at Waterkloof.

Its Mirage IIIEZs, DZs and D2Zs were passed on to No. 85 ADFS (Advanced Flying School).

15

16

15. Uncluttered by armaments or an extra fuel tank, an F1AZ of No. 1 Squadron shows off its clean lines as it goes into a barrel roll at 14 000 feet.
16. Carrying a belly tank for extra range, an F1AZ strike fighter retracts its undercarriage just after leaving the runway at AFB Waterkloof. Because of its shoulder-mounted wing, the F1's main undercarriage members have to be drawn up into the fuselage in a complex sequence of movements.
17. Overleaf: In superb line-abreast formation two F1AZs of No. 1 Squadron and two F1CZs of No. 3 Squadron flash over the bushveld of the north-eastern Transvaal. At the time this photograph was taken No. 1 Squadron did not display its unit emblem on the tail-fins of its aircraft.

18. When a large South African fits himself into the cramped cockpit – jocularly known as the 'Ace cage' – of an F1 Mirage there is not much elbow-room, as can be seen here as this F1CZ levels out during aerobatics.
19. An F1CZ crouches on the apron, the camera's ultra-wide lens giving it an almost Concorde-like appearance. Enhancing its lethally beautiful looks is the pitot tube which measures airspeed;
20. Trailing a shimmer of heated air from the tailpipe of its Atar 9 K engine, this F1AZ thunders down the runway just before taking off, the slats on the leading edges of its wings extended to improve lift.

THE DASSAULT MIRAGE III
Fighter of many faces

21 .A Mirage III R2Z of No. 2 Squadron, carrying two underwing tanks for extended range, touches down at Durban's Louis Botha Airport, its drag chute scooping at the air to slow the aircraft down. Landing lights blaze from above the nose-wheel, for lights-on landings are standard operating procedure to scare off any birds – a potential hazard on many South African runways – and to help the control tower spot the aircraft at a distance.

Its adoring public calls it simply 'the Mirage'; some Afrikaans-speaking pilots affectionately refer to it as 'die Strykyster' (flat-iron) because of its delta wings; and the would-be cognoscenti call it 'the Miracle', enraging the men who actually fly it.

Call it what you will, the Mirage III is a superb combat aircraft which has thoroughly proved itself in battle, though not in southern African skies. It is also an aircraft with as many faces as a quick-change actor. The public see only one Mirage III – 'the plane with the delta wings' – but, in fact, there are more than half-a-dozen distinctly different types flying in the SAAF, each adapted to a specific role in the country's defence.

The Mirage III story started on November 17, 1956 when the prototype designated Mirage 111-001 made its maiden flight in France. It was a success, and 10 pre-production models, designated Mirage IIIA, ironed out all the bugs during the next two years.

The first production Mirage IIIC flew in October 1960, and over the next 20 years gained a well-deserved reputation as one of the finest jet fighters since the almost-legendary North American Sabre. It equipped squadron after squadron of the French Air Force and was exported extensively.

The earliest foreign customers for the Mirage III were Israel – which used it to great effect during the 1967 Six-Day War – and South Africa. They obtained a formidable fighting machine, almost as potent today as it was two decades ago.

The SAAF IIIC is a single-seater all-weather interceptor, capable of Mach 2 (twice the speed of sound), armed with two internally mounted 30 mm cannon and equipped to carry a variety of bombs or missiles on external mounts under its wings and belly. Its nose carries a high-power Cyrano I. bis navigation and fire control radar system.

The SAAF's first Mirage IIICZ (the 'Z' suffix was exclusively applied to the SAAF export versions) arrived, dismantled, in the hold of a C-130 Hercules transport in April 1963. It was assembled and flight-tested by a French team from the Dassault factory and handed over to No. 2 (Cheetah) Squadron which was then flying Canadair Sabres out of AFB Waterkloof, near Pretoria. Other IIICZs followed in due course till all the Cheetah Squadron pilots were flying the delta-winged warbird.

The Mirages – first displayed to a suitably impressed public in July 1963 – provided the SAAF with an awesome increase in strike-power. At last South Africa had a truly supersonic fighter. The Sabre could break the sound barrier, but only in a dive; the Mirage accomplished it easily in level flight.

The acquisition of the new fighter soon led to yet another purchase from the Dassault factory. At that time the only advanced jet-training aircraft in SAAF service was the Vampire T Mk 55, which was hardly suitable for conversion training. Previously, prospective Mirage pilots did their pre-solo training on a simulator, but even the best simulator is no substitute for the real thing, and before long the SAAF ordered a number of the Mirage tandem two-seat training variant, the IIIB.

The SAAF's first Mirage IIIBZ was delivered to No. 2 Squadron in November 1964. Essentially a trainer developed simultaneously with the IIIC, it was slightly longer in the fuselage and featured two tandem seats. Though lacking the IIIC's sophisticated Cyrano radar – for which there was no need in the training role – it carried the same armament and had the same external weapon capability.

In the meantime, Dassault and the French Air Force had developed an improved strike and ground-attack version, the bigger, heavier and longer-ranged Mirage IIIE, which boasted a more powerful engine – the Atar 9C turbojet with improved afterburner – and increased fuel capacity.

The Mirage IIIE – which made its maiden flight as early as 1961 – bore a close family resemblance to the IIIC, but its profile differed somewhat. Not only was the fuselage 300 mm longer, so that its cockpit was moved forward of the engine-intakes, but it had a slightly different tail-fin lacking the IIIC's dorsal fairing.

Less obvious were the changes that made it considerably more versatile than its predecessor. While still as good an interceptor as the IIIC, a much improved Cyrano IIB multi-function radar system made it an all-weather ground-attack fighter as well, with an advanced Doppler navigation system built into the fairing under the cockpit. It also could carry an external war load similar to that of the IIIC.

The SAAF ordered several IIIEZs and the first batch – which saw limited French Air Force service before being shipped to South Africa – was delivered to No. 2 Squadron in 1965.

The 'Flying Cheetahs' did not retain the new aircraft for long; in August 1966 No. 3 Squadron was re-formed and the Mirage IIIEZs delivered at that stage were transferred to it. Not long afterwards a fourth Mirage type came into SAAF service when IIIDZs (the advanced conversion trainer version of the IIIEZ) were procured in the late 1960s.

Before long the SAAF acquired a fifth Mirage variant when it added a tactical reconnaissance element to No. 2 Squadron in the shape of a number of Mirage IIIRZs.

The Mirage IIIRZ was the SAAF version of the Mirage IIIRD, which was essentially similar to the Mirage IIIE and had the same Atar 9C engine. However, the Cyrano radar system in the nose had been replaced by a pack of five cameras positioned so that they could be focused in four different directions for low-altitude, medium-altitude, high-altitude and night reconnaissance missions. The nose fairing contained a Doppler advanced navigational radar system as well.

The inital Mirage IIIRZs were delivered wearing the Nato camouflage scheme adopted by the French Air Force – olive drab/extra-dark sea grey upper surfaces and natural metal under-surfaces – the only difference being the SAAF castle insignia on the engine-intakes. In fact, French-language stencilling could still be seen on the aircraft up to the time they were repainted in the standard SAAF deep buff/olive drab scheme in 1976.

It was not till 1971, in fact, that camouflage was applied first to the Mirage IIICZs and then to other aircraft. Various types of camouflage were evaluated for local conditions before the present olive drab/deep buff/light Admiralty grey scheme was adopted, and in due course all Mirages were painted thus.

Early in 1975, No. 3 Squadron's IIIEZs and IIIDZs moved to Pietersburg to join the former Advanced Flying School there, which had just been renamed 85 Advanced Flying School.

Yet another Mirage variant, the IIID2Z, was acquired by the SAAF in 1974. The '2' in the type-designation signifies that this version has the more powerful Atar 9K-50 turbojet which is also fitted to the Mirage F-1. It was a tandem two-seat advanced trainer version equipped with an arrester-hook – an item usually confined to carrier-borne aircraft – and stood out from its sisters because it lacked the IIIDZ's Doppler fairing under the nose.

Along with the IIID2Zs a small number of single-seat Mirage IIIR2Zs – also powered by the Atar 9K-50 turbojet, but lacking the arrester-hook – were added to No. 2 Squadron as tactical reconnaissance aircraft.

Waterkloof air base has seen the last of No. 2 Squadron and its motley stable of Mirages, at least for the time being. When No. 1 Squadron began receiving its Mirage F1s in the mid-1970s, No. 2 Squadron was transferred to the ultra-modern air base at Hoedspruit in the Eastern Transvaal.

There the Cheetahs screech around the skies, as swift and deadly as the fleet-footed carnivore whose spotted head adorns their fins.

Historical note on No. 2 Squadron SAAF

The 'Flying Cheetahs', best known for their exploits during the Korean War, actually trace their ancestry back to January 1939, when No. 2 (Transvaal) Squadron was formed at Waterkloof and equipped with Hawker Hartbees

The squadron – redesignated a fighter-bomber unit later that year – spent much time in varied and intensive training flights. In the event, No. 2 Squadron was doomed to oblivion, because in December 1939 the unit was renumbered to become No. 12 Squadron.

On October 1, 1940, however, No. 2 Squadron was re-formed in Kenya, its basic cadre being a flight of No. 1 Squadron, and equipped with Fury Is, Hurricane Is and Gladiator IIs. Its first 'kills' were scored on October 29, when two pilots borrowed Hurricanes from 3 Squadron.

The squadron flew many fighter patrols, but much of its time was spent on air defence sorties and, soon, in January 1941, its Hurricanes were taken away, leaving it with only Furies and Gloster Gauntlets.

Then, in April 1941, No. 2 Squadron moved to Egypt and was re-equipped with Curtiss Tomahawk IIBs and, briefly, some Hurricanes. Shipping patrols were carried out for a time, but by July 1941 the squadron was in action against the Luftwaffe in the Western Desert.

No. 2 Squadron's long and famous career as part of the Desert Air Force began auspiciously – in one of its first clashes on July 29 it shot down four Ju-87 Stukas and claimed two Bf-109s as well, for the loss of two Tomahawks.

The squadron flew Tomahawks until May 1942, by which time it had begun to receive Kittyhawk IAs and later Kittyhawk IIIs. None of these were a match for the Luftwaffe's aircraft when it came to speed, however, and the 'Cheetahs' had to fight hard for their victories.

Nevertheless there were bright moments. On September 3, 1941, its Tomahawks intercepted 27 Italian Fiat G-50 fighters and shot down six of them within 90 seconds of being scrambled; and exactly one month later a No. 2 Squadron pilot achieved the distinction of shooting down the first Luftwaffe Bf-109F fighter to fall to the Desert Air Force.

Alternating between strafing missions, bomber-escort duties and fighter sweeps, No. 2 Squadron claimed many victories – and mourned many of its own dead – during the bitter 1942 battles. During one mission on November 11, 1942, it wiped out nearly a whole Stuka *staffel* (squadron) for the loss of two aircraft.

The end of the year found No. 2 Squadron beginning to specialize in fighter-bomber duties and when the war ended in Africa in 1943 it

moved to Sicily and then Italy, re-equipping with four-cannon Spitfire VCs for ground-attack operations, and later, Spitfire IXs.

The squadron spent the rest of the war in attacking ground targets (its score for air victories stood at a total of 108 by the time hostilities ended in Europe) and was on stand-by to serve in the Far East when Japan surrendered, bringing an end to World War II.

Like many other fine SAAF units, No. 2 Squadron was then disbanded, but was re-formed at Waterkloof Air Station on December 1, 1948, flying Spitfire IXe's with O.C. Capt. Keith Kuhlmann.

When the Korean War broke out South Africa pledged to contribute a fighter squadron to the Allied cause, and No. 2 Squadron was selected. It served in Korea from November 1950 to December 1953, first flying the superb but obsolescent F-51D Mustang and later (from February 1953) the stunning new North American F-86F-30NA Sabre.

On its return to South Africa the squadron converted to Vampire F.B. Mk. S2's, and in 1956 to Sabre 6s, which it flew till receiving Dassault Mirage IIIs in 1963 for fighter-recce and fighter-bomber duties.

22. Ground crew hasten to unplug the external Hobart starter from this Mirage III D2Z as it prepares to take off on a night tactical exercise. The furnace-like glow from the tailpipe indicates the big bird's engine is running smoothly.
23. Unstick! The pilot drags back on the stick and his Mirage III CZ of No. 2 Squadron, the 'Flying Cheetahs', is committed to the air. The nosewheel has already lifted off, or 'rotated', as the Mirage flyers say, and in a moment man and machine will be creatures of the air – for a while, anyway. This Mirage is setting off on an air combat manoeuvring exercise, and the air-to-air missile under its port wingtip is clearly visible.

22
23

25
26 27

24. Previous page: A Mirage III EZ from No. 85 Advanced Flying School fires a salvo of unguided rockets at a ground target. The 24 rockets are gone in less than one second, and by the time they hit the target are travelling faster than sound. Some burn later than others: these are known to the Mirage fraternity as 'late flamers'. This III EZ still displayed No. 3 Squadron emblem when this photograph was taken, as can be seen by the wasp insignia, but the squadron has since been re-equipped with F1CZs.

25. A Mirage III CZ streaks across the Transvaal countryside in low-level flight, the high-water marks of Loskop Dam conspiring with the camera to make it appear as if the earth itself has been rearranged into an air-flow pattern by the force of the warbird's passage.

26. Its afterburner glowing a hellish bright orange, a Mirage III D2Z of No. 85 Advanced Flying School leaps into the air from the runway at Durban's Louis Botha Airport at about 150 knots. The D2Zs are two-seaters used mainly for conversion training, but unlike most trainers have retained full operational capability.

27. A Mirage III D2Z hurtles at tree-top level across the once-tranquil bush-veld, the cone of power from its engine whirling leaves and branches into a flurry of helpless movement. (Photo by Charles Norman.)

50

THE HAWKER-SIDDELEY BUCCANEER
The warbird that nearly wasn't

28. A Buccaneer S. Mk 50 of No. 24 Squadron makes a low, slow pass, its massive air-brakes and undercarriage fully extended and the bomb-bay doors open to reveal its load of four brightly-painted 450-kg bombs.
29. Overleaf: To make a Buccaneer's long 'reach' even longer, the name of the game is 'buddy-pack', or air-to-air refuelling. Here a 'Buc' of No. 24 Squadron prepares to link itself to the drogue which will connect its thirsty engines to the fuel pod of a tanker aircraft, also from No. 24 Squadron. Air-to-air refuelling takes less than a minute, but it requires a good deal of navigational and piloting skill.

The Buccaneer pilots and navigators of No. 24 Squadron (unofficial motto: 'Hit the floor, it's 24') refer to one another as 'the Pirates' – appropriate, considering the type-name of the aircraft they fly and their primary task which is to swoop down on and knock out enemy shipping.

The Buccaneer came into SAAF service as a result of the strategic concept, since abandoned, that in terms of the now-defunct Simonstown Agreement, South Africa would guard the vitally important southern tip of Africa with powerful maritime weapons supplied by Great Britain.

One of the requirements was for a heavily armed long-range naval strike bomber which could evade enemy radar by making low-level attacks, and the obvious choice was the Blackburn (later Hawker-Siddeley) Buccaneer, a folding-wing two-seater jet designed to operate from aircraft-carriers. In January 1963 16 of these big, beautiful aircraft were ordered by South Africa.

Two years later the renowned World War 1 SAAF squadron.

No. 24, was re-formed at the Lossiemouth Royal Naval Air Station in Scotland, and there the squadron commander (Commandant Bob Rogers, later Chief of the SAAF) and his senior officers started converting to Mark I Buccaneers. At the same time a technical team was sent to Britain for training.

At first the South Africans trained on British aircraft; but on May 26 that year the first SAAF Buccaneer arrived at Lossiemouth from the Hawker-Siddeley factory, and was soon followed by another seven.

The SAAF version of the Buccaneer, designated the S. Mk 50, was similar to the British S. Mk 2, but incorporated a rocket pack to equip it for operating from Air Force Base Waterkloof, near Pretoria.

Waterkloof is hot and high, and while its runway was considered adequate for Buccaneer operations, it was decided that the rocket-packs – which could generate a massive 3 600 kg thrust for 32 seconds – would provide an extra margin of safety under certain conditions by assisting the aircraft, which had a maximum mass of 28 tonnes, to attain the necessary airspeed in the climb attitude during or soon after take-off.

At first all the SAAF Buccaneers retained the folding wings required on carrier-based aircraft; but these were later fixed – folding wings were not needed for land-based service and maintenance expenses were unjustified.

But a sword of Damocles hung over the newly reborn squadron. In 1964 the Labour Party had come to power in Britain, and the new Prime Minister, Harold Wilson, was determined to enforce the optional United Nations arms embargo against South Africa.

Wilson believed the Buccaneers might be used to suppress internal insurgency – somewhat illogical reasoning since there were many SAAF aircraft better suited for counter-insurgency roles than the Buccaneer.

Nevertheless it was apparent that No. 24 Squadron's new aircraft were threatened. In 1964 India's Minister of Defence arrived in Britain to buy maritime weaponry, and it was reported (though never confirmed) that Wilson was seriously considering diverting the as yet undelivered SAAF Buccaneers to that country.

Following severe pressure from the Republic, however, Britain eventually agreed to let South Africa have its Buccaneers, but summarily cancelled an option the Republic had taken on an undisclosed number of others.

On October 27, 1965, two formations of Buccaneers each left Britain, one led by Commandant Rogers and the other by Major A. M. Muller (now a lieutenant-general and Chief of the Air Force).

Commandant Rogers had an uneventful trip, and led his formation onto the Waterkloof tarmac just after 15h00 on November 3. Major Muller, however, ran into serious trouble. One of his Buccaneers suffered a double flame-out after a high-altitude stall in mid-Atlantic, somewhere between the Cape Verde Islands and Ascension Island. Major Muller sent the other aircraft on to Ascension Island while he and two accompanying SAAF C-130B Hercules (which were carrying the Buccaneers' ground-support equipment) mounted an area search.

Soon Major Muller's fuel began to run low and he had to turn back to Las Palmas, leaving the two Hercules to continue the search. It found nothing, and two Avro Shackletons were sent from Cape Town by No. 35 Squadron SAAF to join the search for the missing aircraft's two crew members. Hampered by bad weather and a low cloud base, they searched doggedly, but fruitlessly, till 22h30 that night, when Shackleton 1722 spotted the downed flyers bobbing in their dinghy.

It dropped them a 10-man dinghy and supplies before returning to base, and the SAAF men were picked up by the Dutch freighter *Randfontein* after spending 13 hours in the water.

Now No. 24 Squadron was one aircraft short almost before it had begun to operate. It stayed that way; the Wilson government applied the arms ban to the letter and refused to replace the lost Buccaneer.

The rest of the Buccaneers were sent by sea in 1966, the first arriving at Cape Town on August 5 and the others on October 17.

Almost at once one of the Buccaneers wrote itself into the record-books. In December 1966 the new OC No. 24 Squadron, Commandant A. M. Muller, took to the air in a Buccaneer and flew 9 600 km in nine hours and five minutes, twice being refuelled by another Buccaneer in mid-air, before landing still with substantial reserves of engine-oil and oxygen. At that time it was the longest Buccaneer flight ever undertaken.

Today, after almost a decade and a half, the SAAF Buccaneers are still an important component of the country's air umbrella, but, sadly, flying accidents have reduced their number. Those that remain, however, have grown steadily more formidable.

For one thing, their range has been stretched even further. Commandant Muller's record of 1966 has been surpassed several times, and since late 1974 all but one of the SAAF Buccaneers have been equipped with bomb-door fuel tanks similar to those fitted to the Royal Air Force's Buccaneer S. Mk2B.

The SAAF Buccaneers have kept pace with the latest weapons developments as well, and are equipped to carry such ship-busting missiles as the Nord AS20 – now withdrawn from service and needed only for training – and the AS30.

So far the SAAF's big birds have not taken part in any big combined manoeuvres since the last of the long series of Anglo-South African 'Capex' exercises was held off the South African coast in November 1973, a few months before the Simonstown Agreement was cancelled.

However, they have twice been called in to sink tankers threatening the coast with disastrous oil-spills.

In February 1971 the huge Liberian tanker *Wafra* ran aground on a sandbank off the Cape coast with 60 000 tonnes of Persian Gulf oil on board. After a tough struggle the *Wafra* was pulled clear, but it was decided to sink her because there was a danger she would break up in the heavy seas and pollute a huge stretch of coastline.

The SAAF was called in and plans were laid to open up the *Wafra's* ballast tank, which was filled with compressed air, and also her bow, so that she would sink in one piece rather than catch fire and explode.

Amid a glare of publicity (the Minister of Defence and a number of high officials were circling the area near by in the SAAF Viscount, not to mention two Shackletons loaded with journalists), two Buccaneers dived on the *Wafra* and fired four Nord AS30 missiles.

The result was not impressive. The first missile, intended for the ballast tank, skimmed the deck, struck the water 20 metres further on and exploded on impact. The second missile was deliberately steered away from the *Wafra* because at the moment of firing one of the observation aircraft was considered to be too close to the target.

The third missile missed the ballast tank, hit the *Wafra* further forward about three metres above the waterline and penetrated, leaving a hole 380 mm across which was insufficient to sink the ship. The fourth was fired at the bow, but missed narrowly.

Next day the Buccaneers fired another eight missiles at the *Wafra*, but she remained stubbornly afloat. In the end, two series of depth-charges dropped by Shackletons from No. 35 Squadron set the tanker on fire and then sank her.

To the public this was rather less than satisfactory. What the armchair aviators did not realise, of course, was that the Buccaneers had been operating with one hand tied behind their backs, so to speak, thanks to the restrictions laid on them.

On an actual shipping strike, one way of sinking the *Wafra* would have been to attack head-on from the bow, with one missile ploughing through her from stem to stern and almost certainly sinking her.

Instead, the Buccaneers had had to aim for the ballast tank – an extremely small target only about 3-4,5 m high above-water – and a specific point on the bow. Throughout the operation, rain hampered visibility and the wind gusted up to 40 knots.

In May 1972, the SAAF's Buccaneers really showed what they could do when the 112 174 dwt Liberian tanker *Silver Castle* collided with a South African freighter, the *SA Pioneer*, off the Cape coast a month earlier. The tanker's stern section was badly damaged and she was towed out to sea, where her cargo of 10 000 tonnes of oil was transferred to another tanker.

She had suffered so much damage by this time, however, that it was decided to scuttle her. After several conventional attempts had failed the SAAF was called in to help. At 09h07 on May 15 five Buccaneers closed in on the *Silver Castle* with another standing by for air-to-air refuelling, and this time they were not hamstrung by pettifogging instructions. They dropped several 1 000 lb bombs on her and she broke in two and sank almost immediately.

Given the opportunity to show what they really could do, the sleek deadly aircraft had silenced the doubters.

Historical note on No. 24 Squadron SAAF

No. 24 Squadron was formed on March 5, 1941 by renumbering No. 14 Squadron, which had operated in Kenya and Abyssinia during the East African campaign, and replacing its Hawker Hartbeestes with Maryland light bombers – subsequently replaced by Bostons during the ensuing Western Desert campaign.

The last Boston mission was flown on November 8, 1943. The squadron was then re-equipped with Marauder Mk IIs from December 1943 onwards, and then with Marauder Mk IIIs.

The last operation of the war was flown on April 25, 1945, after which the squadron was attached to No. 3 Wing SAAF with its Marauders converted to transports. On November 6, 1945 No.24 Squadron was disbanded, but re-formed the following April as a regular medium bomber squadron flying B-34 Venturas out of Air Force Station Bloemspruit, near Bloemfontein.

In 1948 a part-time Active Citizen Force element flying Harvards was added to it, and when No. 24 Squadron was disbanded for the second time, on January 1, 1951, the part-time pilots became the nucleus of No.8 Squadron, flying Harvards till they were replaced by Impala Mk I jets in the early 1970s. No. 24 Squadron itself remained in suspended animation, however, till it was re-formed at RNAS Lossiemouth in May 1965.

30

31

30. Bright orange flames light up the underside of this Buccaneer's wings as unguided rockets spew out from four pods in a salvo burst.

31. A Buccaneer pilot proves that size has nothing to do with surefootedness by making a high-speed pass just 3 m above ground level. The clean profile of its belly indicates this particular aircraft has not yet been modified to accommodate an extra fuel tank on its bomb-bay. The 'flagstaff' on its nose is actually its air-to-air refuelling nozzle.

THE CANADAIR CL-13B SABRE 6
Beautiful Canadian

The long, glorious era of the Sabre in South African Air Force service ended while this book was being written, but it will be many years before the mark this beautiful and well-loved aircraft made on SAAF history fades away.

The Sabre was the first jet fighter South African pilots flew in combat, and by the time the last few still in SAAF colours were withdrawn from service early in 1980 it had become a legend in its own time – as well-loved both by pilots and the man in the street as the Spitfire had been to an earlier generation.

There is no family resemblance between the two, but the Sabre is from the same stable as the North American P-51 Mustang, one of the last and best of the piston-engined fighters.

The Sabre was conceived late in World War II as a result of a US Defence Department requirement for a jet fighter capable of attaining 600 mph (960 km/h).

The North American plant's original design – based on the FJ-1 Fury – was for a new aircraft with the same stubby straight wing as the extremely tough and successful Mustang. But preliminary investigation indicated this would not be suitable in view of the speed required, so the designers on the basis of an evaluation of captured German records, decided to incorporate a swept wing instead.

The new design was accepted by the US government in November 1945, and work started on a prototype, designated the XP-86. Slightly less than two years later, on August 8, 1947, the first XP-86 rolled out of the North American plant at Inglewood, California. Its maiden flight took place two months later.

The great difference the swept wing made became evident during a test flight in April 1948 when the Sabre prototype's pilot put his machine into a shallow dive and exceeded Mach 1 – the speed of sound.

Though this sounds relatively insignificant today, it caused a sensation at the time – only one other aircraft at that time had broken the sound barrier, the Bell X-1. The X-1 was a highly experimental machine, however, while the Sabre prototype was a production aircraft.

The first variant, the F-86A, made its maiden flight in May 1948; and the post-war international power struggle ensured that the Sabre would not rust in its sheath.

In 1950 a Russian-backed Juggernaut swept irresistibly down the Korean peninsula, brushing aside the weak forces in its path. Only desperate fighting by a hastily-assembled United Nations contingent slowed its forward thrust.

In the early stages of the Korean War, the US Far East Air Force, though equipped with a variety of obsolescent aircraft, maintained the upper hand over the even worse equipped North Koreans. Consequently, the piston-engined fighters of World War II – the Mustang F-51s, the Yak-9s, the Chance-Vought Corsairs – had their last fling before the Jet Age relegated them to the scrapyard.

The US FEAF retained command of Korean airspace until the new Russian-built MiG-15 jets of the Chinese Air Force arrived to upset the balance of air power. The US riposte was to despatch its new Sabres to the war theatre.

32. When will we see their like again? Aged but still classically beautiful, some of the last Sabre jets still flying in the world stand lined up on the apron at No. 85 Advanced Flying School at Pietersburg, noses curled up as if smelling the air for the scent of an adversary. One of most famous of the early jet fighters, the Sabre broke new ground with its large canopy, which was stronger and gave the pilot better vision than any previous model. Since this photograph was taken the Sabre in SAAF service has flown into history as well.

33. Landing lights ablaze and nose wheel high after landing, a Sabre continues to roll down the runway at AFB Pietersburg.

33

The first Sabre mission in Korea was flown on December 17, 1950, and the second Sabre to take the air that day achieved the first jet 'kill' of the war when it shot down a MiG-15 deep inside North Korean territory.

South Africa's contribution to the polyglot UN force was No. 2 Squadron, the famous 'Flying Cheetahs', which was attached to the 18th Fighter-Bomber Wing of the USAF and made such a name for itself that it was awarded a presidential unit citation – a high American military honour seldom given, particularly to a foreign unit.

For the major part of the war the 'Cheetahs' flew the tough but definitely outmoded F-51D Mustang. It was not till late 1952 that news came it was to be re-equipped with the latest Sabre variant, the improved F-86F, on loan from the USAF.

The first five F-86Fs (serials 601 to 605) were delivered to No. 2 Squadron late in January 1953, and after conversion training the first missions were flown along the Yalu River in the notorious 'MiG Alley' area on March 12, 1953.

In the remaining four months before the armistice, the SAAF Sabres flew 1 694 sorties. As far as No. 2 Squadron was concerned, the war ended with a bang rather than a whimper – on July 27, 1953, the last day of the war, No. 2 Squadron flew no less than 41 sorties before the armistice came into effect at one minute past 22h00.

Of the 20 or so Sabres flown by No. 2 Squadron, only four were lost on active service, although a fifth crashed after the armistice.

All operational flying ceased on October 1, 1953. Ten days later the Cheetahs' brief but passionate love affair with the beautiful swept-wing fighter ended when the last two Sabres were flown to a USAF base to be handed back. Reportedly, all the ex-SAAF F-86Fs later found their way to the Philippines Air Force which has since dispensed with them.

No. 2 Squadron returned to the Union of South Africa, where it was re-equipped with Vampire F.B.Mk.52s which had recently been delivered from Britain, and for the next three years the Sabre was no more than a memory to the SAAF.

Meanwhile the SAAF was evaluating several other aircraft types as possible eventual successors to its Vampires and finally settled on the Canadian version of the Sabre, the Canadair CL-13B Sabre Mk6.

Destined for No. 1 and No. 2 Squadrons, the Canadair Sabre was the final production version of a long line of Sabre variants. It was a totally modernized and updated form of the original F-86F. Among the improvements was the more powerful Orenda 14 turbojet engine, which could bring it to within an eyelash of Mach 1 at sea-level.

All together 34 were ordered from Canadair (serials 350 – 383). They were test-flown in Canada, then dismantled and shipped to South Africa, where they were re-assembled at No. 1 Air Depot in August 1956. The first to fly was 350, a No. 1 Squadron aircraft, which took to the air on September 4, 1956, and almost immediately Capt. Larry Eagar, flying a No. 1 Squadron Sabre, became the first pilot in South Africa to break the sound barrier.

The Canadair Sabre carried much more muscle than its American

59

ancestor of the Korean days, but the improvements had not spoilt it. It was still a sweet aircraft to fly.

Small boys collected its vital statistics and built models of it. So did older boys ranging well into middle age. At air shows they turned out in their thousands to 'ooh' and 'ah' while the Sabre 'jet jockeys' threw the lovely fighters around the skies.

For seven years the Sabres were South Africa's premier first-line fighters. Then, in the early 1960s, they felt the first chill wind of obsolescence; No. 2 Squadron was re-equipped with the newer, faster and more potent Dassault Mirage IIICZ. All its Sabres were handed over to No. 1 Squadron, which later (in 1967) moved out of Waterkloof to the air base at Pietersburg. There it remained, its Sabres still playing a key role in South Africa's air defences. But their days as first-line SAAF fighters were shortening and, in 1975, when No. 1 Squadron converted to the Mirage F-1, the Sabres were all transferred to Pietersburg's 85 Advanced Flying School.

For the next four years the Sabres soldiered on in the ranks of 85 AFS's motley stable of training aircraft but, after more than two decades of high-stress flying, their age was beginning to tell. In August 1979 all were grounded for the last time.

Their last public appearance was during the SAAF 50th anniversary celebrations in January 1980 when Sabres featured in two air shows – five aircraft at Pietersburg and one at Waterkloof. It was a sad last hurrah: they formed static displays while more modern fighters flew overhead.

One aircraft enthusiast cannot forget the pang he felt when he realized the Waterkloof Sabre had arrived at its former home-base at the end of a tow-rope – an ignominious way for one of the SAAF's great fighters to return home.

Three months later, in April 1980, the Chief of the SAAF, Lieut. Gen. A. M. Muller, wrote the final words in the saga of the beautiful Canadians by announcing that all the Sabres had finally been withdrawn from SAAF service.

One Sabre (No. 361) remains on display at Lanseria at the SAAF Museum Workshop, and is finished in natural metal and markings of a No. 1 Squadron aircraft.

Historical note on No. 85 Advanced Flying School

No. 85 ADFS was formed on August 1, 1972 by renaming the Advanced Flying School, Pietersburg. The unit took over some of the last remaining Vampire FB Mk52s and T Mk55s, but by 1973 was completely re-equipped with Impala MkIs and Mirage IIIDZs.

With the delivery of Mirage F1CZs to No. 3 Squadron during 1975, 85 ADFS took over that unit's Mirage IIIEZs as well as new IIID2Zs. A Sabre Mk6 flight was formed the following year and recently Impala MkIIs have been added to the unit's inventory.

The Sabre Mk6s were withdrawn in April 1980 leaving 85 ADFS operating Mirage IIIDZs, D2Zs, IIIEZs and Impala MkIs and IIs in the advanced jet training role.

34. A denizen of the sky and clouds it might be, but this Sabre cannot entirely ignore its origins, and so it carries a coat of camouflage which helps it to melt into its background of Transvaal bushveld. For the moment, however, the pilot is lord of all he surveys – and thanks to the Sabre's fine bubble canopy there is little he cannot see.

35 36

37

35. With an infernal flare, jet fuel ignites in the tailpipe of a Sabre. At this moment it is still firmly earth-bound, however, the air-brake doors are wide open, and the umbilical cable from the external power starter is still plugged into the port side.

36. As smoothly powerful as any ocean predator, a shark-like Sabre 'goes over the top' during a loop, its grey-white belly blending into clouds in the background.

37. In classic silhouette a Sabre flies low over the Ebenezer Dam near AFB Pietersburg, the pilot riding high in his cockpit to obtain the maximum visibility allowed by his canopy. The Sabre still carries the eagle emblem of No. 1 Squadron, now long since re-equipped with Mirage F1s.

THE ENGLISH ELECTRIC CANBERRA
Friday 13's child

38. Characteristically cockeyed-looking with its off-set canopy, a Canberra B (I).12 of No. 12 Squadron sits on the apron, the hatch on its starboard side open in readiness for its pilot and navigator/bomb-aimer.

At the beginning of its long career, what the South African airman familiarly calls the 'Can', proved that it was a lucky aircraft. What other interpretation can one place on the fact that the first prototype made its maiden flight on Friday the 13th – and not only survived the test but performed beautifully?

The Canberra dates from a 1944 English Electric Company design to meet a specification for a high-altitude bomber with a radar bomb-aiming system (in fact it was meant to be the first jet-propelled bomber capable of carrying an atomic device). As it happened, the radar was not ready for the first production version, which is why some early Canberra variants have 'glasshouse' noses.

No. VN 799, that superstition-busting first Canberra – although it was then known only as the English Electric A.1 – took to the air on May 13, 1949, in the hands of a famed test pilot, Wing-Commander Roland Beamont. To the experts of the newborn 'Jet Age' the A.1 had a curiously old-fashioned look. Its conventional straight wing configuration was in direct contradiction to the already-fashionable swept wing. As observers did not fail to point out, the latest American bomber, the B-47 which had flown 17 months earlier, had a swept wing. Why not the A.1?

In fact, the A.1's straight wing had been chosen after various

options had been weighed. Since the aircraft's maximum speed was to be sub-sonic, the designers opted for a conventional wing – a swept-wing would provide no advantage at the maximum design speed, that would not be offset by various disadvantages.

As a result the A.1's wings were not only straight but rather large, with a total wing area of 950 ft². This enabled a considerable volume of fuel to be carried, giving the aircraft additional ferry-range.

The designers' choice was completely vindicated at the A.1's debut. At the 1949 Farnborough Air Show Beamont amazed his audience with a bravura performance of very fast climbs, slow rolls, high-speed turns and passes (the latter at more than 800 km/h) and slow approaches at less than 160 km/h, with landing-gear down and bomb-doors open, while rocking the aircraft violently with its ailerons, to show its full control at near-stalling speed.

The A.1 proved, in fact, that it was as fast as, and even more manoeuvrable than, most fighters of the day.

The initial production version was designated the B.Mk2 and entered RAF service in 1951. In January that year the aircraft received its now-famous type-name when the Australian Prime Minister, Mr (later Sir) Robert Menzies dubbed it 'Canberra' in nautical fashion by breaking a bottle of Australian champagne over its nose.

In the years that followed, the Canberra saw wide service in many different versions. Apart from the British production version, large numbers – some of them tandem two seaters – were also built under licence by Martin for the United States Air Force, which designated it the B-57. Many of these later saw service in Vietnam, fighting side by side with Canberras built under licence for the Royal Australian Air Force.

As well as the Canberra B.2, there were the photographic-reconnaissance versions, the PR.3; the T.Mk.4 trainer, the B.5, which featured the more powerful Avon 109 engines and integral fueltanks; the B.6, which was a B.2 with the same improvements as the B.5; the PR. 7, a photo-reconnaissance version based on the B. 6; the B (I). 6, with improved armament; the B (I). 8, a B (I) 6 fitted with a fighter-type cockpit canopy; and finally the PR. 9, a development of the PR. 7. There were also numerous additional designations applied to various conversions and export models.

One of the first Canberras South Africans saw was a B.2, numbered WH699 and named Aries IV. 'Aries' was a generic name applied to aircraft used in a RAF Empire Air Navigation School project designed to develop navigational techniques. Some of the project's earlier long-range missions included flights to South Africa. One of the aircraft used thus in March and April 1945 was a Lancaster named Aries, which was followed by two Avro Lincolns named Aries II and III.

Aries IV arrived in Cape Town on December 17, 1953, as part of a long-range navigational exercise undertaken to celebrate the 50th anniversary of the Wright brothers' first powered flight. The flight was made in record time, the Canberra covering the 6 009, 72 statute miles in 12 hours, 21 minutes and 3, 8 seconds.

In April 1958, Aries V, a Canberra PR. 7 numbered WT528, visited South Africa, again on a navigational exercise, and in the next few years South Africa often played host to Canberras of the Southern Rhodesian Air Force , also on navigation exercises. (The Southern Rhodesians acquired 15 ex-RAF Canberras delivered in 1959, and three T.Mk.4 trainers – converted B.2s – in 1961.)

It was not until 1962, however, that the South African Air Force placed an order for Canberras, to be used as tactical bombers and high-altitude reconnaissance aircraft. All of these were B(I). 8s, then in production.

At the time, the final production batch of an order for 12 Canberras was being completed for New Zealand, this export version of the B(I).8 being designated the B(I).12. The SAAF Canberras received the same designation and, according to some reports, were assembled from spare components as production had already ceased. It is a fact, however, that the SAAF Canberras were the last new ones produced by English Electric, though it was later to rebuild and refurbish many others.

The SAAF Canberras were flown out to the Republic – the first two being delivered at Waterkloof air base on September 30, 1963 – to equip the newly re-formed No. 12 Squadron.

The Canberra in SAAF service differs from the earlier versions, having a lengthened nose with fighter-style cockpit canopy – the only other production model with this nose arrangement being the PR. 9. Seen from the front, the canopy gives the Canberra a slightly cockeyed look, since it is situated to port, slightly off-centre.

Only the pilot occupies the cockpit, entering it through a small hatch on the port side of the fuselage; the navigator is in the nose itself, and gains access through a slightly larger door on the starboard side, just forward of the cockpit.

In the B(I).12 Canberra the rear half of the bomb-bay is adapted to carry a detachable pack of four 20 mm Hispano cannon with enough ammunition for one minute's continuous firing. At the same time three 1 000-lb bombs can be accommodated in the forward half of the bomb-bay, as well as a 1 000-lb bomb under each wing. If necessary, the cannon pack may be replaced by a camera pack for high-level reconnaissance missions.

The SAAF also needed trainers for pilot conversion, and ordered three Canberra T.Mk4s. These were no longer in production, how-

ever, so three ex-RAF T.4s were refurbished by English Electric and delivered together with the B(I).12s.

The T. 4 retains the same outward cockpit and nose appearance as the earlier Canberra models like the B. 2, except that it seats the two crew side by side in the cockpit instead of one behind the other (the rearward navigator's seat remains, however, making it in effect the only three-seater Canberra). Entrance to the cockpit is through a hatch beneath the canopy on the starboard side, with a smaller hatch for the navigator further to the rear.

Each of the SAAF T. 4s, all three converted B. 2s of 1953 vintage, had a different pedigree. No. 457 started life as an early production version, B. 2, one of a number built under contract by A. V. Roe in about 1953 when English Electric could not keep up with the demand generated by the Korean War. No. 458 was built by English Electric, while No. 459 was produced by Handley Page under sub-contract. All three saw service with the RAF before conversion into trainers in the mid-1950s.

Initially all the SAAF Canberras were painted silver, while the T. 4s also carried high-visibility Dayglo bands characteristic of SAAF colour schemes of the time. The silver finishes began to disappear in the mid-1970s when the B(I).12s were given an all-over coat of PRU (Photographic Reconnaissance Unit) blue. The T. 4s retained their silver-and-Dayglo scheme till early in 1978, and then also went into PRU blue.

In spite of its long-lived design and peaceful-sounding name, the Canberras remain a potent part of the SAAF, and are well-loved by the crews who fly them for their vice-free and gentlemanly characteristics.

Historical note on No. 12 Squadron SAAF

Without question, No. 12 Squadron can claim that it fired the SAAF's first shot of World War II and, in fact, did so several hours before hostilities had been declared between South Africa and Italy, a late entrant in the war.

No. 12 Squadron was formed a few months after the outbreak of World War II by simply renumbering No. 2 Squadron at Waterkloof air station in December 1939. The new unit was officially designated 'No. 12 Bomber/Fighter Squadron', although at first it was equipped with ageing and relatively harmless Avro Ansons.

This was rectified to some extent when it flew to Cape Town's Brooklyn airfield on May 17, 1940. The day after its arrival 10 ex-South African Airways Junkers Ju-86s (still in their blue-and-grey civil livery) were taken on charge and the squadron returned to the Transvaal post-haste for equally rapid conversion training at Germiston. They had previously operated on coastal patrols.

Such was the speed of this that on May 22 the squadron with its hastily militarised ex-airliners – mostly Ju-86Z-7s, but including one Ju-86K-1 – set off for Eastleigh aerodrome at Nairobi, followed later by others.

The squadron had barely settled in at Eastleigh before seeing action for the first time. At 16h45 on June 10 the Italian government informed Britain that from midnight it would be at war with the Allies and just before hostilities began pilots of No. 12 Squadron were briefed for an early-morning attack on an Italian camp at Moyale. At 07h55 on June 11 a flight of four Ju-86s under Major Danie du Toit (OC, 'C Flight') took off from Eastleigh on the South African Air Force's first bombing raid of World War II – though South Africa's separate declaration of war on Italy had not become official.

This pioneering raid was followed by others during the ensuing weeks, No. 12 Squadron bombing such targets as airfields and other Italian installations.

The squadron suffered its first casualties on September 3, 1940, when anti-aircraft fire at Yavello downed one of the Ju-86s with the loss of its whole crew. Nine days later the squadron avenged this loss by taking off from Lodwar, flying to the outer limits of their range and, in spite of cloudy conditions, destroying nine Italian aircraft on the ground at Jimma airfield.

Operations continued and on occasion the squadron dropped ammunition to the 'shifta' (Abyssinian partisans) and flew various VIPs – among them South Africa's Prime Minister, General Jan Smuts, and General Sir Archibald Wavell – on inspection tours, but its main role remained bombing, and for months it shadowed the swift advance of the South African forces into Italian East Africa.

From March 1941 the squadron could boast a number of Maryland light bombers on temporary detachment from both No. 14 and No. 60 Squadrons SAAF. The Marylands' main role was to fly reconnaissance, but with their superior speed they could also combat the Italian fighters.

By April 1941 No. 12 Squadron's airmen, not to mention the aircraft they flew, were showing signs of strain after almost a year of continuous operations. (One of the air gunners, 'Pikkie' Rautenbach, who was reputed to be only 16, was decorated with the DFM during this period.)

Reinforced by aircraft received from No. 39 Squadron RAF in September 1941, the South Africans pursued their part of the desert war, giving as well as taking when attacked by German fighters.

The unit flew its last Maryland operation on December 23, 1941, when six aircraft of No. 12 and No. 21 Squadrons combined. It was not a happy ending, however; the Marylands were jumped by a formation of Bf-109s, which shot down two of the South African planes.

Three days later the Marylands were handed over to No. 21 Squadron after flying a total of 732 sorties in the hands of their former owners, and No. 12 Squadron moved back to the Nile Delta to re-equip with Boston Mk IIIs.

Within two months the squadron was battle-ready and joined No. 3 Wing SAAF, which was later to become famous during the bitter fighting of that year.

Operations began in March and continued day and night with ever-increasing intensity; on raid after raid Bostons of No. 12 and No. 24 Squadrons pressed home their attacks in such tight disciplined formations, flak or no flak, that they came to be nicknamed 'the 18 imperturbables' by the Germans.

On August 10, 1942, the squadron was pulled out of the line for a brief rest, but on August 22 was back in action with 14 aircraft (at this time it also had an attached flight of B-25Cs of the United States Army Air Force's 12th Bomb Group).

The squadron participated in the Battle of El Alamein, the final turning-point in the desert war, by laying smoke-screens, and then following the Allied advance westwards; by December 16, 1942, it had flown its 2 000th Boston sortie.

But it could not rest on its laurels, and operations continued full-tilt. On March 21, 1943, the squadron took the wing sortie record for the day, with 29 out of 72 flown.

Operations in North Africa ended on May 11, 1943, and the squadron turned its attention to the fortified Italian islands of Pantelleria and Lampedusa. This task completed, July saw it commence with pre-invasion operations over Sicily, carrying out armed reconnaissance as well as bombing raids.

On July 20, part of the squadron moved to Malta; the following month the whole squadron transferred there, and by September was operating over Italy. In October the squadron moved on to Italian soil and began what proved a long association with that

39. He travels fastest who travels alone, but no matter how fast it flies this Canberra T Mk4 will never be able to shake off its own shadow. Specially adapted for training, the T Mk4 differs from the B(1).12 operational version by having a domed canopy so that two pilots can sit side by side in the cockpit. This aircraft is carrying tear-shaped fuel tanks on its wingtips.

campaign, although occasional raids over Yugoslavia were flown.

The last of 3 851 Boston operations was flown on December 22, 1943: a total of 7426 hours over enemy lines which had cost the squadron 17 aircraft and 53 men dead or wounded. By December 27 all the Bostons had gone, and the squadron returned to North Africa to convert to Marauder Mk IIs.

Soon afterwards, on April 7, No. 12 Squadron's personnel proved they were as valiant on the ground as in the air when the airfield's fuel dump exploded. Two members were awarded George Medals and three others were made MBEs for their rescue work.

The year 1944 saw the start of close-in bombing in direct support of the Eighth Army, which was now slogging its way up Italy in spite of ferocious resistance, and the squadron stayed in this role (pausing only in September 1944 to convert to Marauder Mk IIIs) until the end of the war in Europe in May 1945.

The squadron counted the costs of its long war service – 150 men and more than 40 aircraft lost in 8 237 sorties – and its achievements: At least six enemy aircraft shot down and a total of 52 DFCs and four bars, 12 DFMs, one AFC, two GMs, three MBEs, three British Empire Medals, 40 mentions in despatches and two Belgian Croix de Guerre. (As was the case with No. 24 Squadron, it had had a batch of seconded Belgian pilots.)

Several of the Marauders had flown on 50 or more operations, such as 'The Saint' (S-Sugar), which notched up more than 57, and 'Viking' (V-Viking) and 'Aloma' (G-George) each of which had more than 100.

Then, having totted up the figures, the squadron buckled down to its final task, ferrying homeward-bound soldiers of 6th SA Division to Bari in May 1945, on the first stage of their journey home. This done, it was disbanded.

In October 1946 the squadron was re-formed, equipped with Ansons and posted to Gollel for anti-tsetse fly spraying operations

40. As it slides down into a low-level run over its target the bomb-bay doors of this Canberra T Mk4 drop open.
41. Locked into a shallow dive, a Canberra B (I). 12 pops its air-brakes to slow it down for maximum precision in hitting the target.
42. High above the patchwork landscape, a Canberra breaks away into a graceful turn. The broad surfaces of the 'conventional' wing – adopted at a time when a swept configuration was all the rage – contributes to its exceptional stability.

in Zululand. In April 1947 the squadron was moved to Mtubatuba to continue the spraying work. Later the squadron was equipped with Sikorsky S-51 helicopters, but was disbanded again, to become a flight of No. 28 Squadron.

At the end of 1963 No. 12 Squadron reappeared on the active list when it was re-formed as the SAAF's first jet bomber squadron, flying Canberras.

No. 12 Squadron is still flying Canberras today.

41

THE MB-326 IMPALA
Gazelle in camouflage

43.   An Impala Mk 1 of No. 5 (Chaka) Squadron hurtles into a sudden blaze of sunlight as it rounds a huge koppie near AFB Pietersburg during a low-level navigational exercise.

Ask the average South African if he knows anything about the Impala and the chances are that he will reply: 'The Silver Falcons', for the SAAF's renowned aerobatics team has delighted crowds at air shows for more than a decade.

But the two locally-built variants of the Macchi MB-326 which most people know by the generic name of Impala are much more than mere instruments of the SAAF's public relations officers. The 'Imps', as their pilots affectionately call them, play a key role in what is generally acknowledged to be Africa's most efficient air force.

In its oldest role the Impala is a trainer in which newly-minted SAAF pilots get their first taste of flying a jet aircraft. In 14 years of SAAF service it has evolved, however, and the Impala Mark II is a light ground-attack fighter, heavily armed with rockets and cannon with which to strafe enemy positions.

The Impala type occupies a permanent place in the annals of South African aviation because it is the first aircraft to be wholly manufactured in the Republic. Until the ancestor of today's 'Imps' rolled off the assembly line near Johannesburg in 1966, South African airmen were dependent on an increasingly hostile outside market for the aircraft they flew.

The gestation process that culminated in the birth of the Impala began in the early 1960s when the SAAF embarked on a long-overdue expansion and modernization programme designed to lift

it, once and for all, out of the slough of penny-pinching neglect into which it had fallen since World War II.

Part of this programme consisted of a committee chaired by Professor L. J. Roux, then vice-president of the Council for Scientific and Industrial Research. Charged with investigating ways of maintaining the SAAF's more advanced fixed-wing aircraft and helicopters, the committee deliberated from July to December 1963 and produced a report that exceeded its original terms of reference.

A civilian organization should be established, it recommended, that would not only maintain the SAAF's jet aircraft and helicopters, but also undertake local manufacture of a jet trainer to replace the Harvards and Vampires then in use. It was also felt that it would be better if such a trainer were a proven and established type manufactured under licence rather than one designed from scratch.

The committee acknowledged that it would be an expensive venture; building aircraft, even relatively unsophisticated ones, is particularly costly because of the production facilities required. Furthermore, the finished product would be more expensive than its foreign-built equivalent because only a relatively small number could be absorbed by the SAAF.

On the other hand, the establishment of a local aircraft industry would lead to greater self-sufficiency, increased technical know-how and a greater national industrial potential.

It was a far-sighted and daring report. At that time southern Africa was one of the world's more stable regions, and the turmoil of the 1970s was still a long way into the future.

In the event, the SAAF accepted the Roux Committee's recommendations and began to evaluate aircraft produced in a number of countries, among them the French Air Fouga Magister, Britain's Hunting Jet Provost and Italy's Macchi MB-326. On May 9, 1964, the Chief of the South African Defence Force reported the little Italian two-seater to be the most suitable for local production.

The SAAF proposed to adopt the same fine light aircraft that remains in production and development to this day, almost a quarter-century after the prototype made its first flight in Italy in December 1957.

The MB-326 type was the brainchild of Dr I. E. Bazzochi, then general manager of the famed firm of Aeronautica Macchi. His original proposal was made in 1954, less than a decade after Italy's superb engineers had begun to pull themselves out of the decline following World War II.

Three years later the first MB-326 flew – and was an immediate success. It was adopted by the Italian Air Force as a replacement for the piston-engined T-6 (the aircraft known elsewhere as the Harvard), and the MB-326D was selected by Alitalia, the Italian state airline, as its standard pilot trainer. Six aircraft of the MB-326B version were exported to Tunisia in 1962, while the similar MB-326F was built for the Ghanaian Air Force.

In the meantime AerMacchi was still developing the type and eventually produced the MB-326G, which had a more powerful engine and a greater fuel capacity. This development went on to serve in a variety of air forces around the world. The Australians built it under licence as the MB-326H. The MB-326GB has been supplied to countries such as Zaire, Zambia and (as a naval aircraft) Argentina. Brazil obtained a licence to manufacture its own MB-326GC under the name AT-26 Xavante, and also exported some to Togo and Bolivia. Later versions were exported by AerMacchi to the Arab oil state of Dubai and to the company's original foreign customers, Tunisia and Ghana.

But much of that still lay ahead when, in 1964, the South African government obtained a local manufacturing licence and gave the giant Bonuskor conglomerate the go-ahead to set up production facilities as soon as possible.

Bonuskor did not drag its corporate feet. In January 1965 it registered two new companies, Bonaero Beleggings (Pty) Ltd and Atlas Aircraft Corporation, and set about the awe-inspiring task of building a functioning aircraft industry almost from scratch. The Republic possessed the necessary industrial infra-structure but little else: it had no aircraft factory to use as a starting-point; local expertise in aircraft production was minimal; and not only was there a lack of most key technical personnel but there was no time to train them.

Bonuskor bridged the latter gap by importing experts from the French Sud Aviation company to oversee the setting up of a production line, and by launching a world-wide campaign to recruit the skilled technicians South Africa could not supply. These streamed in from all parts of the globe: within five years men of no less than 22 nationalities were working on the Atlas production line, many of them housed in two completely new Bonuskor-built suburbs, Bonaero Park and Impala Park.

The Atlas factory rose next door to Johannesburg's Jan Smuts Airport, the country's largest and most modern air facility, which is conveniently close to SAAF Headquarters and various air bases, and has a number of firms in the vicinity specializing in the production of avionics and radio equipment.

It was decided to prime Atlas's pumps by importing 16 MB-326Ms in knocked-down form. These would be assembled locally, and gradually more and more locally-produced parts would be used until full South African manufacture was achieved.

The first knocked-down MB-326M was shipped to Cape Town by sea early in 1966, little more than a year after the scheme got off the ground. This aircraft, No. 460, was assembled in the workshops of Cape Town's big airforce base, Ysterplaat. It was test-flown in May and formally handed over to the SAAF on June 3.

The first Impala incorporating South African parts flew on November 8 of the same year, but it was not until almost exactly 12 months later that the first Impala of substantially local manufacture first took to the air; and by the time the last MB-326M to be built was handed over to the SAAF on August 29, 1974, the Impala, including its engine, was almost completely South African made.

This was the end of the first chapter in the Impala saga, but another followed on almost immediately. In the years since 1966 the AerMacchi designers had developed their original jet trainer into an efficient single-seater light ground attack/operational trainer called the MB-326K: thus the original Impala became the Mk I and the MB-326K was selected by South Africa for licence manufacture as the Mk II. The first Mk II, No. 1000, was taken on charge by the SAAF on April 22, 1974, and was followed by six more, all of them complete aircraft supplied by AerMacchi; subsequently, however, all have been built by Atlas.

Today Impalas of one kind or another can be seen flying in almost any part of South Africa. 'Pupes' (pupil pilots of the SAAF) who have completed their initial training on the dependable old Harvard go on to the Flying Training School Langebaanweg, near Cape Town, where they hone their skills on the good-natured little jets. Mk IIs serve at the SAAF's 85 Advanced Flying School near Pietersburg, where they are used for operational training. Several of SAAF's Citizen Force squadrons (consisting of part-time fliers backed up by a hard core or regulars) also fly Mk IIs, though each retains some Mk Is for dual training.

From the earliest days of their SAAF service, Impalas have been involved in aerobatics. The forerunners of the Silver Falcons were the whimsically-named 'Bumbling Bees', a more or less ad hoc team formed by Commandant Chris Prins at what was then the Air Operational School at Langebaanweg. The 'Bumbling Bees' disbanded when the Air Operational School was transferred to Air Force Base Pietersburg in the Transvaal at the end of 1967, and Langebaanweg became the Central Flying School, later the Flying Training School.

Commandant Prins re-formed his aerobatic team in late 1968, although the name of 'Silver Falcons' was not adopted until January 1970

Ten years is a long time in a pilot's career, and since the team's formation it has had no less than nine complete turnovers of men and machines. But a decade has not dulled the glamour of the Silver Falcons. Every time they appear in public, they effortlessly steal the show from their winged brethren, as gracefully beautiful as the delicate bushveld antelope for which their aircraft are named.

Historical note on No. 4 Squadron SAAF
No. 4 Squadron was formed at Durban in April 1939 and equipped with Hawker Hartbees, Hawker Furies and a few Wapitis – one of which flew one of the SAAF's first coastal reconnaissance missions after the outbreak of World War II.

The squadron was disbanded in December 1939, but was re-formed at Waterkloof air base on March 24, 1941 with Hurricanes. Equipped with Curtiss Mohawks and a few Furies, it underwent operational training in East Africa before going to Egypt to convert to Tomahawks.

In November 1941 the squadron went into action in the Western Desert and later moved to Italy, by then flying Kittyhawks and finally Spitfires. It was still in Italy when the war ended and was disbanded for the second time in October 1945.

Six years later, however, in January 1951, it was re-formed at Waterkloof from the Active Citizen Force element of No. 1 Squadron, and equipped with Harvards and Spitfires – only to be disbanded yet again on October 10, 1958.

Slightly more than three years later, on November 1, 1961, No. 4 Squadron was resurrected for the third time and based at AFS Swartkop, flying Harvards. This time it had come to stay, and in August 1972 the squadron was re-equipped with Impala Mk Is before moving house to AFB Waterkloof in December that year.

No. 4 Squadron now flies Impala Mk Is and Mk IIs, which it first received in November 1976.

Historical note on No. 5 Squadron SAAF

The pilots of No. 5 Squadron SAAF call themselves 'the Chakas' in honour of the greatest and fiercest of all the Zulu warrior-kings, and they have a solid record of wartime achievement to prove their right to the title.

In its first incarnation – as a fighter-bomber unit formed at Cape Town in April 1939 – No. 5 Squadron lasted only eight months before being disbanded in December.

On May 7, 1941, however, No. 5 was re-formed at Swartkop air station near Pretoria. Now first and foremost a fighter squadron, the authorities intended that the new unit would be trained along improved lines derived from recent lessons learnt in aerial combat.

This scheme did not turn out quite as planned. It was true that the commanding officer and his flight commanders all had recent operational experience (the CO was, in fact, the famous Major J. E. Frost DFC), but most of the pilots were new hands at this deadliest of pastimes.

Nevertheless, intensive training was carried out with the Mohawk IVs allotted to the squadron, and in December 1941 it left for Egypt. Re-equipped with Tomahawk IIBs, No. 5 Squadron was given the task of shipping patrols, late in February 1942, one of these excursions provided it with its first 'kill', a Junkers Ju-88, on March 3.

Some time after this the squadron was taken off shipping duties and deployed in the Western Desert in its primary role, that of a fighter unit. Now its operational career had begun in earnest, and many 'kills' were claimed by what came to be known as 'the Lucky Squadron'. But losses were heavy, too. On June 3, 1942, the Luftwaffe's top-scoring Western Desert ace, Oberleutnant Hans-Joachim Marseille, shot down five of the squadron's Tomahawks and damaged a sixth all in a matter of minutes, during an encounter over Bir Hacheim.

June 1942 brought another heavy blow to the erstwhile 'Lucky Squadron', when Major Frost failed to return from a mission and was never seen again.

Thus battered by fortune, No. 5 Squadron soldiered on with its trusty, but definitely outclassed, Tomahawks (although a captured Bf-109 was acquired at one stage and used as a unit 'taxi').

At the end of 1942 the squadron discarded its Tomahawks for Kittyhawk IIIs and later Kittyhawk IVs, and began to specialize in the ground-attack role, though still functioning as an ordinary fighter squadron when the need or opportunity arose.

When the war in Africa ended, the squadron moved base to Malta for the invasion of Sicily, and in due course moved to Sicily itself for operations over Italy. The squadron was concentrating on ground attack now; its main enemy had become not German fighters but anti-aircraft gunners, and on September 9, 1943, it lost the commanding officer to flak – its fifth CO to be killed in action.

44. Glittering against a sombre seascape, the Silver Falcons aerobatic team goes into a dizzying formation wing-over. Renowned scene-stealers at any air show they attend, the pilots of the Silver Falcons team are not full-time aerobatics specialists, but instructors from Flying Training School Langebaanweg who rehearse in their spare time.

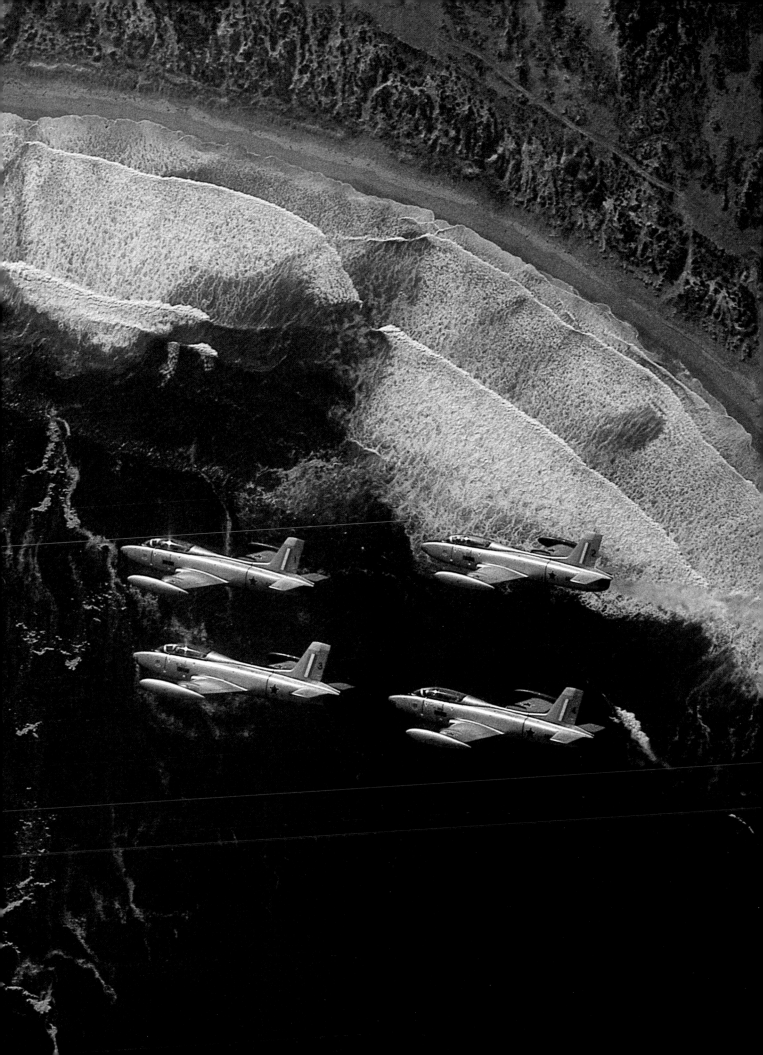

In October that year the squadron moved to Italy for more close-support and general fighter-bomber missions, some of them flown over Yugoslavia. No. 5 Squadron took part in the desperate battles on the Sangro River, at Monte Cassino and along the Gustav and Gothic Lines, finally discarding its Kittyhawks to be re-equipped with Mustang IIIs (and later Mustang IVs). It used these superb fighters to good effect in Italy and Yugoslavia until the end of the war in Europe, by which time it could boast of 69 confirmed 'kills', not to mention hundreds of trains, vehicles and German installations destroyed during ground attacks.

Disbanded when war ended, No. 5 Squadron was re-formed in December 1950 as a Durban-based Active Citizen Force unit flying Harvards and known as 'the Chakas' – a name first carried on a Tomahawk during the Western Desert days.

The squadron was re-equipped with Impala Mk Is in July 1973, and since March 1970 has enjoyed the freedom of entry into Durban – the highest municipal honour any city can bestow on a military unit, and one which dates back to the walled cities of the Middle Ages. The squadron started receiving Impala Mk IIs early in 1981.

45. An Impala Mk 1 of No. 5 Squadron pulls out of a loop above the Albert Dam near Pietermaritzburg, Natal.
46. Displaying its famed agility in the air, an Impala Mk 1 rolls out of inverted flight above Durban Harbour.
47. This is what it looks like from the rear seat of an Impala Mk 1 as a formation's component aircraft team up after individual take-off. In the foreground is the pilot's ejection seat; the 'brackets' are, in fact, canopy-breakers.
48. 'Oh, I have snapped the surly bonds of earth, and danced the sky on laughter-silvered wings . . .' An Impala Mk 1 brings to life the beautiful opening lines of 'High Flight', the famous airmen's poem, as it passes before a sun-tinged cloudscape while on a leisurely sweep over the sea off Durban.

HISTORICAL NOTES ON SQUADRONS 6, 7, 8 AND
FLYING TRAINING SCHOOLS ON PAGES 166-167

49

50   51

49. Sleek and deadly, a South African-made Impala Mk II of No. 4 Squadron swims through the air-oceans high above the winter-brown landscape of the Transvaal.

50. Standing by for a formation take-off, two Impala Mk IIs, armed with rockets and gun-pods, are a photographer's joy and a modeller's delight.

51. This Impala Mk II's pilot is wasting no time in getting down – or up – to business; he is barely off the ground, but his undercarriage is already being retracted. 'Cleaning up fast' is how pilots describe this hasty clearing of the decks.

52 53 54
55 56

52, 53, 56. Even the Citizen Force squadrons such as No. 5 Squadron display superb formation flying.

54. The Silver Falcons in formation.

55. This is the one that makes the children's – and the adults' – eyes pop at the air shows. The Silver Falcons go into a downward bomb-burst, their specially fitted smoke-pots painting huge splashes of white on the endless canvas of the sky.

THE DOUGLAS DAKOTA
Methuselah with wings

57. A sight many soldiers and airmen in many wars have seen at one time or another – the unmistakeable lines of a Dakota silhouetted against the indigo early-morning sky as it stands by to take them home . . . or to the fighting line. This 'Dak' is part of No. 44 Squadron.
58. Overleaf: A Dakota gets in close while flying near the Transvaal's Hartebeespoort Dam, its Pratt & Whitney Twin Wasp radial engines hammering out the hoarse-throated harmony that has been heard all over the world for nearly half a century.

The Douglas Dakota is a latter-day legend in almost every far-flung corner of the earth where men have taken to the air. 'Dakota' is only one of a string of names, official designations and nicknames that servicemen from scores of nations have given her in the past four or five decades. The Americans call her (among other things) the 'Gooney Bird' and the 'C-47'. Elsewhere in the English-speaking world she is generally known simply as the 'Dak', while irreverent South African troopies who have survived long, noisy, bumpy journeys strapped into her back-breaking seats have given her the vulgar yet affectionate soubriquet of 'the Vomit Comet'.
The Douglas Dakota is now nearing its 40th year of service as a South African Air Force transport aircraft, and seems in no danger of being phased out, even though it is by far the oldest military aircraft type still on active duty in southern Africa – the SAAF is one of the world's largest Dakota operators.
The Dakota cannot boast of being bigger, better, faster or more beautiful than anything else in its class. It is neat but distinctly homely; its top speed is a mere 256 km/h or so; and its carrying

capacity is strictly limited – park a Dakota next to a SAAF C-130B Hercules or Transall C-160Z and it is dwarfed.
But it is still up there, slogging away at its unglamorous job, long after transport aircraft of more recent vintage have been relegated to the scrap-heap in other parts of the world. This is partly because of anti-South African boycotts, but mainly because the Dakota has some supremely important virtues. It has few vices, is sturdy enough to stand up to rough handling and bad conditions, is simple to maintain and would cost a great deal to replace in quantity.
For these and other reasons the Dakota remains an important SAAF short-haul aircraft and general work-horse. Military Daks drone into and out of the southern African fighting zones of the 1980s with the same leisurely aplomb they displayed in the dangerous skies over the battlefields of World War II; all that has really changed is that the pilot behind a Dakota's control column is usually many years younger than the aircraft he is flying.
What South Africans know as the Douglas Dakota has been around since December 1935, when it first took to the air in the United States. It was known then as the DC-3 or 'DST' (for 'Douglas Sleeper Transport'), and it created quite a stir because it had bunks in which its 20-odd passengers could snatch some sleep during those long, long pre-jet flights.
The DC-3 revolutionized American air travel, but it did not become a legend till World War II put it into uniform.
Large numbers of DC-3s were built for, or bought by, the United States Army Air Force and the United States Navy. The USN gave

the type the designation 'R4D'. The USAAF allocated several 'C' (for 'cargo') numbers to various types of DC-3s. The basic designation was C-47, but there were also the C-47A and the C-47B, (which were fitted with supercharged engines for arduous flights over the Burmese 'Hump' into China), and the C-53 Skytrooper, which could carry 29 soldiers at a time – a great number by the standards of those days. Other military versions were designated C-68, C-84 and C-117, while ex-civil DC-3s taken over by the USAAF were numbered from C-48 to C-52.

All, however, were just variations on the DC-3 theme, and it seemed at times that there was nothing the stubby little transport could not turn its hand to. It dropped paratroopers and supplies, landed on impossibly short and bumpy jungle strips, ferried VIPs and towed targets. There was an amphibious model with twin floats, and the glider version called the XCG-17.

The 'Gooney Bird' swiftly became famous for its stoutness under almost any circumstances. It could be relied on to fly even after suffering incredible damage. One C-47 serving in China was reported to have been flown to safety after a badly damaged wing had been replaced with a much smaller one from a Douglas DC-2.

The DC-3/C-47 did not just fly on all fronts in World War II, but sometimes served both sides as well. The Russians built more than 2 000 under licence, calling it the Lisunov Li-2; but the Japanese had also acquired a prewar licence and by 1945 they had turned out 487 to fly in the service of the Rising Sun, calling it the L2D (Allied intelligence boffins gave the L2D the code-name of 'Tabby', but it was none other than the old 'Gooney Bird', no matter how you sliced it).

There has not been a new DC-3 built since May 1946 – because at the end of World War II there were so many surplus C-47s around that it was not worth while for the Douglas Aircraft Corporation to go back to large-scale civilian production.

So the years rolled by, and the DC-3/C-47 stayed in harness, tirelessly coursing through the sky all over the world. In April 1965 a DC-3 of North Central Airlines in the United States was reported to have logged no less than 83 000 hours without an accident, which was thought to be a record at that time. Probably it was, but quite likely some old 'Dak' has improved on the record in the intervening years.

The Vietnam War saw the emergence of yet another variation on the DC-3 theme. Fitted with the ultra-rapid-firing General Electric Minigun, the 'Gooney Bird' became a 'dragon ship', and flew out to amble around Vietcong positions, methodically pounding them with bullets.

The DC-3/C-47 entered South African service by way of the Royal Air Force, which acquired a total of 1 951 of the planes during World War II and gave them the later-to-be-famous name of 'Dakota'. Some of these were passed on to South Africa, which had had to struggle through the early war years with a motley collection of ex-South African Airways Junkers Ju-52/3m's, some creaky old ex-RAF Vickers Valentias and a batch of Lockheed Lodestars – ordered for SAA but diverted to military use.

A total of 84 Lend-Lease Dakotas were transferred to the SAAF during World War II. The first of them – still wearing its USAAF serial number, 42-23630, although an RAF serial, FD874, had been allocated to it – was collected at Accra by Captain Johannes Slabbert and his crew on June 21, 1943. Captain Slabbert flew it to South Africa by way of El Geneina, Juba and Kasama. He landed at Germiston, Transvaal, on June 25 after 33 hours and 38 minutes' actual flying time.

The SAAF's pioneer Dakota was given a new serial, 6801, and allocated to No.5 Wing, to start many years of yeoman service.

Little time was wasted in putting 6801 and its successors to work. That same month two SAAF flights were merged at Almaza, Egypt,

to form No. 28 Squadron. At first it was equipped with Ansons and Wellingtons, but on July 29 received its first Dakota. On March 11, 1944, another Dakota squadron, No. 44, was formed at Almaza from elements of No. 43 Squadron, and took over its first 'Dak' at Cairo on April 27.

The two squadrons earned their keep in the long, weary months of war that remained. No. 28 Squadron operated out of Castel Benito until June 1944, and then moved its headquarters to Maison Blanche. No.44 Squadron ended up at Bari in December 1944, dropping supplies to Yugoslav partisans. Elements of both squadrons also operated from other bases as circumstances demanded.

At the end of the war the two squadrons were disbanded and their Dakotas, together with those already in No.5 Wing, began a mammoth task which endeared them to thousands of Springbok soldiers. Unlike its predecessors, Major-General Evered Poole's 6th South African Division did not return to South Africa as a formation at the end of the Italian campaign. A grateful government started repatriating its soldiers while the division was still in Italy, and the Dakotas of No.5 Wing logged thousands of hours ferrying war-weary troops back to their homes and families.

And then, with the war over, the SAAF's Dakotas suffered the traditional fate of the warrior left without a war. The pruning of the vastly swollen SAAF saw many of them virtually given away to civil operators for trifling sums ranging from a ridiculous £200 to an only slightly less laughable £2 750. Numbers of the bargain-basement ex-SAAF Dakotas were converted for civil use and flew in countries as far afield as Canada, Britain and Burma. Some ended up at the 'sharp end' again – however, this time in the 1948 Israeli War of Independence.

One Dakota suffered the bizarre fate of being turned into a restaurant near Johannesburg. Among the Dakotas summarily disposed of was none other than the pioneering No. 6801 Captain Slabbert had collected at Accra in 1943. She and seven others were sold to the SAA, and flew in civil livery between 1946 and 1971. In this time three of them went out of service, but eventually the five survivors found their way back to the SAAF . . . Including old No. 6801, which had spent her time in Civvy Street as ZS-DJB, and then returned to military duties, as 6889. Those Dakotas that never left the SAAF served with Nos. 28, 44 and 60 squadrons during the early post-war period, and later Dakota units included Nos.25 and 27 Squadrons, as well as the SAAF's Multi-Engined Conversion Unit.

The SAAF's Dakotas did not take part in the mammoth Berlin Airlift that saved thousands of Germans from starvation during 1948 and 1949, but their pilots were there flying 'Gooney Birds' borrowed from the RAF's Transport Command.

Dakotas have participated in several wars since then. SAAF 'Gooney Birds' took part in the Angolan War, in which air supply played a large role, and are serving now in the Namibian border campaign. At the time of writing, Mk 3s and Mk 4s are in SAAF service with 44 Squadron at Air Force Base Swartkop, near Pretoria; No. 25 Squadron at Air Force Base Ysterplaat, near Cape Town; and No. 86 Advanced Flying School at Air Force Base Bloemspruit, near Bloemfontein.

Zimbabwe's air force also operates a number of battle-scarred Dakotas (one of them actually dropped paratroops at the Battle of Arnhem in 1944, before ending up in the Central African bush). Like their colleagues of the SAAF, these Dakotas are contributing to the still-growing store of anecdotes about the fabulous 'Gooney Bird'.

Not long ago one of them made a rough landing on a bush airstrip, hit a tree and tore off about a metre of one wing-tip. The air mechanic responsible for repairing it simply trimmed off the rough edges and bound up the wing-tip with some masking tape . . . After which the Dak carried out the rest of its programme for that day,

apparently none the worse for damage that would have grounded many another aircraft. Small wonder, then, that the writer who first revealed this classic Dak story could not help but quote an airman's poem:

'. . . They patch her up with masking tape,
And paper clips and strings;
And still she flies and never dies,
Methuselah with wings . . .'

Historical note on No. 25 Squadron SAAF

A layman might find it strange that a transport unit like No. 25 Squadron should have as its motto the warlike Xhosa words 'Laduduma Ezulweni' (Thunder from the Sky), but this was its motto in an active fighting career during World War II and, in fact, it flew the last raid undertaken by the SAAF in that conflict. Today its motto is the milder *Adiuvamus* (We help).

It would be fair to say that No. 25 Squadron got off to a bad start in life when it was formed on July 1, 1942 from No. 33 Flight.

To begin with, its base near Port Elizabeth was called Cemetery Camp, and in the early stages the only aircraft it had to fly were some ageing Ansons belonging to No. 33 Flight SAAF, from which it was formed, and an even more obsolete Wapiti.

Officially it was classed as a torpedo, bomber and reconnaissance squadron, and in due course it received more pilots to bring it up to strength for the day when it would become operational with B-34 Venturas.

The Venturas began to arrive on September 12, 1942, before any conversion training had been done. This problem was overcome by retaining the Venturas' ferry pilots till the Anson experts had undergone a somewhat hurried course to accustom them to their temperamental new machines.

During this formative period coastal patrols – the now-defunct No. 33 Flight's task – were still being carried out with assistance from No. 42 and No. 44 Air Schools.

The squadron's first submarine sighting was made in November 1942, but the subsequent attack was unsuccessful.

In February 1943 the squadron left its ominously-named base and moved to an airfield at St Albans, also in the Port Elizabeth area, where it was reinforced by the attachment of a flight of Dutch naval Catalina amphibians from No. 321 Squadron RAF.

A satisfactory modus vivendi was envolved, in terms of which the

Venturas flew the daylight patrols and the Catalinas operated at night. This state of affairs lasted till late in the year, when the Catalinas were withdrawn and the Venturas took over the night patrols as well. A detached flight operating from East London also carried out night patrols, using Ansons because the airstrip from which it operated was too short to accommodate Venturas after dark.

In January 1944 the squadron's establishment was reduced to such an extent that it had to operate in conjunction with other coastal units. This led to its aircraft venturing far from their home base, and also its first loss.

In March 1944 the squadron was warned to stand by for a move to the Mediterranean, and by June that year – having lost its new PV-1 Venturas and been reissued with the B-34 version – it was in Italy. The intention had been to employ it on maritime patrols, but now its role was abruptly changed and the unit was attached to the Balkan Air Force for operations against shipping and harbours along the Dalmatian coast.

No. 25 Squadron's first raid in its new role took place on August 30, 1944, and during September 40 missions – a total of 243 sorties – were flown.

In November the squadron began to convert to Marauders, but without interrupting its B-34 operations which now included strikes against German lines of communication in Yugoslavia – in spite of the foul weather characteristic of that time of the year.

Operations in support of Tito's partisans continued to the very end of the war; on May 4, 1945, while taking part in the last SAAF raid of the war, a Marauder was shot down by German ground fire.

Disbanded in July 1945, the squadron was re-formed on January 1, 1951 from No. 21 Squadron SAAF, as a part-time transport unit flying Dakotas, and continued in this role till it disappeared when it was renumbered to No. 44 Squadron in November 1953.

In February 1968 the squadron was re-formed from the long-standing Ysterplaat Station Flight and again equipped with Dakotas.

59. A Dakota of No. 44 Squadron wends its way over the bright Western Transvaal veld en route to the operational area. It is slow at the best of times and given a strong headwind is downright plodding, but the 'Dak' remains as reliable as a well-tuned grandfather clock.
60. An aircraft's camouflage and its background need not have the same pattern – what matters is how they blend, as this No. 44 Squadron Dakota in full war-paint proves so conclusively.

THE DOUGLAS DC-4 SKYMASTER
Old fiddle, new tune

61. A suit of camouflage has replaced the eye-catching silver trim of its civilian days, but this Skymaster of No. 44 Squadron still has something about it that recalls the early days of luxury as it drones through the southern African sky, carrying – what? A party of VIPs? A load of war-weary troopies? At one time or another the Skymasters have handled both.

Old fiddles can make fine music, whether the tune is a delicate concerto or a rousing jig – and a parallel of this adage can be found in the story of the five venerable Skymasters of No.44 Squadron.

There was a time when the Skymaster was South Africa's premier passenger aircraft, initially on overseas and later on internal services. But times change and so do aircraft, and the days when Skymasters plied between Johannesburg and London are long past. Today's Skymaster passengers are usually soldiers and airmen in battledress, travelling between Pretoria's Swartkop air base and remote, heavily-protected landing strips in the border operational area.

In a sense the wheel has turned full circle. The DC-4 type started off as a wartime aircraft, even though it had been designed as a civil airliner in the first place.

It saw the light of day on a designer's drawing-board at America's Douglas Aircraft Company in February 1936, and if it bears a startling resemblance to the SAAF's veteran Dakotas, this is no coincidence. The DC-4 was intended to be the Douglas company's eventual replacement for its spectacularly successful DC-3.

It was a much more ambitious venture altogether. It was considerably larger than the DC-3, had four engines instead of two and

boasted many innovations, among them a retractable tricycle undercarriage, three fins and rudders, in addition to a pressurized passenger-cabin.

The new venture – designated the DC-4E – flew in June 1938, slightly more than two years after designing began. But it was not a success, being too large and uneconomical for the small post-depression airline market of the time.

The Douglas company cut its losses by selling the unprofitable prototype to Japan and then redesigned the DC-4 as a smaller, unpressurized aircraft with a single, instead of a triple, fin and rudder.

The new design, called the DC-4A, had no chance to prove itself on the civilian market. American participation in World War II loomed, and the United States War Department took over all provisional orders for the type, redesignating it the C-54.

The first C-54 flew in February 1942 and, in the years that followed, various versions such as the C-54A, the C-54B and C-54D ferried military cargo and passengers to and from many parts of the war-torn world. By the end of World War II a total of 1 165 C-54s had been built, including two experimental ones designated the XC-114 and YC-116.

As soon as the war ended, Douglas returned to peacetime production with a purely commercial variant called the DC-4-1009. Altogether 79 of these were built before production ended two years later, in August 1947.

Among the Douglas company's earliest post-war customers was

South African Airways, which took delivery of three DC-4-1009s at the end of 1945. Registered as ZS-AUA, ZS-AUB and ZS-AUC, the DC-4s soon became familiar to thousands of South African and foreign passengers as they droned to and from Johannesburg and London on the 'Springbok Service' which SAA ran in co-operation with the British Overseas Airways Corporation.

The Springbok Service's traffic soon became so heavy that SAA bought three more DC-4-1009s, ZS-BMF, ZS-BMG and ZS-BMH, just before production of the type ceased in 1947 – ZS-BMH was, in fact, the last DC-4 to come off the Douglas assembly line (now 6904 in the SAAF).

Augmented by an ex-USAAF C-54 registered as ZS-BWN, the SAA Skymasters stayed on the South African-Britain run till they were replaced by Constellations in 1950. Thereafter they were used on internal routes, and many will remember flying in them on the popular reduced-rate 'Skycoach' service SAA ran for some years.

The Skymaster fleet was diminished by two at the end of 1959, when ZS-AUC and its ex-USAAF stablemate, ZS-BWN, were sold to UAT French Airline, flying later for the Ivory Coast's Air Afrique and thereafter for Air Chad and Air Comores. The other five stayed in SAA service for another seven years and were then transferred to the SAAF – ZS-AUA, ZS-BMF, ZS-BMG and ZS-BMH in January, and ZS-AUB in October 1966.

On June 30, 1962 in cloudy conditions, a Harvard of No. 5 Squadron sliced through the tail-fin of an SAA Skymaster on finals to Louis Botha Airport. It is a tribute to the aircraft's strength and durability that it landed safely with no injuries to its passengers. The Harvard lost part of its right wing but the pilot, Lieutenant Paul Sinclair and his passenger then managed to parachute to safety seconds before it crashed.

The Skymasters – properly speaking, the name 'Skymaster' should apply only to the C-54 military version – were allocated to No. 44 Squadron at Swartkop, and 14 years later they are still there, slogging away at their unglamorous but essential task of supplying the men engaged in the border war. Now and again a party of VIPs arrives at Swartkop to be taken on a visit to the operational area, and for a while the Skymaster reflects something of its heyday as South Africa's finest airliner, but this does not happen very often. Its passengers are mostly civil servants burdened with fat briefcases or young soldiers with the angry dust of the fighting zone still on their boots as they clamber aboard, and the leisurely approaches of the SAA days have been replaced by breath-taking swoops to earth to foil any insurgent who might be lying in wait with a heat-seeking missile.

It seems likely that the Skymasters of No.44 Squadron will go their dependable way from Swartkop base for some time to come. Their sturdy airframes are far from exhausted by the endless journeys to the far corners of southern Africa, and each aircraft has been fitted with modern avionics, radar and navigation systems. Like their older brothers, the Dakotas, the SAAF's Skymasters are not yet ready to bow out.

Historical note on No. 44 Squadron SAAF

No. 44 Squadron came into the world full-grown, as it were, when No. 43 Squadron was renumbered at Cairo West on March 12, 1944. A transport unit, it started off with Ansons, but within a month of its formation was engaged in intensive training and conversion to Dakotas, assisted by veterans from No. 267 Squadron RAF and No. 28 Squadron SAAF.

From April 27, 1944, the squadron began to take its own Dakotas on charge, and on May 20 the pilots soloed for the first time. By July the squadron was up to strength and became operational, its first scheduled flights taking it to the Levant, Arabia and the Persian Gulf area by way of the Sudan.

It also made special unscheduled flights to destinations as far apart as Takoradi on the Gold Coast (now Ghana) and Karachi, India (now in Pakistan); during August 1944, the first full month on operations, the squadron logged 1 500 flying hours (and also suffered its first loss).

Scheduled 'runs' soon expanded to Italy, Cyprus and north-west Africa, with special trips to numerous places in the Middle East and neighbouring areas, ranging from Rome to Sharjah.

By September 1944 the squadron was well into its stride, transporting a total of 3 305 passengers and 549 130 kg of freight – a very good show for a new unit – and its performance was not a flash in the pan: in October it flew 1 069 hours on scheduled flights and 1 006 hours on special missions, including a trip to Russia.

Some detachments of the unit operated separately, while four of No. 44 Squadron's Dakotas reinforced No. 267 Squadron RAF in the Balkan Air Force. The vital but hard and unglamorous work continued into the new year, one unusual mission in December 1944 being the ferrying of British troops to Greece to quell faction-fighting among the various national liberation movements.

In February 1945 the squadron moved to the Italian port of Bari for operations in the Balkans and elsewhere, and in spite of bad weather conditions, carried out transport flights in support of the Yugoslav partisans; in March it evacuated some 1 000 partisans from what the pilots jocularly called 'Jug-Land' – in spite of the fact that at one stage a temporary halt had to be called because the airfield in use was occupied by the Germans for 24 hours.

Supply drops were also carried out, the first night drops being made on April 1, and the squadron's pilots found themselves landing on perilously crude airstrips behind the German lines to evacuate casualties.

The squadron's activities were not confined to the Balkans. Throughout this time its aircraft (now numbering 30, and including a few Ansons from the Cairo days) were still undertaking general transport flights to such places as the south of France, Turkey, Egypt and even Britain – the cargo carried including VIPs, passengers, wounded and freight.

The squadron continued daylight supply drops to the Yugoslav partisans till May 5, 1945. The end of European hostilities did not drop the curtain on No. 44 Squadron's activities, and flights to Britain and various destinations in the Middle East continued until it was disbanded at Bari on December 6, 1945.

In November 1953 the squadron was re-formed as an ACF Dakota transport unit at AFS Swartkop by renumbering No. 25 Squadron. Since early 1963 it has been staffed partly by regulars, but its work has not changed. Strengthened by the addition of Skymasters in 1966, it still carries freight and passengers of all kinds.

It has also carried out supply-dropping and paratroop missions, and has a special ambulance Dakota always on stand-by

The squadron received its colours from the State President, Jim Fouché, on November 16, 1968.

62. There can be no doubt about their family relationship as this Dakota of No. 44 Squadron closes up on its younger and bigger Skymaster brother. Both are from No. 44 Squadron.
63. Stately, but quite capable of cutting a couple of sedate capers, a Skymaster of No. 44 Squadron banks away from the camera. In the background are the foothills of the Magaliesberg Mountains.
64. A Skymaster begins its landing approach at Air Force Base Swartkop near Pretoria, showing its extraordinary amount of flap and outsize nosewheel.

THE LOCKHEED C-130B HERCULES
Aircraft for all seasons

65. A C-130 Hercules retracts its sturdy undercarriage just after taking off from AFB Waterkloof. Its distinctive dolphin-shaped nose carries a large area of glazing to provide excellent all-round vision – an important advantage to the pilot of an aircraft which is designed to land on airstrips that are often considerably less than perfect.

66. Overleaf: Its four engines and their paddle-blade propellors perfectly synchronized, a Hercules of No. 28 Squadron goes into a gentle banking turn over Hartebeestpoort Dam. But, when the occasion demands it, a Hercules can carry out considerably more violent manoeuvres than this.

Whoever gave the C-130 type the generic name of 'Hercules' made an inspired choice. If ever an aircraft deserved to be named after the strong man of mythology, capable of incredible labours, it is this big, mottled-brown bird.

The Hercules is neither glamorous nor speedy; if ever a 'kite' was built for carrying capacity and brute strength, it is the C-130. Which is not to say it does not have a certain appeal. In the eyes of a lot of people, a Hercules has the chunky, indomitably tough good looks of a fine Afrikander trek-ox. Nor are the looks deceptive. Like the trek-ox, the Hercules is a go-anywhere, do-anything, carry-anything, damn-the-distance creature which can absorb a lot of punishment before it balks.

This is why it has been deeply involved in dramatic 'boondock' rescues without number, not to mention such ventures as the Isrealis' successful Entebbe raid, and the equally daring, but ill-starred, attempt to free the American hostages in Teheran. Its many virtues have made the Hercules the most widely-used transport aircraft of its type in the world. So far more than 1 600 have been

produced by the Lockheed plant at Marietta, Georgia – two-thirds of them for its original customer, the United States armed forces.

The Marietta plant has produced king-sized warbirds since World War II, when it was built to turn out the famous Boeing B-29 Superfortresses. And a new legend was born there in July 1951, when Lockheed's design to a specification for a United States Air Force tactical medium cargo transport aircraft was accepted by the US government.

Three years later, on August 23, 1954, the first of two Hercules prototypes (both designated YC-130) made its maiden flight at Lockheed's plant in Burbank, California. After that the Marietta plant took over, and in December 1956 the first batch of production aircraft, designated the C-130A, was delivered to the USAF Tactical Air Command.

Within two years, in 1958, the Royal Australian Air Force placed the first foreign order – for 12 C-130As to replace some of its C-47 Dakotas. These were the last C-130As built, for in the same year the first of several improved Hercules versions appeared.

This was the C-130B, whose more powerful engines (Allison T56-A-7 turboprops) and strengthened undercarriage gave it an increased operating mass. The payload remained the same as that of the C-130A, but instead of being fitted for carrying under-wing fuel tanks, the C-130B had more integral fuel-tanks placed in the wings, giving it a considerably increased range.

By mid-1959 the C-130As in USAF service had chalked up a massive 500 000 flying hours for only three aircraft lost (one had been shot down and one crashed after a mid-air collision). Thus it was hardly surprising that when, in the early 1960 s, the SAAF decided to augment the Dakotas which were its only transports at the time, it turned to the Hercules. Only 29 C-130Bs were built for export, and seven of these were delivered to 28 Squadron SAAF in January 1963 to replace the Dakotas it had operated for 20 years. That it was a good choice, the events of the ensuing 17 years have proved.

The Hercules' secret lies in the superb design which gives the C-130 family its incredible versatility. The high-wing configuration that contributes to the C-130's ungainly looks makes it easy to load bulky cargoes into the hold, which can digest a mind-boggling amount – at one go a SAAF Hercules can carry three Alouette III helicopters, or two Bedford three-tonners and a Landrover.

The strong undercarriage is mounted on to the fuselage, rather than on fragile legs protruding from nacelles under the wings, making it capable of very rough landings without damage – the history of military aviation is studded with daring descents that turned out to be futile because the aircraft concerned damaged itself so badly it could not take off again – and the four Allison turboprops give it an excellent short take-off performance.

Having hit the dirt, the C-130 needs little nursing to get it back in the air. Its auxiliary power unit in the port undercarriage fairing provides complete independence of ground support vehicles.

The SAAF C-130s have proved themselves in many roles. It will be a long time before details of South Africa's involvement in Angola in 1975 and 1976 are made public, but is no secret that the 'Herks' played a major part in that semi-clandestine venture. The South Africans' hardest fighting took place at the worst possible time – in the rainy season, when vast stretches of landscape turn into sheets of water or large expanses of deep, glutinous mud. Consequently it was a roadbound war in many places, with the interventionists constantly battling against the clock. In these circumstances air-supply and air-trooping assumed paramount importance, and in the forefront of both were the C-130s.

As well as their military role, they were used for humanitarian purposes to help the authorities cope with the seemingly endless flood of refugees who fled the fighting. At one stage, 28 Squadron's C-130s ferried no fewer than 1 604 of these people from Angola to AFB Waterkloof outside Pretoria.

SAAF C-130s have taken part in many search-and-rescue operations and 28 Squadron's pilots are permanently on round-the-clock stand-by so that within two hours of receiving a call they can be airborne. On sea rescue missions the C-130s normally carry Lindholme gear to drop to the survivors.

An early example of the C-130's search-and-rescue work dates to November 1965, when two of the aircraft, Nos. 403 and 405, took part in the search for the crew of the SAAF Buccaneer that crashed in the Atlantic Ocean near Ascension Island. In this case the C-130s did not have to be summoned from the Republic; loaded with ground-support equipment, they were accompanying the Buccaneers on the flight from England.

Four years later, in October 1969, a C-130 took part in another search for a missing Buccaneer, lost at sea north of Durban.

In recent times C-130s have flown several long-range search-and rescue missions. One mission South Africans will remember well was the search for the yacht *Girasol,* lost in 1975 in the Indian Ocean south of Madagascar. More recently, in late-1979, C-130s searched for the coaster *Induna,* also lost south of Madagascar.

No. 28 Squadron also runs a regular shuttle service between Pretoria and Cape Town, using not only its C-130s, but also its Transall C-160s. Accommodation on this 'milk-run' is spartan. Between pallets of baggage can be crammed some 90 passengers on webbing seats that grow steadily more back-breaking with each passing minute. There are more comfortable ways to travel, but the shuttle service never lacks for 'customers' who prefer it to a day-and-a-half on a train or the hefty price of a commercial air ticket.

SAAF C-130s switched from a natural-metal and white finish to the standard olive drab-dark earth camouflage some time ago, the first appearing in early 1975. An unusual feature of this camouflage scheme is that although the belly of the fuselage is painted an uninterrupted dark sea grey, at the time of writing, the undersides of the wings retain the olive drab-dark earth arrangement.

Another unusual feature of the 'Herk' is that the SAAF prefers to call it the 'C-130' instead of insisting on its bearing a name rather than a manufacturer's designation. (In other cases, such as the AerMacchi AM3C and the Piaggio P166S, aircraft were actually given local names because their makers had not done so.)

And what of the C-130 today? In various guises it is still rolling off the production lines at the Marietta plant. The version of which the most were built was the third production version, the C-130E. The C-130E was very similar to the C-130B, but was given under-wing strong points for carrying long-range fuel tanks, to meet a USAF requirement specifying the carrying of adequate payloads across the Atlantic and Pacific Oceans. The C-130B's heavy fuselage side-door has been omitted from all subsequent versions to provide extra range.

There is also a civil version, the possibilities of which were being evaluated at Lockheed as early as 1964. Eventually a civilian C-130E, designated the L100-10, went into service, and apart from those used by US airlines, four were used by Zambia to ferry oil from Dar-es-Salaam, after Rhodesian UDI in 1966.

A stretched-fuselage version, the L100-20 was produced and sold in limited numbers, one example going to a South African airfreight company, Safair. The L100-20 was then further extended and designated L100-30, and Safair bought several of these – in fact, at one stage Safair was the world's largest operator of civil 'Herks', with 16 on its books.

In June 1979, there was an unusual – and impressive – display, at the Greenham Common International Air Tattoo in England. No less than 25 'Herks', ranging from an early production USAF C-130A to a brand-new RAAF C-130H, came together to mark the 25th anniversary of the first flight of the prototype YC-130. Will there be another in 1997? It is a moot point, but the way things are, the strongman of the sky will quite likely still be around to flex its muscles.

67. Standing easy after hours in the air, the red tags hanging from the covers of this Hercules's air intakes indicate it has finished work for the day . . . but that does not necessarily include the mechanics or the ground crew who have to keep it in flying condition.

68. This is what it looks like from the cockpit of a C-130 when it is accompanying one of its stable-mates to a distant dropping-zone with a load of paratroopers.

69. 'Geronimo!' That is not quite what the South African 'parabats' shout (they have a slightly earthier cry than their American counterparts) when they step out into thin air from the door of a C-130, but the effect is the same. The lower paratroopers in this photograph were dropped a little earlier by a C-160 Transall.

THE TRANSALL C-160Z
South Africa's pocket Hercules

70. Its main undercarriage housings give this Transall C-160Z of No. 28 Squadron a look of bow-legged menace as it drones over the Transvaal.
71. Overleaf: A Transall claws itself into flight, vortices of moist air blooming along the propellor-tips. The multi-wheeled undercarriage helps to spread the mass of the heavy loads this SAAF work-horse often carries.

Seen for the first time by the layman, a Transall C-160Z coming in to land proves something of a shock. Surely a Hercules has four engines instead of two? Yet it *must* be a Herk – there is that characteristic inverted banana tail and cumbersome appearance. But what has happened to the other two engines?

The answer is simple: The 'Hercules' is a Transall, and in spite of what might seem a strong family resemblance, it has never had more than two engines because it does not need them.

The Hercules and the Transall seem to resemble one another, but they neither share a common designer nor the same role. The Hercules is an all-American long-range transport; the Transall a medium-haul machine designed and built by two European nations. Its very name is a hybrid consisting of the first few letters of two German words.

Although the two aircraft are more or less the same size, the Hercules can carry a much heavier load than the Transall because it has four engines instead of two, and therefore a greater lifting capacity The Transall makes up for this, however, by having a slightly larger internal capacity than the Hercules, which means it can carry bulkier cargo.

Like many other modern military aircraft, it is the product of international co-operation – an ever more familiar phenomenon as research and development costs rise and standardization becomes increasingly important, particularly among Western Europe's anti-communist allies.

Its birth-processes go back to 1959, when representatives of France and Germany met to draw up preliminary operation requirements for an aircraft which would replace the Nord Noratlas, a widely-used veteran which at that time was the work-horse of both countries' transport fleets.

A bilateral working group known as '*Trans*porter *All*ianz' was formed and proceeded to design an aircraft which would satisfy French and German requirements. Both governments approved the resulting design, and by early 1960 construction of the prototype Transall was in progress.

In terms of the agreement, three major aircraft companies – France's Nord Aviation (later incorporated in Aérospatiale), and Germany's Weser Flugzeugbau (later VFW-Fokker) and Hamburger Flugzeugbau (later Messerschmitt-Bölkow-Blohm) – shared the project's development costs and were each responsible for the construction of specific parts of the airframe. Each plant had its own assembly line, however, and as it happened the prototype, which first flew on February 25, 1963, was assembled at the Nord plant in France.

The Transall already had a name: now it received a type-number as well – though in a rather unusual way. As well as five prototypes and six pre-production aircraft, France ordered 50 and the Germans 110, making a total of 160. An American-style 'C' (for 'Cargo') was added, and the Transall became the C-160.

Further prototypes were assembled by the German participants in the venture, and it was not until May 1965 that the first pre-production Transall took off on its maiden flight. The first five production samples, designated C-160F (for 'France'), did not follow until 1967.

By this time some discord had been sown among the production alliance by Germany's decision to reduce its 110-aircraft production order. After vehement French protests the Germans backpedalled, but were now landed with more Transalls than the Luftwaffe required. They solved the problem by finding a foreign customer – Turkey, which bought 20 of the earlier C-160Ds for its air force.

This export order was not followed by others, however, and at the time of writing the only other foreign military operator of Transalls is the South African Air Force. The SAAF expressed an interest in the Transalls almost from the time they began to fly – reportedly, although this has never been confirmed – because it had been deprived of buying more Lockheed C-130 Hercules transports as a result of the mandatory United States arms embargo.

Be that as it may, in the late 1960s the SAAF ordered nine Transalls, all of which were assembled at the Nord plant in France. This violated the agreement that the three partner-firms were to take turns at assembling the new aircraft, and was almost certainly a political decision, since the Nord plant was already lagging six months behind the German partners at the time production of the first SAAF Transall was due to start in late 1968.

The decision stood, however, and on January 28, 1969, the first SAAF C-160 was test-flown. Like other SAAF aircraft produced in France, it was given a 'Z' suffix, although there was no difference between it and the other production C-160Ds and C-160Fs.

SAAF crews were sent to France for conversion training, and towards the end of August 1969 the first South African Transalls were delivered. Delivery was completed in 1970, the earlier ones arriving in time to make their public debut at the SAAF 50th anniversary celebrations in February and March of that year.

Since then the big bird has had a busy time. Like its heftier colleague, the C-130 Hercules, the Transall is a versatile machine First and foremost, of course, it is a transport aircraft. It has large loading doors in the rear and another on the port side of the fuselage. The undercarriage can be made to 'kneel' backwards to facilitate loading through the rear doors; and its two British Rolls-Royce Tyne turboprop engines give it an exceptional aerial manoeuvrability and short take-off and landing capability which have delighted the crowds at air shows since 1970.

In a direct warlike role the Transall is used for dropping paratroops (it can accommodate up to 80), but it also flies a regular shuttle service between Pretoria's Waterkloof and Cape Town's Ysterplaat air bases, as well as a 'milk run' from the giant Grootfontein base in Namibia to others in the border operational area.

Transalls were also the heroes of a sensational sea-rescue in January 1980, after a Danish freighter named the *Pep Ice* had run firmly aground on the murderous Bassas da India reef in the Moçambique Channel.

For five days the plight of the stranded freighter's crew (which included a girl) grew increasingly perilous. Then the Danish government appealed to South Africa for help. This was followed by some speedy talking between the South African and Mocambique governments, which maintain a fairly solid working relationship.

The upshot of it was that three SAAF Transalls took off from Waterkloof air base, one of them carrying a partly dismantled Puma helicopter which had had its tail rotor, main rotor-blades, engines and firewall removed, together with such other protrusions as the main undercarriage fairings, to allow it to fit into the transport's hold.

After a refuelling stop at Maputo – probably the first for any SAAF aircraft since Mocambique became an independent Marxist state in 1974 – the Transalls landed on Europa Island, a flyspeck on the map, 65 km from the Bassas da India reef.

It was a perilous enterprise, since the Europa Island airstrip was uncomfortably short, only partly prepared and completely unknown to the SAAF aviators.

The Transalls put down safely, however, the Puma was assembled and the task of ferrying the *Pep Ice's* crew back to Europa Island commenced. That same night one of the Transalls arrived back at Waterkloof with all the rescued sailors; the other two aircraft followed the next day with the Puma and support equipment.

Production of the Transall ceased in October 1972, but that is not the end of its story. Five years later, in October 1977, the production line was re-opened as a result of a French Air Force order. The first of the 'new' Transalls rolled off the line in late 1979, and production will probably continue till the mid-1980s, since about 40 aircraft are to be produced in order to make the re-opening of the line an economically viable proposition.

Will some samples of the reborn Transalls end up in SAAF colours one day? It is an open question – a lot has happened since the first batch of the big French birds were ordered by South Africa. But no one can say that the SAAF's pocket Hercules has not earned its keep.

Historical note on No. 28 Squadron SAAF

No. 28 Squadron has been a transport unit ever since its formation at the South African Air Force's base depot at Almaza, Egypt, on June 1, 1943, though immediately afterwards it was split in two, with A Flight based at Castel Benito in Italy and B Flight based at Ras-el-Ma in Morocco.

Initially the two flights were equipped with Avro Ansons taken over from No. 34 and No. 35 Flights SAAF, but by August 1943 the aircraft on strength had diversified into two Vickers Wellingtons, five Douglas Dakotas and seven Ansons.

The squadron spent much of its wartime existence serving in detachments stationed not only in Italy and Morocco but also in Sicily and Algeria. It was not until near the end of the war in Europe, in fact, that it was consolidated at Maison Blanche, Algeria. Two Beech Expediters were delivered in February 1945.

In September 1945 the squadron returned permanently to South Africa and was based at Swartkop, near Pretoria, from where it did yeoman service in shuttling South African troops home during late 1945 and early 1946; its work-horses at this stage being Dakotas, with a handful of Ansons reserved for VIP duties. The squadron also maintained an ACF element at Baragwanath, flying Harvards until January 1, 1951 when this was renumbered No. 3 Squadron.

VIP flights remained an important part of No. 28 Squadron's duties for some years, and as time went by the Ansons were supplanted by larger and more modern aircraft.

At first these comprised two Dakotas named 'Fleur' and 'Rustig and a few Ventura light bombers, all fitted out with improved accommodation. Then, in 1949, nine De Havilland Devons were acquired for the VIP flight, which were further augmented in 1955 by the acquisition of two larger De Havilland Heron 2s.

The Venturas were retired in the late 1950s, and in 1958 a Vickers Viscount named 'Casteel' was added to the VIP element, because Dakotas were obviously no longer suited to transporting important passengers on long journeys to places as far distant as Britain or Europe.

The early 1960s saw the Devons and Herons retired as well, because of their poor performance at high altitudes, and when No. 28 Squadron was re-equipped with C-130 Hercules transports and moved to Waterkloof air base, it also divested itself of its Dakotas, which stayed behind at Swartkop to join No. 44 Squadron. During 1969 several Transall C-160Zs were delivered to augment its C-130Bs.

In February 1968 the VIP flight was reconstituted as No. 21 Squadron, leaving No. 28 Squadron a purely transport unit again, flying C-130s and C-160 Transalls.

72

73 74

72. Pulling up sharply, a C160 displays surprising agility for so large an aircraft. Designed for tactical transport work, the C160 can take off and land in remarkably short distances.
73. Spilling out rapidly from the two side doors of a C160, 'parabats' take part in a training exercise in the northern Transvaal.
74. Leading two C130s, stable-mates from its squadron, a C160 sets the pace during a low-level fly-past.

THE AVRO SHACKLETON MR. 3
St Bernard of the sky

75. A Shackleton of No. 35 Squadron sets off on a long-range reconnaissance of South Africa's sea-lanes. As it thunders out to sea, members of its crew test the operation of its radome and bomb-bay doors. Out there, where it is going, there is no-one to help if something goes wrong.

The classic World War II look of the Avro Shackletons flown by No. 35 Squadron SAAF is hardly surprising, for they are directly descended from the dam-busting Lancaster bombers.

The Shackleton was born soon after the war's end, when the Liberators flown by the Royal Air Force's Coastal Command had to be returned to the United States in terms of Roosevelt's Lend-Lease scheme.

In place of the Liberators the RAF took the Avro Lancaster GR-Mk 3, but these were not really suited to their new role as maritime patrol aircraft, and in 1946 a production order was placed with Avro for a new model, the Shackleton, combining a wider fuselage with the older Avro Lincoln's wings and undercarriage.

The new aircraft took a long time to develop, but in 1949 the prototype, known as the Avro 696 Shackleton GR-1, made its first flight. It was a distinctive aircraft with its four Griffon engines turning contra-rotating propellors and short, fat fuselage with chin-mounted radar and dorsal turret.

Seven RAF squadrons were equipped with the Mk 1 and Mk 1A, but the 'Shack', as South Africans know it, did not appear on the scene until the Mk 2 – with its ventral radar installation, longer fuselage, twin 20 mm cannon and extended tail-cone – made its first flight in June 1952.

South Africa became acquainted with the Shackleton in May and June 1953, when four RAF Mk 2s visited the country. At this time the SAAF was seeking replacements for its ageing Short Sunderland flying-boats – which No. 35 Squadron was operating out of Congella sea-base near Durban – and the visitors were thoroughly evaluated. The SAAF obviously liked what it saw and in January 1954 announced that eight were to be acquired for the SAAF – the only export order ever placed for this aircraft.

The SAAF wanted its Shackletons to be capable of a secondary role as bombers; they were to incorporate attachment points for underwing rocket rails, and to carry a Saro Mk 3 airborne lifeboat under the bomb-bay when used in an air-sea rescue role. These three Saro boats were later replaced by Lindholme-type rescue gear – one of the three was accidentally destroyed during a dropping trial, while the other two were presented to the SAAF Museum and the SA National Museum of Military History.

Partly as a result of the SAAF order, the A.V. Roe factory undertook some redesign of the aircraft, and the result was the Mk 3, which had a nose-wheel undercarriage to improve cross-wind landings; a stronger main undercarriage, with dual main wheels; permanent wingtip fuel tanks; clear-vision cockpit canopy; and improved equipment and crew facilities.

The planned switch from seaplanes brought upheavals for No. 35 Squadron. Because the Shackletons were landlubbers, the squadron moved from the Congella base to Cape Town. Here, the existing air base at Ysterplaat was overcrowded and the runway inadequate, so a special section of the D.F. Malan civil airport was set aside as a Shackleton operational base – with Ysterplaat being used as a headquarters and maintenance facility. No. 35 Squadron has remained at D.F. Malan to this day.

In February 1957, a 41-man team from No. 35 Squadron was sent to the A.V. Roe factory at Woodford for an intensive training programme. Meanwhile the first of the redesigned Mk 3s had flown, and on May 21, 1957, No. 35 Squadron formally took over its first two MR Mk 3 Shackletons, No. 1716 and No. 1717, at Woodford – three months before any of this variant were taken into RAF service.

Soon joined by a third, the SAAF 'Shacks' took part in a combined British-American-Dutch exercise in the North Sea and then flew to their new home. The first two arrived at Waterkloof air base near Pretoria on August 18, 1957. The next day 1718 arrived as well, and together they flew to Cape Town.

The Shackletons were newsmakers from the start. In mid-February 1958, with No. 35 Squadron still awaiting its last three aircraft, one Shackleton hit the headlines by setting what was then a local record: a non-stop 14,5-hour flight that took it from Waterkloof base to Cape Town by way of Beit Bridge, the Bechuanaland (now Botswana) border, Katima Mulilo in the Caprivi Strip, and to the Cunene River mouth on the South West African northern border.

About 10 days after this flight, the latecomers – 1721, 1722 and 1723 – arrived, and the squadron became fully operational in its main task of patrolling the sea-route around southern Africa. Today, almost a quarter-century later, they are still doing just that, although only seven of them are left – 1718 lies shattered in the Cape's Steynskloof Mountains where she crashed after encountering bad weather during an exercise on August 8, 1963, with the loss of all 13 crew on board.

Day after day the Shackletons lumber gracefully up and down the long, long coastline of South Africa and Namibia, carrying out their assigned tasks. First among these is long-range maritime reconnaissance, and few of the ever-growing number of Russian warships and supply vessels that have circumnavigated the Cape in recent years have escaped the Shackletons' prying eyes and ready cameras.

But the Shackletons are also birds of peace and have carried out many air-sea rescues and other mercy missions. A much-publicized search carried out by two of them was on October 30, 1965 when a SAAF Buccaneer crashed into the Atlantic while being flown from Britain. Helped by a distress call a commercial airliner relayed to one of the searchers, 1722, the Shackletons were able to find the Buccaneer crew in their dinghy and pin-point their position so that a passing ship could pick them up.

Thousands of refugees of the 1975 phase of the Angolan War have reason to remember the trusty old 'Shacks' as well. Many of them suffered extreme distress as they poured southwards into Namibia. Ill-equipped for the journey along the barren, terrible Skeleton Coast, many of them might not have reached safety, had it not been for the Shackletons' keeping a regular eye on them, reporting their progress and, when necessary, dropping supplies.

Few people disagreed with the Cape Town newspaper which in 1978 described the Shackletons and the men who flew them as 'the St Bernards of our skies'.

A civilian observer wrote fondly of the Shackleton: 'It's big, noisy and shakes like a drunk with the DTs – but to a lost yachtsman or an Angolan refugee trapped in the harsh Namib Desert, a Shackleton must look like an angel of mercy, floating down on huge ungainly wings . . .'

Now and again the Shackletons have shown their teeth. In March 1971 the damaged tanker *Wafra* – condemned to be sunk but still afloat in spite of the attempts of SAAF Buccaneers to sink her – was despatched with depth-charges dropped by a Shackleton.

What of the future? The Shackletons cannot go on forever. Over the years their avionics and electronic equipment have been kept up to date, but sooner or later they are going to reach the limit of their safe endurance. As it is, their contemporary Mk 3s in RAF service were retired a decade ago, although this was due largely to a 1963/64 modification programme which added so much to the overall mass that a Bristol Siddeley Viper jet engine was installed in each outboard nacelle to improve take-off performance.

This extra mass and the resultant stress shortened their flying lives so drastically that they were retired. Older converted Mk 2s linger on in the RAF in the airborne early-warning role, but even these are soon to be replaced by specially adapted BAe Nimrods.

Improved South African technological expertise has helped keep the 'Shacks' flying. In the mid-1970s the SAAF embarked on an extensive refit and re-sparring project. Of all the requirements, the re-sparring was the most difficult; a task of this magnitude had never been tackled locally.

The first Shackleton to be overhauled was 1716. It was entirely dismantled because the re-sparring had to be done overseas. When 1716 was completed it was 1717's turn, and great difficulties were experienced because relations between South Africa and Britain were particularly chilly at the time. Eventually it was decided that 1717's refit, including the re-sparring, would be carried out completely by the SAAF.

This took the technical staff about a year of working time, and they were plagued as much by technical problems as by what some felt to be British obstructionism. Certain vital replacement parts ordered from Britain did not arrive, or were sent in insufficient quantity; the SAAF responded by manufacturing what it could not obtain. In one instance, lacking an essential part which could neither be bought, nor made locally, the SAAF sent a technical party hiking into the almost inaccessible Steynskloof Mountains to cannibalize the remains of 1718. They found the part concerned in perfect shape, and it duly ended up serving again in 1717.

The project was completed late in 1977, and on October 13 that year 'Seventeen', as 1717 is known in the squadron, was rolled out of the workshops and put on display for the media by her justifiably proud rejuvenators.

So the 'Shacks' will stay in the air for the time being. But there is little doubt that they do not have a long future ahead of them, and under present circumstances it seems unlikely that the SAAF will soon be able to acquire any replacements such as the Lockheed Orion, the BAe Nimrod or the Breguet Atlantic. Nor is it an economic exercise for the SAAF to attempt to manufacture so large and complicated an aircraft.

Some of the Shackletons' tasks have been taken over by the shorter-range Piaggio Albatross aircraft of No. 27 Squadron SAAF, but the need for a new long-range maritime patrol aircraft remains unfilled. The SAAF is now one of the last operational users of Shackletons; it is just as well that old 'Seventeen' and her sisters are good for a few years yet.

Historical note on No. 35 Squadron

This squadron – motto: 'Shaya Amanzi' (Strike at the Water) – was formed on February 2, 1945 by renumbering No. 262 Squadron RAF, which had operated Catalina flying-boats from Congella, with detachments at St Lucia, on the eastern Natal coast, and Langebaanweg on the western Cape coast.

The renumbering of No. 262 Squadron as a SAAF unit was logical, since it had received drafts of SAAF personnel as early as 1943 and from July 16, 1944 had had a SAAF commanding officer.

It was awarded the battle-honour 'South African Waters', granted for operations within a 1 600 km radius off the South African and South West African coasts in 1944 and 1945.

On April 24, 1945, less than two months after its birth, the new squadron received the first of 16 Short Sunderland GR.5 flying-boats and was earmarked for an operational tour of the Far East where fighting was still in progress.

But before this occurred, peace came to the eastern theatre of war and the Sunderlands were diverted to shuttling South African troops home from Cairo. Both squadron and aircraft responded magnificently, and the Sunderlands ferried 1 786 troops as well as 55 tons of equipment back to South Africa without a single cancellation as a result of unserviceability.

No. 35 Squadron made two entries in the record books in the early post-war years. One of its Sunderlands, NJ262, made the first South African and South West African round trip (Durban-Cape Town-Walvis Bay-Johannesburg) in July 1948, taking 20 hours; and an Avro Anson on unit strength was fitted with floats taken from a Blackburn Roc and used as a seamanship trainer – the only Anson, it is believed, ever to have been turned into a float plane.

In 1948, No. 35 Squadron took on a distinctly heterogeneous appearance when a Citizen Force element flying no less than four different types of land-based aircraft – Harvards, Venturas, Oxfords and Spitfires – joined its complement. The part-time airmen, operating out of Stamford Hill aerodrome near Durban, gradually whittled down the number of types they were using, and when they were detached from No. 35 Squadron to become No. 5 (Citizen Force) Squadron in December 1950, they were flying only Harvards.

The last Sunderland flight took place on September 27, 1957, after which the squadron was re-equipped with Shackletons and moved to Cape Town, and all the Sunderlands were scrapped in Durban.

In 1959 and 1960 the squadron also operated the last Venturas in SAAF service – mostly leftovers from Nos. 17 and 22 Squadrons SAAF – as part of Maritime Group, before these were withdrawn.

76. A Shackleton can drone along on a patrol like this for 12 hours at a time, rising and falling in the air-currents, its great wings flexing till the skin wrinkles noticeably. The contra-rotating propellors on each engine are clearly visible in this photograph.

77. The nose gunner, his twin 20 mm cannon shrouded to protect them from the corrosive sea air, peers out of his 'greenhouse'. No SAAF Shackleton has ever fired its guns in anger, but there is a first time for everything, and they are always ready, even on routine patrols.

78. The Shackleton's vast bomb-bay yawns empty, ready to swallow up anything from a load of air-sea rescue equipment to a cluster of bombs or depth-charges. Just to the rear is the 'dust-bin', or radome, in its lowered position.

79. Taking off, the forward-retracting undercarriage members of a Shackleton whine towards their housing, unheard in the general din kicked up by the four great engines.

80. A Shackleton co-pilot goes through his pre-flight checks. His concentration is total, so that he does not even pause to marvel (as even pilots must do sometimes) at the great Rolls-Royce Griffon engines with their twin contra-rotating propellors.

THE PIAGGIO P-166S ALBATROSS
Unseen but not unheard

81. Dwarfed by the famous Twelve Apostles that mount vigil along the Cape coast near Cape Town, an Albatross of No. 27 Squadron heads for its base at D. F. Malan Airport after a long patrol along the western littoral.

The pilots of Cape Town's No. 27 Squadron SAAF like to joke that their unit's unofficial motto is 'We come unseen – but not unheard', a reference to the undeniable fact that the Piaggio P-166S coastal patrol aircraft they fly day in and day out announces its presence far and wide by the penetrating nasal roar of its twin Lycoming engines.

Most South Africans refer to the Piaggio P-166S by its official local name, the Albatross; a few talk about the 'pig', a dreadful nickname imported from Australia. The men who fly it tend to be friendlier and call it the 'trossie'. But by whatever name it is known, there is no doubt that the P-166S is a bit of an odd bird, with its high gull-wings and backward-facing 'pusher' propellers.

Popular legend claims it got its name more or less by accident. The story goes that when the first SAAF P-166S was put through its public paces, a sudden panic ensued at the announcer's microphone when it was realized the aircraft had no type-name that would not reveal its ancestry – a distinctly uncomfortable state of affairs for a semi-clandestine purchaser of arms like South Africa. A certain SAAF officer came to the rescue, however, by arbitrarily calling it by the first name that came into his head.

The provenance of this story is doubtful, but the choice of name is singularly appropriate. What bird better symbolizes the eternally wakeful role of the SAAF's maritime air patrols than the soaring, ever-watchful albatross?

It is a fact, however, that for years after it went into service with the SAAF no photographs of the Albatross could be published in terms of defence legislation, apparently as a precaution against embarrassing the makers.

The Albatross is an only child, the sole current offspring of Italy's Piaggio company. Piaggio is not one of the best-known aircraft manufacturing concerns in the world, but it has been in business for about 65 years – a long time in the aircraft industry.

Although it builds only one type of aircraft at its plant in Genoa, it produces sub-assemblies for the new Panavia Tornado fighter and has a very active aero engine division devoted to licenced production of Rolls-Royce Viper turbojets and various Lycoming powerplants.

Several Piaggio aircraft types have been built since the Italian aircraft industry rose from the ashes of World War II, notably the P-148 and P-149 basic trainers, but the Albatross is descended from one of its parent company's earliest post-war designs, the P-136, which first flew in 1948.

The P-136 was a five-seat amphibious flying-boat featuring the same gull-wing and pusher propellers as today's Albatross, and it was moderately successful, about 20 being exported to the United States and Canada.

In 1955 a team consisting of a designer, Prof. Giovanni Casilaghi, and an engineer, Alberto Farabioschi, took the P-136 a stage further by developing it into a multi-purpose land-based aircraft designated the P-166.

The P-166 was seen mainly as an aircraft for the executive market in the same general class as the American Aero Commander, but with a roomier interior. So generous were the dimensions allowed by the design team that when the P-166 finally appeared, its cabin had so much head-room – not usually a feature of aircraft in this class – that a person of average height could stand upright.

At the same time there was little doubt about its ancestry, since the new aircraft retained the P-136's gull-wing configuration and pusher engines, as well as the older machine's undercarriage, the only difference being that it had a nose-wheel instead of one in the tail.

The prototype, registered as I-RAIF, flew for the first time on November 26, 1957, powered by twin 340-hp (253,5 kW) Lycoming piston engines. Testing continued till July 1958, when certification was obtained and production of the first version, the P-166-AL1, could begin.

Several of these were ordered by small operators, some as far afield as Australia, and were driven hard from the start (by 1977 one of the Australian 'pigs' had chalked up 12 000 flying hours, a record for a single P-166 aircraft at that time). Other P-166s of this first batch were sold to the USA's Northrop aircraft company, which uses them for shuttle flights – sometimes four a day – between its various plants.

Interest in the hard-working little aircraft was soon shown by the Italian Air Force, which needed logistic support aircraft for its Fiat G91R jet fighters. It settled for a special version of the P-166 which featured a cargo door and strengthened cabin capable of transporting the G91R's Orpheus turbojet engine, and ordered 51, the largest single order for the type to date.

The G91R is no longer a first-line Italian Air Force fighter, and the Piaggios are now used essentially for multi-engine conversion training, casualty evacuation and general communications duties.

Meanwhile development of the type continued. After 32 models of the orginal P-166 had been built for the civil market, Piaggio introduced the P-166B Portofino, which was fitted with more powerful 380-hp (283 kW) engines and a lengthened nose which could house extra avionics.

The Portofino first flew in March 1962 but was not very successful, only six being produced. Development continued, however, and October 1964 saw the first flight of a 'stretched' version designated the P-166C. The fuselage was not lengthened, as is usually the case in a 'stretched' aircraft; instead, a high-density layout cabin was obtained by means of a new undercarriage which retracted into fairings under the fuselage rather than fitting into the fuselage itself.

Sadly the P-166C did not catch the market's fancy either and, apart from the prototype (a converted Portofino), only two were built, with all subsequent P-166s reverting to the original undercarriage arrangement.

About this time the SAAF was shopping for a close-inshore maritime patrol and fishery surveillance aircraft to replace the Dakotas then operating in this role. Several aircraft were evaluated but nothing came of them (it was reported at the time that the SAAF had wanted to buy a number of Cessna 411s, but had been thwarted on political grounds) and the Republic then settled on the Piaggio.

There were a number of distinct advantages in the P-166. Firstly there were no obvious political strings attached, but above all the little aircraft was ideally suited to its role. Not only did it have a high wing, but also was blessed with a strong undercarriage which permitted operation from roughly-surfaced airfields. In addition, the hot exhaust fumes, being vented high up on the wings, did not fog the lenses of the cameras that would have to be fitted to the floor and sides of the fuselage.

The SAAF version, designated the P-166S, was an adaptation of the Portofino, but had a slightly longer nose for extra radar equipment, larger wing-tip fuel tanks, containing 323 litres each, which stretched endurance to between eight and nine hours, and two pilot-entry doors, one on either side of the fuselage instead of only a single door.

It also had an emergency escape-hatch in the cabin's roof in the event of a ditching at sea, it being a P-166 virtue that it would float on its wings for a short while even with the fuselage submerged.

The first ordered by the SAAF made its maiden flight in October 1968 and was certified in February 1969. Soon afterwards the first models were shipped to Cape Town, assembled and despatched to No. 27 Squadron at Ysterplaat air base.

There they stayed, becoming a familiar sight – and sound – to the residents of the surrounding suburbs, till the mid-1970s, when No. 27 Squadron moved to the military section of D.F. Malan Airport.

The Albatrosses have been at D.F. Malan ever since, their pilots operating alongside their colleagues of No. 35 Squadron, who fly the big Avro Shackletons on long-distance maritime patrols. It might be thought that flying Albatrosses on long coastal patrols is a boring job – but only by those who do not know the details of No. 27 Squadron's chosen task.

The Cape of Good Hope was once also known as the Cape of Storms by the old Portuguese navigators who braved the worst of its weather; and the pilots of No. 27 Squadron – some of them regulars, others business and professional men who sacrifice large slices of their spare time to guard the Cape coastline – know only too well that often they fly on the edge of darkness.

As well as facing some of the worst weather along the southern African coast, they must often fly at wave-tip height to get the best possible photographs of ships using the Cape sea-lanes. As it is, an Albatross disappeared at sea in 1976 and neither it nor its experienced crew were ever seen again.

Perhaps a better unofficial motto for the Albatross pilots of No. 27 Squadron would be 'Unseen – but not unappreciated'.

Historical note on No. 27 Squadron SAAF

If there is one task No. 27 Squadron knows intimately it is maritime patrolling. Barring two relatively short periods of inactivity, it has been watching the wave-tops since it was formed from No. 8 Squadron at Eerste River, near Cape Town, on August 24, 1942.

Officially designated No. 27 (TBR) Squadron – the initials standing for 'torpedo, bomber and reconnaissance' – the unit was equipped with Ventura Vs and became operational on South Africa's west coast in January 1943, flying convoy escort and anti-submarine patrols from rural Cape bases such as Rooikop.

A detachment also operated with No. 23 Squadron at Darling, and in November 1943 the relatively even tenor of the two units' daily existence was interrupted by a fruitless attempt to lay by the heels a Japanese submarine, carrying supplies and technicians from Germany.

In October 1943 the Squadron moved to Phesantekraal and anti-submarine operations continued into March 1944, after which it became No. 27 Squadron's turn to go 'Up North'; by June – still operating Ventura Vs – it was based in north-west Africa, carrying out air-sea rescue duties and flying shipping and maritime reconnaissance patrols in the Western Mediterranean and Spanish coastal areas.

By August 1944 the squadron had a detachment operating from Malta as well, and in that month the unit's aircraft logged 278 hours 57 minutes of operational flying.

Enemy activity in the Mediterranean was declining steadily, however, and October 1944 saw the squadron closing up shop. The following month it began to move back to Swartkop air station near

Pretoria, although a rear party remained in Egypt to begin converting to Wellingtons and Warwicks.

At that stage the Warwick had been selected as the replacement for No. 27 Squadron's Venturas, but for various reasons training on the Warwick G.R.V. did not begin until May 1945, and was still in progress when the war in Europe ended.

The squadron did not return immediately to South Africa, as was the case with some other SAAF units, but stayed on in Egypt and in July 1945 resumed air-sea rescue duties in the eastern Mediterranean area, using airfields in Palestine and along the North African coast. (In November its Warwicks helped to rescue survivors from a burning British steamer.)

In November 1945 the squadron handed over its ASR duties to No. 621 Squadron RAF, reassembled in Egypt and finally returned to South Africa with its 16 Warwicks. There it was disbanded in December 1945.

In January 1951 it was re-formed at Ysterplaat, near Cape Town, as a part-time maritime patrol unit equipped with Venturas. After

seven years it was disbanded again, but in October 1962 entered its third incarnation when it was re-formed at Ysterplaat as an ACF inshore maritime reconnaissance squadron flying Dakotas.

In 1969 the squadron was re-equipped with Albatrosses, which it still flies on medium-range maritime patrols.

82. Hundreds of metres below, Capetonians do not even have to see the gull-wings and rearward-facing pusher propellors to know an Albatross is passing overhead – the nasal roar of its engines is a distinctive enough signature tune.

No. 88 Advanced Flying School

No. 88 AFS was formed on May 7, 1976 from the Maritime Operational Training Unit (MOTU) at AFB Ysterplaat, taking over the latter's duties and personnel. It trains aircrews for the various maritime air units, principally Nos. 27 and 35 Squadrons. It has no aircraft of its own, but uses operational squadrons' aircraft.

This training role has been its sole function throughout its existence and its motto is singularly appropriate: *Custodes Litorum Docemus* (we teach the guardians of the shores).

THE WESTLAND WASP
Below them the waves

83. Its rotor-blades blowing up a fierce miniature sandstorm, a Wasp prepares to set down on its four spraddled wheels at Milnerton, on Cape Town's outskirts.
84. Overleaf: Wasp by name, Wasp by nature . . . Like a great sea-grey insect, one of South Africa's anti-submarine helicopters skims over waves brushed with gold by the late afternoon sun.

One certain way of irritating the pilots and flight engineers of No. 22 Squadron is to refer to the machines they fly as 'naval helicopters'. Close as their co-operation with the South African Navy's helicopter-carrying vessels may be, No.22 Squadron's men are 'blue jobs' through and through.

The South African Defence Force has no naval air arm as such, and until the 1960s possessed no ships capable of including aircraft in their armoury. About 20 years ago, however, it became clear that some naval air capability was needed if the Navy was to carry out its duties in terms of the Simonstown Agreement with Britain.

As a result of this need it was decided to comprehensively refit and modify the SAN's two old destroyers, SAS Simon van der Stel and SAS Jan van Riebeeck, among other things equipping each with a helipad and storage hangar.

At this time the Westland factory was preparing to build its new anti-submarine helicopter, the Wasp, a marine version of the Scout general-purpose helicopter, then serving in the British Army's air corps.

Modified to allow its operation from the cramped and unstable

facilities of a small warship, the Wasp has a folding tail-boom and rotor-blades, and a special four-wheel castor undercarriage which allows the wheels to be adjusted to a 45-degree angle to assist it when landing on the pitching, rolling helipad in rough seas.

The first production Wasp flew in October 1962, and soon afterwards the SAAF placed an initial order for six. Delivery was completed early in 1964, the new helicopters being formed into No.22 Flight at Ysterplaat air base, at the same time as the revamped Simon van der Stel was recommissioned and work began on the Jan van Riebeeck (this was completed in April 1966).

The Wasps – the fifth helicopter type to go into SAAF service – encountered both setbacks and successes in the early stages of their South African service. Two were lost soon after No.22 Flight was formed, but another which was operating off the Simon van der Stel became the first helicopter ever to land on Bouvet Island, a bleakly inhospitable piece of rock rearing up out of the Atlantic more than 3 000 km south-west of Cape Town.

Four more Wasps – the last South Africa was to obtain from Britain for some time – were delivered early in 1966 making up for the 1964 losses.

This fact was brought home late the following year when on August 8, Wasp No.82 ditched into the sea off Cape Town's Milnerton beach. This time there was no question of the SAAF buying a replacement from Westland, since Harold Wilson's Labour government had made it quite clear it would veto any arms sales to South Africa.

But No.82 did not end on the scrap-heap. Salvaged after a night on the bottom by the guano-ship, *Gamtoos,* she was dismantled, carefully rebuilt by No.22 Flight's technicians, and was back in service by 1975. At the time of writing she was still in operation.

In the late 1960s new fields of activity were opened up for the Wasps. By then their profiles had altered, for the SAAF had followed the example of the Royal Navy and others by fitting inflatable flotation bags on either side of the cabin roofs to assist crew evacuation in the event of a ditching. The new development arose from a decision to provide the South African Navy's three Whitby-class anti-submarine frigates (the *President Kruger, President Steyn* and *President Pretorius)* with an air capability.

The *SAS President Kruger* was recommissioned on August 5, 1969, the *SAS President Steyn* in 1970, and the *SAS President Pretorius* in 1976. Each of the modified frigates has a helipad and a small hangar to accommodate one helicopter.

On May 23, 1972, the Wasps' activities were further extended when the SAN's new hydrographic survey ship, *SAS Protea,* was commissioned. Like the frigates, the *Protea* is equipped to carry a single Wasp for aerial surveys, and it carries out such mundane but essential tasks as placing markers in inaccessible locations.

It had become clear that No.22 Flight's five operational Wasps were too few for the tasks demanded of them, but there seemed no chance to acquire more. Then help came from an entirely unexpected quarter. British voters replaced the Wilson government by a Tory administration under Edward Heath, who announced his willingness to lift the arms embargo on weapons and equipment to be used to maintain the South African end of the Simonstown Agreement. The SAAF wasted no time in ordering seven more Wasps.

But production of the Wasp had stopped, for the Royal Navy had adopted a newer anti-submarine helicopter, the Westland WG-13 Lynx. The SAAF decided that, in the long run, it would be more economical to bear the extra costs of re-opening the production line than to remodify its ships.

This reasoning could not be faulted, but unforeseen delays in re-opening production at the Westland plant resulted in one of the seven Wasps, No. 97, remaining undelivered when Heath was replaced by Harold Wilson, who reimposed a total arms ban without further ado. Instead of roaming the Southern Atlantic skies, No.97 stayed at the Westland factory, reportedly as a test rig, before being broken up late in 1976.

Whatever the official chagrin at the loss of No.97, the arrival of the others brought joy to No.22 Flight, which now achieved full squadron status.

The Wasps' prime function – though sometimes obscured by their regular rescue and scientific exploits – is anti-submarine warfare. In an operational situation, the long-range sonar equipment on the warship locates the enemy submarine, whereupon the ship launches its Wasp sending it out to the enemy's position. Circumstances dictate the next move since a Wasp can carry either depth-charges or two homing torpedoes.

Fortunately, there has been no need for anti-submarine operations off the South African coast. But Wasps have logged many flying hours on more peaceful – though sometimes extremely hazardous – missions.

In 1970 they took part in a widely-publicized search for two Department of Transport personnel who disappeared on remote Gough Island, and rescued two seamen from the crane barge *Shir Yib,* which had gone aground off Cape Point. In June 1978, Wasps lifted 26 Japanese fishermen from a trawler stranded on Namibia's fearsome Skeleton Coast.

Frequently Wasps have fetched injured or critically ill sailors from merchant ships rounding the Cape of Good Hope and brought them ashore for treatment. They have travelled far and wide in the performance of their duties; for instance, in 1972 they made the first SAAF landing on the distant Atlantic island of Tristan da Cunha, almost 3 000 km west of Cape Town.

In 1978 a Wasp from *SAS Protea,* which was engaged in a fisheries research programme off the South American coast, brought a new twist to an old sailor's tale by flying around Cape Horn, thus becoming the first SAAF helicopter to operate in the Pacific Ocean. At a later stage of the meandering voyage the Wasp also became the first SAAF helicopter to operate in Antarctic waters.

The *Simon van der Stel* and the *Jan van Riebeeck* were withdrawn from service years ago, but the Wasp crews sailor on. But remember not to call them 'seamen'.

Historical note on No. 22 Squadron SAAF

The No. 22 Squadron of today co-operates extremely closely with the South African Navy, but there is nothing new about this – since its earliest days this unit has had an intimate association with maritime warfare and rescue work.

It was formed as No. 22 (Torpedo-Bomber-Reconnaissance) Squadron in Durban on July 1, 1942, from the SAAF's 31 Flight, its assigned role being coastal reconnaissance, air-sea rescue operations, convoy escort and anti-submarine patrols.

For these demanding tasks it was equipped with such of the SAAF's militarized Junkers Ju-86 converted airliners as still survived, and 31 Flight's ageing Avro Ansons. In spite of its second-rate equipment, from its earliest days the squadron embarked on training and operational flights – some lasting up to five hours.

The position began to improve in August 1942, when eight Lockheed Ventura light bombers arrived to replace the Ju-86s. One of the new arrivals brought No. 22 Squadron its first success when it detected and identified a Vichy French ship which was subsequently captured.

Both 1942 and 1943 saw much German submarine activity in the Indian Ocean, and the squadron flew many Ventura and Anson patrols on convoy duties. More Venturas arrived to keep pace with the expanding convoy duties, and by November 1942 the squadron had no fewer than 23 of the stubby little bombers, all of them in constant use, particularly from May 1943 onwards.

It was hard work, with little to show for all the trouble taken. No. 22 Squadron never actually managed to sink a U-boat, but it certainly cramped the style of many by forcing them to stay off the surface – an important factor in the non-nuclear submersibles of those days.

In July 1944 the squadron moved to Gibraltar to operate in its assigned role in the Mediterranean, and at one stage late in 1944 was in sole charge of all anti-submarine patrols from the famous mountain fortress.

During this time only three aircraft were lost on operation, in spite of day and night patrols – some lasting almost nine hours – alone or in co-operation with British or American forces; in one month, January 1945, more than 1 000 hours of operations were flown.

The war in Europe over, the squadron lingered on at Gibraltar for a little while and on June 4, 1945, made its last official appearance when some of its members tried their hand at a traditional 'army' pastime – by providing the troops for the ancient Ceremony of the Keys. In July 1945, No. 22 Squadron was posted to Gianaclis, in Egypt, and in August moved to Idku, where it was disbanded on October 24. It was re-formed with Venturas in 1954 but later disbanded once more. Then, in the early 1960s, the SAAF acquired a quantity of Westland Wasp helicopters and a unit known as No. 22 Flight was formed on January 1, 1964. This became a full squadron in May 1976 when enough additional Wasps were received to bring it up to full strength. The squadron also operates a number of Alouette III's.

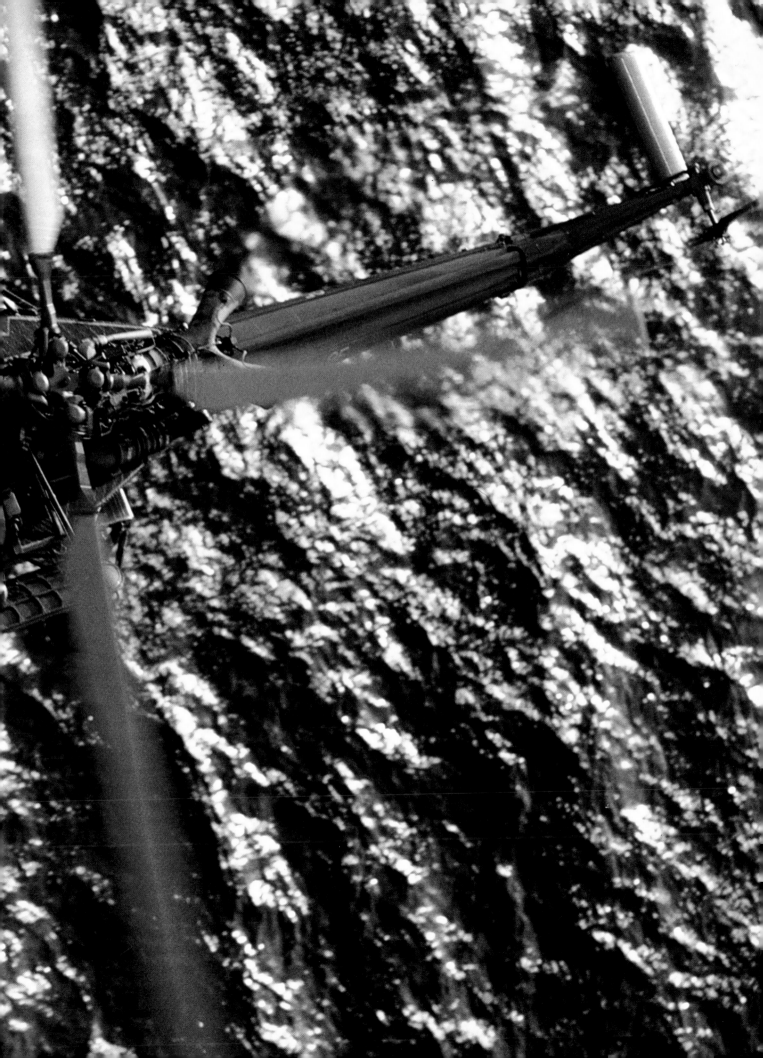

85. A storm is brewing and this Wasp's tail boom has been locked into the folded position before it is towed to the shelter of a hangar.

86. The weather is atrocious, but along the Cape coast that is nothing new, and the crew of this Wasp take it all in their stride as they slog through the meteorological muck towards Bloubergstrand, across the bay from Cape Town.

87. A Wasp heads out to sea, its engine's heat roiling the air into a haze.

88. A Wasp retrieves a diver from the chilly waters of Table Bay, the wash from its rotor-blades beating the sea below into a whirlpool pattern. The oddly canted wheels help to stabilize the helicopter when it has to land on the small, heaving helipad of a frigate battling through heavy seas.

THE AEROSPATIALE ALOUETTE III
From shipwrecks to drugs

89. Two Alouette IIIs of No. 16 Squadron return to base at sunset. The oldest of the SAAF's helicopters, they have seen service in many places and in a variety of roles.

Before 1960 the South African Air Force's helicopter component was very small – three piston-engined Sikorsky S-55Cs and one surviving Sikorsky S-51, all of them operated by No. 17 Squadron, which was then based at Langebaanweg in the Western Cape.

That undesirable situation changed from July 1961, when No. 17 Squadron moved to Ysterplaat air base near Cape Town and began to take delivery of a number of five-seater Alouette IIs from France.

In more ways than one it was an historic change-over. The five-seater Alouette II and its bigger brother, the seven-man Alouette III, were the world's first successful turbine-engined helicopters to attain large-scale production.

The SAAF cut its teeth on the Alouette II, but the somewhat beefier Alouette III was chosen as its standard general-purpose helicopter, and the first of these began arriving in 1962.

When enough of the new helicopters had arrived, the SAAF decided to split No. 17 Squadron into three flights. A Flight was based at Swartkop, near Pretoria; B Flight found itself sent to Bloemspruit air station in the Orange Free State; and C Flight stayed at Ysterplaat, operating Alouette IIs as well as IIIs in its extra role as the SAAF helicopter training flight.

Like other helicopters of the SAAF, the Alouette IIIs in various parts of the country have made a name in a hundred different rescue operations at sea or on land. The most famous during their

first decade in SAAF colours occurred when the freighter *SA Seafarer* ran aground off Cape Town's Mouille Point in the early hours of July 1, 1966.

In a way there have been more spectacular wrecks than that of the *Seafarer.* For one thing, she lay within hailing distance of the shore and not on some remote reef hundreds of kilometres from the nearest rescuers. But she ran aground during typically foul winter weather, with great waves crashing around her, breaking her back and making any surface rescue attempt extremely hazardous.

So C Flight at Ysterplaat was called in, and, in an intense glare of publicity, three Alouette IIIs braved the bad weather conditions and ferried all of the 76 people on board back to dry land. The *Seafarer's* owners were so grateful for this arduous rescue task that they paid for the cost of No. 17 Squadron's unit colours.

Like their colleagues of No. 19 (Puma) Squadron, the pilots of No. 17 (and later No. 16) Squadron have also snatched countless lost and injured climbers from the formidable mountains of the Western and Southern Cape, as well as the Drakensberg in Natal.

Before the arrival of the Piaggio P-166 Albatross maritime patrol aircraft in the late-1960s, Alouettes also carried out close inshore patrols along the Skeleton Coast of South West Africa. During this time they carried out several spectacular rescues from ships that had fallen victim to the inhospitable coast.

Late in 1967 more Alouette IIIs were delivered to South Africa and C Flight blossomed into a full-strength unit, designated No. 16 Squadron. Two years later No. 16 Squadron departed from the

Cape for relocation at Durban, leaving behind several Alouette IIIs and all its Alouette IIs, which became the Helicopter Conversion Unit until being renamed No. 87 Advanced Flying School in 1974, soon before all its Alouette IIs were withdrawn from service.

No. 16 Squadron remained at Durban till B Flight of No. 19 (Puma) Squadron arrived in July 1972, and then moved house to Bloemspruit. In 1973 the squadron was split into two widely-separated sub-units, B Flight remaining at Bloemspruit while A Flight was established at Port Elizabeth (No. 17 Squadron was still at Swartkop, but components or personnel of it and No. 16 Squadron were now in action in the border operational area).

In April 1978 the Alouettes of B Flight, No. 16 Squadron, played a major role in rescue operations in the flood-stricken Transkei. This sub-unit, being the only helicopter operator permanently stationed in the Port Elizabeth area, also maintains close co-operation with the National Sea Rescue Institute.

More Alouette IIIs have been delivered, and of those arriving in 1975, some were fitted with plush VIP interiors.

In January 1978 No. 87 AFS moved to Bloemspruit, and No. 16 Squadron (A Flight) simultaneously upped stakes and returned to its original home, Ysterplaat.

Alouettes often perform special duties for other government departments, notably the Department of Forestry and the South African Police. In the latter role they have helped the police anti-drug unit to raid and destroy millions of rands worth of dagga grown in remote inaccessible mountain plantations.

Often the only way these plantations can be reached is by helicopter. During one such raid in March 1972, in the Lebombo Mountains, one of two 16 Squadron Alouette IIIs involved, made no less than 110 hoists in a single day to drop police into the area.

Often Alouettes have assisted the police in their search for escaped convicts or wanted criminals. On one occasion, in 1971, an Alouette was even used to search for escaped lions from the Hluhluwe Game Reserve in Northern Natal.

Less pleasant tasks performed by Alouette IIIs in the past were searches for missing civilian and military aircraft.

Assisting the Department of Forestry with fire-fighting is another facet of helicopter flying. Often in the past fire-fighters have had to be lifted to forest fires inaccessible by road. The smoke and unpredictable up-draughts from the hot air in the vicinity of these fires make the missions difficult, with flying conditions varying greatly from those normally encountered in mountain areas.

Historical note on No. 16 Squadron SAAF

Because it spent decades In suspended animation, No. 16 Squadron cannot claim any great seniority in today's South African Air Force. But it has eight solid battle-honours won during World War II, and can boast of three decorations for gallantry won in the present border war.

No. 16 Squadron was a war baby, and an impoverished one at that. Formed at Germiston on September 14, 1939, it was transferred to Walvis Bay a week later, and all it had to carry out its designated role of patrolling the South West African coast were three ex-South African Airways Junkers Ju-86Zs.

Not surprisingly, perhaps, the squadron lasted only until December 1939 as a separate entity, and then became B Flight of No. 32 Squadron.

The squadron reappeared on May 1, 1941, a long way from Walvis Bay – at Addis Ababa in Italian East Africa. The revived squadron's equipment still consisted of Ju-86s, but at least it had eight of them (even though serviceability was low) and two Maryland light bombers taken over from No. 12 Squadron SAAF, as well as the temporary use of two Fairey Battle light bombers.

Operational flying began immediately, with bombing and recon-

naissance missions being undertaken in support of the South African ground forces' advance across the Omo and Didessa rivers. In June 1941, a month after its re-formation, the squadron carried out 28 raids, during which it dropped 56 840 lbs of bombs.

July was also a heavy month for the new squadron. Its aircraft dive-bombed the Italian General Gazzera's last headquarters at Dembidollo and fought off at least two attacks by CR-42 fighters, with damage being done on both sides. In one clash the Ju-86 gunners involved fired 5 400 rounds at the attackers.

In August 1941 the squadron was abruptly disbanded, a number of its personnel being formed into a sub-unit called No. 35 Flight SAAF. An attempt to re-form No. 16 Squadron at Germiston in March 1942 failed due to a scarcity of aircraft, but a second attempt early in September 1942 succeeded when No. 20 Squadron SAAF (then taking part in the somewhat anti-climatic invasion of Madagascar) was renumbered.

The squadron, which was equipped with five Marylands and seven Beauforts, flew bombing, reconnaissance and leaflet-dropping operations against the Vichy French forces still holding out on the island. Meanwhile some of its personnel were undergoing training for conversion to Blenheim light bombers, and, when the fighting finally wound down in November, the unit converted to the Blenheim V, popularly known as the Bisley.

For some months the squadron occupied itself with training flights, and in April 1943 moved to Egypt for anti-submarine patrols, losing its Blenheims and converting to Beaufort IIs soon afterwards.

Then, in November 1943, equipment improved when No. 16 Squadron was issued with the formidable Beaufighter and its arsenal of cannon and rockets.

The squadron flew anti-shipping strikes in the Aegean Sea from February 1944 before moving to Italy in August to join the Balkan Air Force, supporting Tito's Yugoslav partisans by attacking German land and sea communications, strong-points and installations.

Two well-remembered operations in which the squadron took part were the sinking of the Italian liners *Rex* and *Guilio Cesare* to prevent their being used as blockships.

No. 16 Squadron was disbanded on June 15, 1945, by which time it had earned eight battle-honours.

On February 1, 1968, the squadron was re-formed at Ysterplaat as a full-time unit flying Alouette III helicopters, and on January 6 of the following year moved to Durban. Here the squadron flew on many peacetime 'operations', taking part in relief work during serious floods and lifting policemen into the mountains to destroy dagga plantations.

On July 5, 1972, the squadron moved to its new home at Bloemfontein, but just under a year later found itself split down the middle when A Flight was stationed at Port Elizabeth, B Flight remaining at Bloemfontein, but later moving to Ysterplaat. During December 1980, B Flight moved to Port Elizabeth to join A Flight.

Historical note on No. 17 Squadron SAAF

No. 17 Squadron was formed on September 1, 1939, in the last days of peace before the fury of World War II burst on the world. For a few months it formed part of the Airways Wing at Swartkop, flying ex-South African Airways Junkers Ju-52/3ms, but was then disbanded on December 1, to amalgamate with Nos. 18 and 19 Squadrons to form No. 50 Squadron.

After this unpromising start, it languished in the SAAF files till October 8, 1942, when it was re-formed at MAF Depot, Voortrekkerhoogte as a general reconnaissance squadron. In December that year the Squadron left for the Middle East. It arrived at Aden in January 1943, for training and to carry out convoy escort duties, and conversion to Blenheim Vs took place.

In May 1943 the squadron moved to Egypt and in August converted to Ventura G.R.V. light bombers. In October No. 17 Squadron moved again, this time to Palestine for convoy escort duties and anti-submarine patrols.

It stayed in Palestine for the next seven months, acquiring the distinction of having the lowest accident-rate in the entire Middle East – it did not suffer an operational casualty till January 1944, when one of its aircraft failed to return from a convoy escort in bad weather.

In May 1944 the squadron returned to North Africa and flew anti-submarine patrols in co-operation with surface vessels until July 25, 1944, when it moved to Sardinia, where it was reinforced by several crews from the disbanded No. 608 Squadron RAF.

By this time World War II was nearing its end, but the pace showed no signs of slackening and there was certainly no diminution of No. 17 Squadron's workload – in August 1944 it notched up a record 1 281 flying hours, 899 of which were operational and 705 at night.

Late in 1944 the squadron returned to North Africa, although it still maintained some detachments in Italy and, in 1945, now based in Egypt, it began training for conversion to Wellingtons and Warwick G.R.Vs.

In September 1945 it returned to South Africa, where it was eventually reassembled at Brooklyn, near Cape Town, flying 16 Warwicks for a few months until its disbandment on March 31, 1946.

Unlike some of the other squadrons disbanded just after World War II, No. 17 spent only 13 months in mothballs before being re-formed on June 1, 1947, as a mixed regular and part-time unit, equipped with Venturas and Harvards in its familiar maritime role.

Known as the City of Cape Town Squadron, No. 17 was a top-line unit, and proved it in 1950 when it won the efficiency award for regular squadrons while attending a weapons camp held at Langebaanweg.

In 1955 this fine squadron was disbanded, but on December 1, 1957, it was re-formed at Langebaanweg as the SAAF's first purely helicopter unit, flying three Sikorsky S-55s and the Air Force's sole surviving S-51, on air-sea rescue duties.

The helicopter's versatility, as demonstrated by No. 17 Squadron, soon brought it added tasks, and among other things No. 17 co-operated with the South African Police in a major internal-security operation in 1960.

In December that year the squadron received its first Alouette IIs, and seven months later moved to Ysterplaat air base near Cape Town. In time it received Alouette IIIs, and A and B Flights were stationed in Pretoria and Bloemfontein, while C and Training Flights remained at Ysterplaat.

No. 17 Squadron and its Alouettes built a solid reputation for flying in many different situations and conditions – in November 1964, B Flight hit the newspaper headlines when one of its machines picked up the wife of the lighthouse-keeper on remote Bird Island and flew her to Cape Town for an emergency operation. Nor has C Flight's memorable rescue of the crew of the wrecked *S A Seafarer* in 1966 been forgotten.

On October 30, 1970, while the squadron was parading at Ysterplaat to receive its unit colours, one of C Flight's pilots, Lieutenant D. Foote, was actually engaged in a mountain rescue-flight not far away.

The squadron presence at Ysterplaat is no more. Soon after Lieutenant Foote's exploit, C Flight became the nucleus for the re-formed No. 16 Squadron, while Training Flight was turned into the Helicopter Conversion Unit.

90. An Alouette III pilot engaged in a mountain-flying exercise hovers watchfully in the foreground as one of his colleagues carries out the final stage of a virtuoso stunt: touching the tip of a phantasmagoric column of rock with his nosewheel, before lifting away again.

91. Like a dragon-fly settling on a stalk of grass, an Alouette III lowers itself gently on to the summit of the Drakensberg mountain range's awe-inspiring Devil's Tooth – a task for a steady hand . . . and even steadier nerves.
92. The pilot cuts his power, and the Alouette III drops down past the sheer surface of the Amphitheatre, another famous feature of the Drakensberg that is beautiful to the eye but perilous for any but expert airmen.
93. An Alouette goes into a high-speed dive past a cluster of precipitous Drakensberg crags. Ordinary flying situations hold little fear for a 'chopper jockey' who has cut his teeth on the Mountains of the Dragons.
94. The Alouette looks more authoritative head-on, when it shows the extensive ribbing in the cabin area which has earned it the nickname of 'draadkar' ('wire car') among its pilots.
95. Flying over the orange groves of Citrusdal in the Western Cape, the three whirling rotor-blades of an Alouette III are frozen by the camera into momentary visibility.

No. 87 Advanced Flying School

No. 87 AFS was formed from the Helicopter Conversion Unit (HCU) at AFB Ysterplaat, which itself was formed on February 1, 1968 from one flight of No. 17 Squadron. Equipped with Alouette IIs and IIIs, it provided basic helicopter training for pilots and flight engineers. Advance training was carried out by B Flight of No. 16 Squadron from September 1974 until January 1975.

Later the unit divested itself of the earlier Alouette IIs and on January 1, 1978 moved to AFS Bloemspruit, No. 16 Squadron's A Flight taking over at Ysterplaat.

The unit continues to operate Alouette III helicopters in its training role.

THE AEROSPATIALE PUMA
Samaritan with teeth

96. A Puma of B Flight, No. 19 Squadron, nears the apex of a stall turn. It is fitted with flotation gear in case it has to make a forced landing in the ocean.
97. Overleaf: Helicopter pilots cannot travel at the same speeds as their cousins the Mirage merchants, but the stunts they get up to are equally hair-raising. Here a Puma pokes its nose into the awesome Hole in the Wall, another famous formation in the Drakensberg.

The twin-engined Puma was designed in the mid-1960s by France's famous Sud Aviation firm (now Aérospatiale) in response to a French Air Force requirement for a medium-sized, general-purpose all-weather helicopter. The first prototype flew in April 1965.

In 1967 the Puma went international, so to speak, with the signing of an Anglo-French agreement in terms of which Britain agreed to buy large numbers of Pumas and Gazelles in return for French co-operaton in developing the Westland Lynx general-purpose and anti-submarine helicopter.

The first production Pumas were delivered to the French armed forces early in 1969, by which time one had already been shipped to Britain for evaluation. The Puma's first foreign buyer, however, was the South African Air Force.

The first ordered by the SAAF (the precise quantity is not known) were shipped to the Republic late in December 1969 and assembled at No. 11 Air Depot – now a separate entity, but at that time still located at Ysterplaat air base near Cape Town – in January 1970 ... almost a year before the first operational Pumas reached Britain.

A new SAAF unit, No. 19 Squadron, was formed at Swartkop air base near Pretoria to accommodate the new 'choppers', but even before all its Pumas had been delivered it was decided that the new squadron would be split in two, A Flight being located at Swartkop and B Flight at Durban. B Flight was consequently brought into being at Natal's major port, and the first Puma was delivered to it in July 1972.

The decision to station B Flight at Durban was based on a search-and-rescue requirement for which the Puma is eminently suitable; not only is it designed for all-weather flying, but it can safely operate with only one of its two engines.

This soon proved a wise move. South Africa's east coast is a killer of men and ships, notorious for its catastrophically bad weather and huge freak waves, and virtually from its inception B Flight was involved in various daring sea-rescue operations.

One of the most famous of these was the *Neptune Sapphire* mission on August 1, 1973. The 12 000-tonne *Neptune Sapphire* was on its maiden voyage to Singapore from the builder's yard in Finland when it was broken in half by a freak wave off the Pondoland coast, far south of Durban.

B Flight was immediately called, and early that morning Major James Sclanders of the SAAF set off with several Pumas which had been specially fitted with long range fuel tanks in their crew compartments. In spite of extremely adverse weather conditions the Pumas winched off and flew to safety every man of the *Neptune Sapphire's* crew.

On occasions the Durban Pumas also take part in less spectacular missions, such as going out to passing ships to lift off sick or injured seamen, but they are not only seabirds; more than once they have been called in to rescue mountaineers trapped on the crags of the great Drankensberg mountain range.

Most of their work is done at sea, though, and the B Flight now flies later-model Pumas tailored to their special role, with squared-off main undercarriage fairings so that flotation-bags can be attached, in case they have to make a forced landing in the water, (Pumas, incidentally, are the only SAAF helicopters which have a retractable undercarriage to boost maximum speed).

Another of the Puma's structural features which often puzzles laymen are the box-shaped dust filters often fitted over the engine-intakes to ensure that foreign objects are not sucked in. Recently some Pumas have been seen with twin cylindrical multi-purpose air-intake filters which give them an undeservedly bellicose look.

Swartkop-based A Flight, while used more for overland missions, has also gotten its feet wet on occasions. The most spectacular recent mission of this kind was the flight to remote Europa Island in the Mocambique Channel to rescue the crew of the stranded Danish freighter *Pep Ice* (see also *'The Transall C-160: Pocket Hercules of The SAAF'*).

Even more recently, in April 1980, A Flight had its first taste of work in sub-zero temperatures when a member of South Africa's SANAE research base in Antarctica developed tuberculosis and it was decided to evacuate him to South Africa.

Two Pumas were sent to Cape Town and sailed for Antarctica with the supply vessel *SA Agulhas,* which has a helipad of suitable size on the stern as well as a hangar large enough to accommodate the two helicopters. The sick man was successfully lifted off and the *SA Agulhas* sailed for Cape Town, one of the Pumas flying him to a waiting ambulance at Ysterplaat air base while the *SA Agulhas* was still at sea.

SAAF pilots love the Puma and know it affectionately as the 'Pum' It is easy to understand why when one sees this rather attractive helicopter being put through its paces. Its auto-stabilizer dampens out the yaw and roll so prevalent in older helicopters to provide smooth flight, and its abundance of power provides a performance envelope which, when compared to the Alouette III, is akin to driving a high powered sports car as against a nippy economy version.

The Puma has been one of the most successful helicopters to date and about 600 have been sold to operators all over the world. For instance, negotiations are in progress to build the Puma under licence in Indonesia. In time to come the Puma may be as widely operated and well known as its smaller stable-mate, the Alouette III.

Aérospatiale has taken the basic Puma and, with more powerful Turboméca Makila turboshafts, modified air intakes, wider-track undercarriage, improved and lighter rotor headgear, changes to the transmission and improved de-icing on the rotor blades, created the Super Puma. Given the type No. SA332, the Super Puma has the same capacity as the older Puma (three crew and 16 passengers), but its performance has been improved remarkably. The AS332L with 'stretched' fuselage made its first flight on October 10, 1980. The Super Puma has generated intense interest throughout the world and time will tell if it will surpass the impact of its earlier namesake. Some Pumas were allocated to the newly formed No. 30 Squadron at Ysterplaat in January 1981.

Historical note on No. 19 Squadron SAAF
These days No. 19 Squadron flies Puma helicopters, but it first appeared on the SAAF scene on September 1, 1939, as part of the so-called 'Airways Wing' at Swartkop air station, which was equipped with hastily militarized Junkers Ju-52/3ms. The squadron lasted only a few months before being disbanded on December 1, and did not reappear on the scene until August 12, 1944, when No.

227 Squadron RAF – which had had a SAAF detachment for some time – was renumbered and South Africanized at Biferno in Italy.

The new squadron immediately commenced operations, flying Beaufighter VIs on bombing and strafing attacks on German lines of communication in Greece and Yugoslavia.

There was no lack of work on hand for No. 19 Squadron, which was eventually converted to Beaufighter Xs. Targets included trains, vehicles, radio-stations, barracks and oil-dumps; ships were also attacked on occasion, and No. 19 Squadron flew in the anti-flak role for No. 16 Squadron's Beaufighters on several joint operations.

September 1944 saw the squadron introduced to the 60-lb rocket projectile, which it used to devastating effect in support of Yugoslav partisans, even when the coming of winter reduced the number of sorties that could be flown.

The squadron never quite shook off the after-effects of the peculiar way in which it was re-formed, and during all this time some British aircrew remained with it, so that some Beaufighters' two-man crews were all-British, while others were totally South African and still others an amicable mixture of the two.

The squadron fought hard through to the last months of the war: in January 1945, for instance, it flew 90 sorties in spite of persistent cloud cover and snow.

The sort of tenacity with which the squadron pressed home its attacks can be seen in the records for February 24, 1945, when it attacked a 4 260-ton minelayer in Fiume harbour which had survived all previous attempts to sink it.

Four of the squadron's Beaufighters, each armed with six 25-lb armour-piercing rockets, made a low-level approach, diving down a mountain-slope and then turning out sharply over the water. They scored numerous hits below the waterline and raced out to sea at extremely low level before the German flak could stop them, leaving the diehard minelayer sinking at last.

The busiest month of No. 19 Squadron's war was yet to come, however; in April 1945, with the war nearly over, its Beaufighters logged 836 hours in the air, hitting bridges, strong-points and even an E-boat base in the course of 38 missions – a total of 263 sorties.

Early May 1945 brought the end of hostilities in Europe, and No. 19 Squadron's comparatively brief but heroic wartime career came to an end when it was disbanded. It was not until the dawn of the 1970s that the unit's honoured name was resurrected and granted to a new squadron formed from a flight of No. 17 Squadron and equipped with Pumas.

The proud traditions of World War II have been maintained and members of the squadron have won several awards for gallantry. In 1973 Captain A. P. Möller was awarded the Honoris Crux for the part he played in an attack on terrorists. Two years later, in 1975, this honour was won by Flight-Sergeant P. O'Neill during operations in Angola and in June 1978 it was awarded to Captain J. Church, also for operations in Angola.

At the time of writing, No. 19 Squadron's Pumas are as heavily engaged in the Namibian operational area as its Beaufighters were in Italy and Yugoslavia.

100

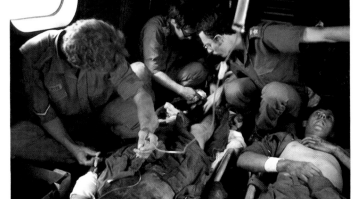

98-102 Operations in Namibia

103, 104, 105, 106, 107. The ancient Romans might have been thinking about the Puma when they coined the phrase *multum in parvo* – a lot in a little. The Puma's versatility is as legendary as its manoeuvrability. It can pluck an injured seaman from a passing ship and bring him ashore for treatment; land on – and take off again from – the snowy winter-bound wastes of the Drakensberg; skim in tight formation at zero feet over the dense bush of the operational area in search of insurgents; meet – and master – the buffeting up- and down-draughts that eddy around a mountain waterfall; and squeeze its way between hair-raisingly crowded cliff-faces with the ease of a cat insinuating itself through the bars of a garden gate.

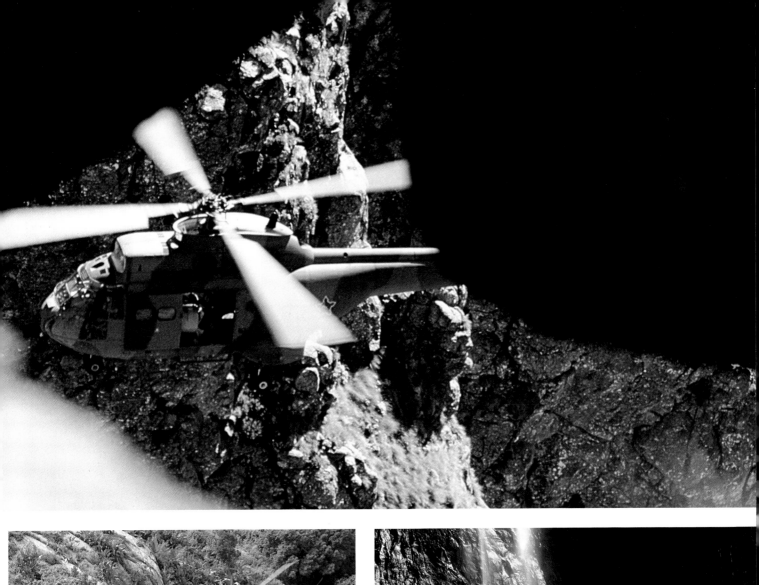

THE SUD AVIATION SA-321L SUPER FRELON
Landbound flying-boat

108. A Super Frelon of A Flight, No. 15 Squadron, scissors past the starkly beautiful memorial to the SAAF dead which stands on Bay's Hill, near Swartkop. Motionless memorial and moving machine symbolize the airman's code: Honour your dead of today – but tomorrow morning you fly again.

If the gracefully curved hull of the Super Frelon, the largest helicopter in SAAF service, reminds you vaguely of a old-time flying boat, rest assured that it is not just a deceptive sense of nostalgia. For the Super Frelon ('frelon' in French means 'wasp') started out as a naval anti-submarine helicopter capable of landing on the sea if necessary, and the boat-shaped hull is a reminder of that fact – even though those serving in SAAF colours are definitely land-bound.

The Super Frelon first saw the light of day in response to a French requirement for a heavy-lift naval helicopter. In proverbially thrifty French fashion, Sud-Aviation did not start designing from scratch but used an existing development, the smaller twin-engined experimental SA-3200 Frelon, which had first flown in June 1959.

The resulting Super Frelon took to the air for its maiden flight on December 7, 1962. It was considerably larger than its parent, featured three Turbomeca Turmo IIIC engines and was fully amphibious, with a hull suitable for landing on the water and stabilizing sponsons on the main undercarriage legs.

Four pre-production aircraft were built and, after they had been successfully evaluated, the French naval air arm ordered 17 in October 1965, mainly as anti-submarine warfare craft (at the time of writing some of these are deployed on the aircraft-carriers Cle-

menceau and Foch, and others on the helicopter-carrier Jeanne D'Arc).

At about this time the South African Air Force had also drawn up a requirement for a heavy-lift helicopter, and in May 1966 it was announced that 16 Super Frelons, designated SA-321L, had been ordered for the SAAF at a cost of R1 013 791 each.

This was the first foreign order for the type, and to date remains the largest. (Of the 98 Super Frelons built up to September 1978, some have also gone to Libya, Israel, Iraq, Iran, Red China and Zaire, the latter, an SA321J, serving as President Mobuto Sese Seko's personal aircraft.)

The first SAAF Super Frelon, like all that followed, was test-flown in France and then shipped to Cape Town, where it was reassembled at AFB Ysterplaat in June 1967. It was then flown up to AFB Swartkop near Pretoria, where it made its official debut on July 27 of that year.

The SAAF had a long wait before its order was completed, because production was in parallel with that of the initial French naval order, and it was not until November 1969 that the last of the Republic's Super Frelons was delivered.

The SA-321L as seen in SAAF service was, and is, a strictly non-amphibious version, and lacks the characteristic sponsons on the main undercarriage legs. It also has a dust filter fitted to the engine intakes which gives it an unmistakable profile.

The Super Frelon is classed as a short/medium-range tactical helicopter and has seen service in a variety of roles. It can carry about 27 fully-equipped soldiers or may be used for 'casevac' (casualty evacuation) or dropping paratroops.

Since it is roomy enough to accommodate sizeable entourages, the Super Frelon has been used to transport VIPs on several occasions, and the present Prime Minister, Mr P W Botha, has used a Frelon several times when making trips to remote areas.

Many disaster-struck southern Africans have good reason to thank the Super Frelons for their work in relief operations – sometimes in neighbouring countries which officially are hostile to the Republic.

A case in point occurred in August 1973, when heavy snows struck the bleakly beautiful Maluti Mountains of Lesotho. Two SAAF Super Frelons, 302 and 304, rescued 58 stranded Basotho from almost certain death, while supplies were flown in to other isolated mountain villages.

No. 15 Squadron initially operated the Super Frelons alone with A Flight at Swartkop and B Flight at Bloemspruit. In January 1981 No. 15 Squadron A Flight moved to AFS Durban and B Flight was reformed at AFB Ysterplaat as No. 30 Squadron.

Historical note on No. 15 Squadron SAAF

The pilots of No. 15 Squadron can claim a history as 'Jacks of all trades', for in their time they have done everything – from bombing a U-boat to rescuing ailing crocodiles and suppressing a naval mutiny.

No. 15 Squadron was born rather inauspiciously on September 14, 1939 at Germiston, one of several SAAF units hastily assembled soon after the outbreak of World War II found South Africa almost totally unprepared.

The degree of national unreadiness was reflected in the equipment initially issued to the squadron: three former South African Airways Junkers Ju-86 airliners, which were expected to carry out long-range maritime patrols even though they had neither modern navigation gear nor 'ditching' equipment other than some tractor inner tubes. It was transferred to Wingfield on September 18, 1939.

In spite of such deficiencies, many patrols were carried out; among other missions was a long and fruitless search – flown in co-operation with the Royal Navy – for the German pocket battleship *Graf Spee* in October 1939. A rather more successful search two months later ended in a Ju-86 of No. 15 Squadron intercepting the German liner *Watussi*, whose crew then scuttled her to prevent her from falling into Allied hands.

Soon after the Watussi incident No. 15 Squadron lost its identity, becoming absorbed as A Flight of No. 32 Squadron, and apparently taking over the establishment of the recently disbanded No. 5 Squadron.

June 1, 1941 saw No. 15 Squadron, its identity regained, sent to Italian East Africa, where on June 1 it absorbed the surviving personnel and equipment of No. 11 Squadron during the Omo River battle and proceeded to carry on with that unit's operations.

The Fairey Battles inherited from No. 11 Squadron were worn out by many months of action, and serviceability was low. Nevertheless, the squadron continued to operate until its last sortie had been flown on August 15, 1941, and it was ordered back to Pretoria, where by October it had begun conversion training to Maryland light bombers.

February 1942 saw the squadron heading northwards for service again, first to Aden for a brief stay and then to Egypt, where it converted to Blenheim Mk IV bombers.

In April a detachment of the squadron was stationed at the later-to-be-famous Kufra Oasis in the Western Desert for reconnaissance operations . . . only to be involved in a tragedy that was all the most ghastly for being accidental. Three Blenheims flying on a mission in early May became lost over the featureless desert and eventually force-landed, only one man surviving.

In July 1942 the squadron was re-equipped with Blenheim Mk Vs (Bisleys), and on August 8 started shipping patrols from the unit's new base at Mariut (the Kufra detachment remained *in situ* until November, 1942, however). In their new role the squadron's Bisleys attacked German coastal communications on land and sea.

On October 26, 1942, the squadron joined forces with RAF Beauforts and Beaufighters on a shipping strike against a vital Axis convoy steaming from German-held Tobruk with supplies for the Afrikakorps, which was then engaged in the Battle of El Alamein. Among the ships was the 9 000-ton tanker *Proserpina,* carrying desperately-needed fuel for the German forces.

The Allied forces fell on the convoy, No. 15 Squadron losing three of its Bisleys but seriously damaging the *Proserpina,* which was subsequently sunk by the RAF. Three of the squadron's pilots were later decorated with the DFC for their part in the attack.

By January 1943 the squadron had moved to Cyprus to fly anti-submarine patrols, and on February 17 a No. 15 Squadron Bisley, while escorting a convoy near Apollonia, witnessed a depth-charge attack by the Royal Navy destroyer *HMS Paladin*. The *Paladin's* efforts forced a Type VIIC submarine, U-205, to the surface, and it was promptly bombed by the Bisley. At this final blow the U-boat surrendered and was taken in tow by *HMS Paladin,* though the submarine sank six hours later.

By May 1943 the squadron had extended its range of operations to include the Palestinian coast, and in July handed in its trusty Bisleys to be re-equipped with Baltimore IIIA light bombers.

Thus equipped, it continued with its convoy escort duties, anti-submarine patrols and shipping reconnaissance missions. There were also occasional bombing raids against Crete and targets in the Aegean Sea, in the course of which small Baltimore formations engaged Luftwaffe fighters several times.

These activities carried on well into 1944, by which time the Baltimore Mk IIIAs had made way for Mk IVs. April of that year saw the squadron engaged in the most unusual of all its wartime tasks – making dummy runs over a Greek cruiser at Port Said to quell disturbances among its ship's company.

In August 1944 the squadron moved to Italy for bombing operations in support of the 84th Army, but late in the year took part in some shipping sorties when again a number of missions were flown over the Balkans.

No. 15 Squadron – equipped by now with Baltimore Mk Vs – stayed on in Italy for some months after the end of the war in Europe in May 1945. Many other wartime SAAF squadrons had been disbanded by now, and on August 15, 1945 it was No. 15 Squadron's turn. While in transit for home, although still on Italian soil, the squadron was disbanded and was not seen again till 1968.

On February 19 that year it was re-formed at Swartkop air base near Pretoria, as a regular SAAF unit flying the newly-acquired Super Frelon, the air force's largest helicopter.

Detachments of Super Frelons soon performed a range of tasks and duties in various parts of the country. In Pretoria in May 1968 two were used to lift air-raid sirens onto their mountings. Soon afterwards the squadron took part in Operation Sibasa, a large-scale military exercise in the northern Transvaal. In the years that followed, the squadron took part in other exercises and carried out flood-relief work in several areas.

A distinctly unusual task fell to its lot in 1970, when one of No. 15 Squadron's machines was used to rescue moribund crocodiles from St Lucia Lake on the Natal coast after the lake had become unduly saline – the strangest mission since its low-flying Baltimore IVs had dampened the ardour of the mutinous Greek sailors at Port Said.

109. When heavy lifting has to be done, the Super Frelons are called in. Here one of them easily hoists a three-tonne military vehicle off the ground.
110. A Super Frelon prepares for a stall turn above the Hartebeestpoort Dam, its six rotor-blades a whirling star above its cabin. Super Frelons have three turbine engines.
111. A Super Frelon beats its way across the endless plains of the South African hinterland. Clearly visible behind the cockpit are the filters designed to combat a traditional South African hazard: dust – lots and lots of it.
112. A Super Frelon pilot plays a perilous game of follow-my-leader with a colleague at low altitude, the six-wheeled undercarriage of his big helicopter spread like talons.

109

110

111

Historical Note on No. 30 Squadron

The squadron was formed by re-numbering No. 223 Squadron (RAF) at Pescora, Italy, on August 12, 1944, operating Martin Baltimore Mk IVs and Mk Vs. (A new No. 233 Squadron was formed in the United Kingdom soon afterwards.) The Squadron converted to Martin Marauder IIIs almost immediately and flew its first operations during August. Between then and the end of April 1945, 1 400 operational sorties were flown from Pescora and later Jesi. After moving to Biferno in June 1945, the squadron disbanded on July 15, 1945, remaining dormant until 1980 when it was decided to form a second Super Frelon squadron.

Posting of personnel commenced on December 8, and on January 6, 1981, Super Frelons of No. 15 Squadron's B Flight at AFB Bloemspruit were transferred to the new No. 30 Squadron at AFB Ysterplaat.

113. Overleaf: Built to fight human enemies, SAAF Super Frelons often find themselves battling an equally formidable adversary – old Mother Nature herself. Here a Super Frelon makes it way across a flooded landscape towards a partly submerged farmhouse.

THE NORTH AMERICAN HARVARD
Schoolmaster of the sky

114. A diving Harvard unleashes a burst of rockets at a ground target. Still a primary SAAF trainer in spite of its age, the Harvard teaches pupil pilots the finer points of 'steam' flying they cannot pick up if they start out on jets.
115. Overleaf: A flight of 'old-and-bold' T-6Gs from the Central Flying School at Dunnottar in the Transvaal thunder past the Durban waterfront in perfect formation while on a courtesy visit to the coast. Because of their training role, Harvards are the only aircraft in the SAAF which wear a high-visibility scheme of silver and dayglo instead of camouflage, not to mention extra-large serial numbers.

For generations of schoolboys it was, in its way, the South African Air Force's best recruiting agent. They would stand open-mouthed and watch the burly silver beast with its stripes of eye-catching Dayglo paint go through some ponderous evolution overhead and then pull out with a blattering 'Waaah' from its big, blunt-nosed engine, and in their hearts would say· 'That's *me* in there, *me* . . .'

That is the way pilots – or would-be pilots, anyway – are born. And it is a process in which the Harvard is second to none.

The Harvard is the best-known of all American training aircraft produced during World War II and is undoubtedly the most widely-distributed trainer of them all. No less then 10 000 were built by the parent North American company, with many more produced elsewhere under licence.

Certainly no-one would dispute that the Harvard, in its many configurations, has taught more fledgling pilots to fly than any other trainer, before or since.

The type-name 'Harvard' is not world-wide; originally it applied only to the models supplied under the wartime Lend-Lease scheme, to British and Commonwealth air forces.

In the pre-World War II United States Army Air Corps (USAAC) it was generally known as the Texan, at first bearing the prefix BC (for 'Basic Combat'). Later the prefix was changed to AT ('Advanced Trainer'), and then from 1948 to T (for 'Trainer'). The US Navy, on the other hand, used the prefix SNJ.

Originally built as a private venture, an early version known as the NA-26 won a USAAC design competition for a new kind of basic combat trainer with the equipment and attributes of operational combat aircraft of the day.

The USAAC designated the NA-26's production version the BC-1, but this was soon followed by an improved version called the BC-1A. This differed from the BC-1 in having squared wingtips and straight rudder trailing-edges – external characteristics which have remained in all subsequent versions.

In 1940 the BC-1A was redesignated the AT-6, although the aircraft was not modified in any way. The AT-6 was followed by two improved versions, the AT-6A and the AT-6B, the latter specifically for gunnery training.

Then came the AT-6C (which, like all subsequent USAAC versions, was known as the Texan). Produced at a time when a scarcity of strategic metals was anticipated, the AT-6C had a rear fuselage and tailplanes made of bonded plywood, and wings and fuselage side-panels of spot-welded low-alloy steel. This, it was calculated, would save some 565 kg of aluminium in each aircraft.

As it turned out, no strategic metal scarcity developed, and when the AT-6D appeared in 1943 it was an all-aluminium version, its main improvement on earlier models being a 24-volt instead of a 12-volt electric system. The final production version of the Texan was the AT-6F.

The aircraft's foreign service also dates from pre-war days. The Royal Air Force showed an early interest in the BC-1, and took delivery of its first models in December 1938, naming them the Harvard Mk I, the BC-1As it received later becoming the Harvard Mk II.

The outbreak of World War II and the institution of the Lend-Lease scheme resulted in a greatly increased flow of the aircraft, so that more than 5 000 eventually found their way to Britain and the Commonwealth. These Lend-Lease aircraft comprised several versions of the Texan: the AT-6C became the Harvard Mk IIa, the AT-16 became the Harvard Mk IIb, and the AT-6D became the Harvard Mk III.

South Africa came by its Harvards in World War II as it was part of the Commonwealth Joint Air Training Scheme. In terms of this, South Africa combined forces with other Commonwealth countries to train pilots. There were many air schools in South Africa where basic training was given on Tiger Moths and advanced training on variants of the old Hawker biplane (Hart bombers, Hart and Hind trainers, Audaxes and the locally-produced Hartbees) and Miles Master Mk IIs.

None of these aircraft was completely satisfactory. The Hart variants were reasonably reliable, but were showing their age and required a good deal of maintenance to keep them airworthy, while the Miles Master had a poor serviceability record, particularly as regards the engine and front spar. It was also very demanding to fly – an important reason, perhaps, why only 107 of the 310 Masters on strength in February 1943 were in flying shape.

As a result, the Harvard was selected as a replacement, the first three Mk Is being delivered in February 1942. Many Harvard Mk Is were being shipped to Rhodesia at this time, and originally these three were also destined for the Southern Rhodesian Air Force. It is assumed that the three were diverted to South Africa so that the SAAF could evaluate the type before receiving the improved Harvard Mk IIa.

The three Mk Is were assembled at Durban and flew with No. 6 Squadron, No. 10 Squadron and the No. 62 Air School. Five other Mk Is were delivered for use as instructional airframes.

For actual training, the Mk IIa was selected. Supplied from the USA by way of the RAF, the first Mk IIa Harvards arrived during the latter part of 1942, and by the time the first Harvard course started at No. 27 AS, at Bloemspruit in the Orange Free State, in February 1943 (replacing the troublesome Miles Master), 135 had been delivered to the air schools. The other air schools now receiving Harvards were No. 22 at Vereeniging and No. 23 at Waterkloof, both of which had been flying Hart variants. Later, many Harvards also were delivered to No. 62 AS at Bloemfontein for instructor training.

Late in 1943 No. 25 AS at Standerton also gave up its Masters in favour of Harvards. Eventually 105 Harvards were delivered to the unit, and in contrast to the Master, the new aircraft's serviceability record was excellent. For three weeks in December 1943, for example, there was 100% serviceability – a rarely-achieved ideal, the significance of which only an airman can fully appreciate.

Harvards continued to flow into the country (some with plywood fuselages, although these were later replaced by metal), and by the end of hostilities 633 Mk IIa and Mk III models had been delivered.

The war over, a great number of these had to be returned to the USA in terms of the Lend-Lease scheme, many subsequently being sold, inter alia, to the Belgian Air Force, while others went to the Air France apprentice training school.

However, a large number of Harvards remained in South Africa to become the backbone of the post-war SAAF'S training units. In some cases they were also the auxiliary – or only – equipment of regular units such as Nos. 1, 17, 24, 28 and 35 squadrons.

In January 1953 the part-time elements of these units were formed into a series of independent Citizen Force squadrons – Nos. 4, 5, 7, 8 and 40, followed in due course by No. 6 Squadron – all equipped with Harvards. Other Harvards were used by the Air Operational School at Langebaanweg.

The SAAF received another batch of Harvards in 1952 and 1953 – about 65 direct from the USA. These were refurbished AT-6As or SNJ-3s, and AT-6Cs or SNJ-4s, all with metal rear fuselages and modified to AT-6D standards with 24-volt electric systems.

In the meantime, the Harvard type was undergoing a resurgence in the United States. In 1949 it was decided – because no new trainer had been selected by the renamed United States Air Force – to have some 2 000 AT-6s rebuilt with various modernizations which, among other things, involved changing the cockpit layout, increasing the fuel capacity and providing a steerable tailwheel.

Many of these rebuilt T-6Gs, as the version was designated, were supplied to foreign air forces in terms of the US military assistance programme, and about 30 were delivered to the SAAF in 1953 and 1954. At the time these latest Harvards were easy to spot among their older brethren because of the propellor-spinners and the egg-shaped direction-finding loop on the rear fuselage, but since these features have been removed, only an expert eye can tell them apart.

The last Harvards acquired by the SAAF arrived in a rather strange way. Four Belgian Air Force Harvards (two Mk IIs and two Mk IIIs) made their way to South Africa in 1961, from the turmoil in the newly-independent Congo. Sadly, they were never put to use because they differed so much from the types in SAAF service; instead, several ended on display at various military institutions. One of these can be seen at the Fort Klapperkop military museum outside Pretoria – where it is eminently eligible for display for it actually saw SAAF service during World War II before being shipped home to Britain and from there disposed of to the Belgian Air Force.

In the late 1960s a batch of SAAF Harvards left the country, being sold to the FAP (Portuguese Air Force) when the Impala trainer was taken into service. Recently the survivors of this batch were sold by the FAP and several are now flying under private civil registration in Britain and the USA. When these Harvards arrived there they still wore large amounts of Dayglo maximum-visibility trim, which the Portuguese had taken over from the SAAF. No doubt inspired by all this, at time of writing one of the British owners intended to repaint his Harvard in an authentic reproduction of its original SAAF scheme.

The Harvard is not as common in South African skies as it used to be. Since the early 1970s many Citizen Force squadrons have been re-equipped with Impala Mk Is, their Harvards being transferred to Central Flying School at Dunnottar and its Citizen Force element, 40 Squadron.

But it will be a long while before that familiar old rasping drone vanishes totally from the flying scene in this country. The Harvard remains the SAAF's ab initio training aircraft on which pupil pilots cut their teeth before graduating to the more modern Impala.

As an SAAF officer once explained it to a layman: 'Before you can fly a jet, you should know how to handle a prop plane. It's like learning to drive on a car with manual gears before going on to an automatic transmission.'

116. A Harvard goes into a banked turn above CFS Dunnottar, its big engine letting out the blatting roar that used to be a familiar sound at almost every air base before the SAAF's part-time Citizen Force squadrons converted to Impalas.

117. A Harvard of No. 40 Squadron rolls into a vertical bank, the spatless wheels tucked in under its wings peering down like a pair of huge pop-eyes.

118. In a Harvard you can still land in traditional fashion with the wind blowing on your cheek. Here a Harvard pilot slides back his canopy as he turns into his final approach. The No. 41 Squadron emblem on the cowling is a relic of the brief period in the early 1970s when that squadron flew Harvards as station aircraft.

119. Harvards are reliable old aircraft which lend themselves to fine flying. Here a formation of T-6Gs makes a text-book take-off from Durban's Louis Botha Airport.

120. Ask a young SAAF flyer of today what the Harvard's nickname is and he will say 'the Spammy', not knowing it is derived from the disrespectful soubriquet 'Spam can' bestowed on the Harvard's distinctive fuselage by wartime airmen. And what is 'Spam'? Ah, if you are old enough to remember it was a species of American ration, you are probably a member of the Harvard generation yourself.

THE AM-3CM BOSBOK and
THE ATLAS C-4M KUDU Children of a Mexican dream

121. Tail up, a Bosbok from No. 42 Squadron trundles down the grass runway at Potchefstroom – once the home of the SAAF's short-lived army Air Recce Squadron – preparatory to take-off. The sturdy little Italian-made aircraft is designed to use far rougher facilities than this well-barbered strip.
122. Overleaf: Seen from some angles it may resemble a tomato-box, but the South African-built Kudu does not fly like one – and this machine of No. 41 Squadron proves it with a steep bank to port.

If there were to be an aerial reincarnation of the tough little Bushveld pony on which the Boers of 1899 ran rings around General Buller's 'Tommies', it would probably be in the form of a Bosbok or Kudu.

They are designed to 'go anywhere and do anything', and though they have not been around for long, these two closely-related but very different aircraft carved out an important place for themselves in the current operational area on the border.

There are few frills on the Italian-built Bosbok and its South African cousin, the Kudu. They are no-nonsense aircraft, designed for 'bush-bashing' in areas where facilities are conspicuously absent and a landing-strip may consist of a stretch of more or less virgin bushveld.

At times they have needed every ounce of the strength and versatility that is engineered into them. A Bosbok may be asked to weave back and forth with a forward air controller who is directing artillery fire by radio; it may be ordered to ferry people or messages in and out of tight spots; a Kudu perhaps will be called on to evacuate wounded soldiers or drop supplies or paratroops. The two aircraft may not look prepossessing when compared with sleeker

and more sophisticated machines, but they can carry out all these tasks and other as well.

As one newly respectful SAAF pilot was reputed to have said after seeing what the ugly little fellows could do: 'Never look a Kudu in the mouth . . .'

Yet the basic concept developed into these essentially South African aircraft was formulated a long way from home base – in the mind of General Luis Azcarate of Mexico 20 years ago, in fact, who dreamt of a four- to six-seater high-wing monoplane, with fixed tricycle undercarriage, capable of operating in extremely rough terrain.

Unlike many dreams, the general's came true, and the result was the LASA-60, which went into production at the Lockheed-Azcarate plant at San Luis Potosi, Mexico, in the early 1960s.

The first link in what might be called 'the SAAF Connection' was forged soon after, when the Italian firm of Aeronautica Macchi – designer of the original MB-326 from which South Africa developed its Impalas Mk 1 and 2 – obtained exclusive manufacturing rights to the LASA-60 for all countries except the United States.

The Italians' first production versions were called the AL-60B-1 and AL-60B-2, and were exported to a number of countries, including South Africa's neighbour, Lesotho. Others appeared on the South African civil register, while the Rhodesian Air Force bought some in 1967, gave them the local name of Trojan, and were still using the survivors in 1980.

AerMacchi development did not stop with the production of the two AL-60B variants. Engines were changed, undercarriages modified and extra freight-doors added. With every major change the AL-60 type became tougher, handier, more powerful.

Then, in the mid-1960s, the Italian army drew up a requirement for a multi-purpose aircraft suitable for such tasks as forward air controlling, observation and liaison work and casualty evacuation. AerMacchi came forward with a concept it called the MB-335, and detailed design work as contracted out to another Italian company, Aerfer Industria Aerospatiali Meridionali (later changed to Aeritalia). The result was the AM-3C, consisting basically of a new fuselage mated to the well-tried AL-60 wing, and the first of three prototypes, I-AEAM, flew at Varese in May 1967.

After an evaluation programme, the SAAF settled on the Italian development, and in May and September 1970 ordered two batches of the AM-3CM version, giving them the local type-name 'Bosbok'.

The first Bosbok to be produced for the SAAF made its debut at the Turin Air Show in 1972, although it still wore an Italian civil registration (I-TAAA) at the time. (For some reason, it did not arrive in South Africa till after the second Bosbok, No. 921, had been taken on charge in March 1973.)

The others followed in due course and the last was delivered in December 1975, by which time many of its predecessors had already seen action during the first phase of the brief South African intervention in the Angolan war.

At the time of its introduction, the Bosbok encountered a good deal of consumer resistance, with some SAAF pilots decidedly unimpressed by this untried and almost crudely simple newcomer, but eventually the 'Bossie' started making friends and generating the first of the layers of anecdotes that build up around every aircraft that sees a lot of use.

A stunt that reportedly melted many hearts is the one about two madcap young lieutenants who went up in a Bosbok to carry out a night mission. At that time the book stated the little aircraft's endurance was 2,5 hours. The lieutenants decided they could improve on this and staggered around for an unconscionable length of time with the aircraft on its lowest power settings. Exactly how long they spent in the air depends on who tells the story – but it is a fact that the Bosbok's official safe endurance is now set at 4,5 hours.

In a sense the SAAF's Bosboks had been overtaken by developments before they had even been delivered by AerMacchi, because late in 1971 South Africa decided to produce a locally-designed light transport aircraft tailored to African conditions: this was to result in the Kudu.

Hard-headed financial considerations led the SAAF to ignore later and more powerful developments in favour of the basic AL-60C-4, since this used the same engine and wing as the AM-3C (Bosbok) variant and meant many components would be common to both.

A design team from South Africa's Atlas Aircraft Corporation went to Italy and eventually came up with what was known as the AL-60C-4M. Basically this was a revamped AL-60C-4 incorporating a maximum number of AM-3CM components, a single sliding door suitable for paratroop-drops instead of freight doors, and a hatch in the floor for supply-drops.

Technicians at the Atlas factory near Johannesburg started work on the AL-60C-4M prototype in 1973, and on February 14 of the following year it was test-flown at Jan Smuts Airport under the civil registration ZS-IZF.

Civil pilots and technicians put the new aircraft through extensive ground and flight tests to check its strength, stability, control and performance. It passed them all, qualified for the United States Federal Air Requirement No. 23, and was duly declared an approved type by the South African Directorate of Civil Aviation.

ZS-IZF's successor, ZS-IZG, went into service as the first Atlas C-4M Kudu in the SAAF, numbered 960.

At the time of writing the Kudu is still being built at the Atlas factory, with all production taken up by the SAAF; the only civil Kudu in existence is the prototype, ZS-IZF, which is used by Atlas as a communications and test aircraft.

The Mexican general's dream differs from what he envisaged: he certainly could not have guessed that the descendants of his brainchild would one day operate over the vast bushveld of southern and central Africa.

Historical note on No. 41 Squadron SAAF

The wheel has turned full circle for No. 41 Squadron, which was originally formed as an army co-operation squadron, then went on to fighters and came all the way back to army co-operation again.

Formed at Waterkloof air base in October 16, 1940, the unit let no grass grow under its wheels and was on the way to join in the Abyssinian campaign by the end of the month.

At first the squadron's Hartbees saw little action, being used mostly for photo-survey work, but in December 1940 offensive operations got under way and there was plenty of hot work until the end of the year, ranging from photo-reconnaissance sorties and strafing vehicles to bombing, artillery spotting and leaflet-dropping. Often heavy enemy anti-aircraft fire was encountered, and on April 10, 1941, one of the squadron's aircraft returned to base showing no less than 33 hits.

In June of the same year the full equipment inventory of No. 40 Squadron was taken over, but the ravages of fighting soon made inroads on this new material – of 18 aircraft serviceable in early August 1941, six were shot down by the end of the month.

During September and October 1941 B Flight of 3 Squadron was transformed for a short time into No. 41 Squadron 'Fighter Detachment', flying Mohawks, but the honeymoon did not last long, and after two months the unit reverted to 3 Squadron.

Things quietened at the end of the year, and by early 1942 No. 41 Squadron was engaged in communications flying and rounding up recalcitrant Italian colonial troops.

The squadron remained behind in a garrison role when the South African war effort rolled on to the Western Desert, and in mid-year began to convert to Hurricane Mk Is and, later, Hurricane Mk IIBs.

The squadron did not arrive in the Middle East until May 1943 and was given air-defence and convoy patrol duties, flying from North African bases – spiced, from July onwards, with long-range operations against Crete.

In February 1944 the squadron began receiving Spitfire Mk IXs (it also operated some Spitfire Mk Vs during that year), and in April 1944 it provided long-range escorts for raids on Crete by Martin Marauders of No. 24 Squadron SAAF, using long-range fuel tanks on its Spitfire Mk IXs. Engagements were few, however, although detachments operated from Cyprus and Palestine and two Spitfire Mk IXs were stripped of all excess weight and paint to prepare them for high-altitude interception.

The squadron did not survive the war; it was disbanded at the end of October 1944, its personnel going to other SAAF units or returning to South Africa.

It was re-formed in January 1963 as the first part-time army co-operation unit, flying Austers, but in 1968 – by which time it was operating Cessna 185s from Grand Central Aerodrome, Johannesburg – it was transferred back to the SAAF in October 1968. In the mid-1970s it was equipped with Bosbok (February 1974) and Kudu (July 1976) aircraft.

Historical note on No. 42 Squadron SAAF

Its men wear Air Force blue today, but there is a glint of Army khaki woven into No. 42 Squadron's heart, because it is the direct descendant of the only army aviation unit to serve in the South African forces during World War II.

No. 42 Squadron's immediate ancestor is No. 42 AOP Flight, which was formed at Bari, in Italy on January 23, 1945, to give the Sixth South African Division's gunners a much-needed aerial observation post capacity. Organization and procedures were taken over from similar British units, and an officer of the South African Artillery was placed in command.

Most of the pilots were drawn from the SAAF, however, and to prepare them for artillery-spotting duties they were given special training that lasted so long the fighting was nearly over by the time they joined the flight at Lucca on March 13, 1945.

The flight became operational on April 15, 1945 – less than a month before the end of the war in Europe – flying Austers from a strip near Grizzana. There was still plenty of work for them to do, and the flight earned its keep by directing artillery fire, locating the division's forward elements and reconnoitring the axis of advance.

The grim stop-go slogging that had characterised the Italian campaign had now turned into a fast-moving follow-up operation as the Germans retreated, and the flight seldom stayed long in one location. At the end of April it moved to Treviso; on May 2 it was at Verona, following the division all the way to Milan, where it stopped for the last time.

With the long war over, only one pleasant duty remained – celebrating the end of more than half a decade of fighting. On May 14 the Sixth Division held a monumental victory parade on the famous motor-racing track at Monza; leading the march-past was one of the flight's Jeeps, while its Austers flew overhead. The Austers were shipped back to South Africa and No. 42 Flight was not disbanded, but was placed under the since-vanished II Armoured Brigade and based at Potchefstroom, the home of the South African Artillery. Its first two purely Army pilots were trained at the SAAF's Central Flying School in 1949, and No. 42 AOP Flight stayed on, flying Austers of various marks.

Inter-service priorities had not been finalized at this stage, and for a while the flight was placed under SAAF control. In 1953 it reverted to the Army again, though not for long, and after only a few years in khaki it was passed back to the SAAF as No. 42 Squadron This time the change-over proved permanent.

During this time the Austers were phased out and the squadron was re-equipped with Cessna 185s in May 1962 and with the Bosbok in 1974. From February 1981 all training of pilots on Kudus, Bosboks and Cessna 185s was to be conducted by a new unit, No. 84 AFS at AFS Potchefstroom.

123   124   125

126

123. By the very nature of its duties, the Kudu is much more intimately connected to the ground than some of its colleagues, and this one seems to prove the point by melting away into the landscape.
124. A SAAF triplane, à la the famed 'Red Baron'? Not quite – three Kudus are photographed in extremely tight formation.
125, 126. Cousins they might be, but the svelte lines of the earlier Bosbok (above) are unmistakable when contrasted with the bulkier fuselages of the three Kudus (below) engaging in a fighter-style break to starboard.

THE CESSNA 185
Odd-job man of the SAAF

127. A formation of trusty work-horses of the SAAF, Cessna 185s of No. 11 Squadron, takes to the air. Appropriately, there were 11 aircraft in the formation when this photograph was taken.

The days when the Cessna 185 was the South African Air Force's premier aerial observation post aircraft are long gone, but a large number of these handy and extremely economical little aircraft still serve in SAAF colours.

The use of aircraft as aerial observation posts (AOPs) is a time-honoured practice dating back to World War I – in fact, aircraft first became involved in the military role because of their ability to see far more than even the keenest-eyed ground soldier.

During World War II an even more important role was played by such AOP aircraft as the American Piper Cub, the British Taylorcraft (known in military guise as the Auster I), and Germany's Fieseler Storch. The Royal Air Force's famed Westland Lysander was an AOP, too, among many other things, and at times even Spitfires were used for aerial observation.

In the early post-war years the South African Air Force acquired a small number of Auster AOP-6s for use in artillery fire control, which is more colloquially known as 'artillery spotting' – at that stage the responsibility of pilots drawn from the army rather than the SAAF.

The SAAF bought more Austers in the ensuing years – five AOP-6s in 1953 and two AOP-9s in 1957 – but in 1958 acquired two Dornier Do-27s, both of which were based at Swartkop air base. They operated from there for some years, until one of the Dorniers crashed in the early 1960s.

Some mystery surrounds the Dorniers. Presumably they were acquired for evaluation purposes but did not come up to scratch, for no further SAAF orders materialized; instead the Cessna 185A was selected to replace the Austers.

It was a good choice, for the 185A – a development of the 1953-vintage Cessna 180, featuring a larger cabin, a strengthened structure for cargo-carrying and a more powerful engine – has proved to be a long-lived aircraft. The first one rolled off the production line in 1961, and at the time of writing the type is still being made.

Basically a utility aircraft designed for the civil market, the Cessna 185 proved from the start that it was a willing recruit to military use. Several air forces adopted it, and many were built under United States Air Force contract and designated U-17, for delivery to foreign nations participating in the American military assistance programme.

The initial SAAF order for 24 Cessna 185As was delivered in May and June 1962. The Austers they replaced were moth-balled until 1964 or 1965, after which they were sold to civilian owners, who are still flying them.

Most of the new Cessnas went to No. 42 Squadron at Potchefstroom base in the Transvaal, home of the School of Artillery, but others were supplied to No. 41 Squadron, a Citizen Force unit then based at Grand Central Aerodrome near Johannesburg. At the time the Army still had its own aviation section, and the Potchefstroom Cessnas were, in fact, flown by army pilots until the late 1960s, when they were placed under Light Aircraft Command SAAF.

The SAAF Cessnas were augmented by 12 185Ds in December 1965, four 185Es in February 1967 and five 185Es in 1968, and for several more years they continued to be the backbone of Army air reconnaissance.

Then the Cessnas faded a little as the first of the SAAF's Italian-made Bosbok aircraft began to be delivered to No. 42 Squadron in 1973. All but one of the SAAF Cessnas, including those of No. 41 Squadron, were transferred to the newly re-formed No. 11 Squadron at Potchefstroom, the lone exception being used for communications duties by No. 6 Squadron at Port Elizabeth until April 1976.

The Cessna in SAAF service has not been relegated to the scrapheap by the appearance of the Bosbok and the locally-produced Kudu. It remains the most economical aircraft flown by the SAAF, and at the time of writing continues to serve as a very useful liaison and communications aircraft.

In its normal configuration, the cabin seats the pilot and five passengers, but if necessary the seats can be removed in order to load cargo.

Historical note on No. 11 Squadron SAAF

No. 11 Squadron was formed in April 1939 as a fighter-bomber unit based at Durban, its A Flight being equipped with Wapitis, but existed only till December that year before being disbanded.

However, it was re-formed at Waterkloof on December 11, 1939 by the simple expedient of renumbering No. 1 (Bomber/Fighter) Squadron to No. 11 (Bomber) Squadron, and by May 1940 it was equipped with 24 Hartbees.

The same month the commanding officer, Major R. H. Preller, took the squadron to Nairobi, and on June 12 led it on its first offensive operation, an armed reconnaissance over the Northern Frontier District.

Later that month the squadron handed all its Hartbeestes over to No. 40 Squadron, preparatory to re-equipping with Fairey Battles. At the time the squadron already had one Battle, No. 901, on charge, but this came to a sad end the day after the hand-over.

Major Preller was flying it on a photo-reconnaissance sortie over landing-grounds in the Kismayu area on June 19 when it was hit by ground fire and he had to force-land. The three-man crew set out on foot for the long slog back to base, but after a while Preller left his two subordinates behind while he went for help on a camel, in company with two Somalis they had met. Preller finally reached help on July 1, his men being picked up on July 4, suffering badly from privation.

Preller's crew were the first SAAF members to be posted missing during World War II (although in this case, of course, there was a happy ending to their disappearance), and Preller himself received a DFC, the SAAF's first decoration of the war.

While all this was going on, 21 members of the squadron had returned to South Africa to fetch the Battles, and by August 12, 15 of the machines were established at Archer's Post, Kenya.

Operations began on August 19 in the form of an armed reconnaissance, and it was a foretaste of things to come: bombing and photographic tasks – usually both on the same mission – were to be No. 11 Squadron's principal duties for the rest of the campaign in Italian East Africa.

The squadron destroyed many Italian aircraft on the ground in the course of the campaign – on August 21, for example, five of its Battles made a low-level attack on the Mogadishu airfield, destroying five Caproni Ca-133 bombers. During this raid one observer, Lieutenant W. J. B. Chapman, was wounded by ground fire as his Battle made its third pass over the airfield, but although incapacitated he successfully directed the gunner, Air-Sergeant Wright, in the operation of his F24 camera.

The squadron also destroyed many Italian vehicles and on occasion even dropped propaganda leaflets. Often its aircraft met stiff opposition; on September 12, for instance, two Battles were shot down in flames by CR-32 fighters.

The first night raid of the campaign, on Mogadishu, was flown by No. 11 Squadron's Battles on October 18 in bright moonlight.

Operations continued into the new year, with March 1941 enlivened by a daring 'stunt' which was much talked about at the time. Forced to land in the bush on March 27 as a result of combat damage, a Battle pilot, Lieutenant Snyman, talked about 50 members of the local population into hacking out a makeshift runway from which he and his crew were duly evacuated by Major Irvine of No. 11 Squadron, flying a Wapiti.

The squadron stayed close behind the Allied advance, attacking enemy installations and vehicles. But the pace was beginning to tell and various members were exhibiting unmistakeable signs of battle fatigue.

On May 23, three Battles attacked a convoy of 30 vehicles near the Omo River, scoring about 40 hits with their bombs. It was one of the last operations flown by the squadron, which was then based at Algato; before the month was out it had been renumbered to become No. 15 Squadron SAAF.

In its short life the now-defunct squadron had posted quite a creditable score. It had lost more than a dozen Battles – four to enemy fighters and five or six to anti-aircraft fire – but it had destroyed at least 19 enemy aircraft on the ground and wiped out or damaged innumerable vehicles, buildings, and other installations, and had dropped a large number of propaganda leaflets – 53 000 in one mission in January 1941.

No. 11 Squadron was re-formed in the Middle East on June 29, 1944 on Spitfire Vs, taking over some equipment from No. 9 Squadron SAAF. Having completed its training it moved to Italy in September, being based initially at Perugia to convert (much to the pilots' surprise and, no doubt, chagrin) to Kittyhawk Mk IVs.

The first operation was flown on October 30, when six of the 'Kittybombers' scored two direct hits on a German stores dump, and from then on until the end of the war in Europe the squadron was kept fully engaged as part of No. 8 Wing SAAF, serving briefly in support of the US 5th Army late in 1944. In April 1945, their final month of operations, No. 3 and No. 11 Squadrons flew a combined total of 1 025 sorties.

The squadron was disbanded after the Axis collapse, and was not re-formed until January 2, 1974, based at AFS Potchefstroom and equipped with Cessna 185s taken over from other SAAF units which were converting to newer types.

128. **Its camouflage blending with the ground far below, a Cessna of No. 11 Squadron wings its way across the geometric pattern of an agricultural landscape.**

NO. 21 SQUADRON
Quart in a pint pot

129. No. 21 Squadron shows what it has tucked away in its VIP taxi fleet in this formation of three aircraft which for variety cannot be matched by any other SAAF unit. Leading is *Casteel,* the squadron's lone Viscount, with a Merlin and a Mercurius as its No. 2 and No. 3.

No. 21 Squadron of the South African Air Force does not have an unusually high number of aircraft, but, as far as variety goes, this élite transport wing flies no less than three different types of passenger aircraft, mainly ferrying the civilian and military leaders of the country from one destination to another.

There is no mistaking the machines it flies; of all the aircraft in the SAAF, they are the only ones which are decked out in a civilian-style trim – white topsides and silver underneath, with a nose-to-tail blue cheatline separating the two.

The queen of No. 21 Squadron's fleet is *Casteel,* the only Vickers Viscount in South Africa still in official hands. If *Casteel's* various crews wished to, they could drop more names than a gossip columnist. In her time she has played hostess to four State Presidents and numerous cabinet ministers, generals and important officials, as well as scores of prominent foreign visitors such as Dr Kurt Waldheim, Secretary-General of the United Nations, and his special representative for Namibia, Martti Ahtisaari.

And the chances are that *Casteel* will carry a good many more before she is grounded for the last time, because the Viscount type is another of those old-timers like the Dakota and Skymaster that are so useful and long-lived there can be no thought of retiring them in the foreseeable future. *Casteel* is also probably the fittest Viscount

flying anywhere in the world today; sturdily built for the constant slog of civil airline work, her comparatively low rate of utilization as a SAAF VIP aircraft has added years to her life.

Viscounts have been flying since 1948. The most successful of Britain's post-World War II export airliners, they are still in use as civil and military passenger aircraft in many parts of the world.

Numerous series of Viscounts were built before production ended. An early customer for some of the original production batch, the Series 700, was Central African Airways (now Air Zimbabwe), but South Africa did not acquire any for some time, until it bought seven of the later Series 813 aircraft and, much later, contracted to buy two Series 818s from, of all places, Fidel Castro's Cuba. (Somewhere along the line the deal went sour, however, and only one Cuban Viscount served in South African Airways livery.)

All the SAA Viscounts have long since been replaced by more modern aircraft, and are still flying overseas. Various other Viscounts are still active in southern Africa, but *Casteel* is the only one left in government service.

The jet-propelled component of No. 21 Squadron consists of Hawker-Siddeley HS-125 executive jets, which in the SAAF are known by the type-name 'Mercurius'. The HS-125 was conceived about 20 years ago by the now-defunct De Havilland aircraft company and went into production as the DH-125.

The first British-designed business jet, it has proved popular in many parts of the world – particularly in the United States, where the De Havilland name was held in such respect that for years after the firm had been absorbed by Hawker-Siddeley, the aircraft was still marketed as the DH-125. After two decades it continues to be produced, albeit with a lengthened fuselage and improved turbofan instead of turbojet engines.

For all its obvious virtues, however, the HS-125 was not the SAAF's first choice when in the early 1960s it began shopping for VIP transports to replace its fleet of ageing De Havilland Herons. The SAAF preferred the French Dassault Mystère 20, and placed an order for three. All had been completed and at least one had actually been painted with the SAAF VIP trim, when the United States government stepped in and blocked the sale on the grounds that the Mystère was powered by US-manufactured General Electric CF700 turbofans.

Eventually the US government decided that the Mystères were unlikely to be used in a combat role and belatedly lifted the embargo, but by then the SAAF had lost interest and ordered four HS-125 400Bs from Hawker-Siddeley. The almost-SAAF Mystères were disposed of to other buyers and at least one ended up in the Royal Norwegian Air Force.

The four SAAF HS-125s, dubbed 'Mercurius' because Hawker-Siddeley had given them no type-name, were delivered during the first half of 1970 – only to be virtually wiped out less than a year later in one of the most tragic flying accidents in South African aviation history.

On May 26, 1971, three Mercuriuses carrying a total of 11 SAAF personnel were rehearsing a mass fly-past over the Goodwood Showgrounds near Cape Town which was to be part of the 10th Republican anniversary celebrations five days later. Because aircraft of various types were taking part, split-second timing and control were called for.

It was a dull, sullen day. Visibility was estimated at between 1,5 and 5 km; the cloud-base varied between 600 m and 760 m above ground, and in some areas it was raining. The three Mercuriuses took off from Flying Training School Langebaanweg, near Saldanha Bay, rendezvoused at Koperfontein, about 50 km from the showgrounds, and then headed for the showgrounds.

The formation's leader, Commandant L. F. Henning, had been ordered to bring the aircraft over the showgrounds at 250 m and 250 knots, maintain direction and height for 30 seconds and then turn sharp right while climbing to 300 m. This done, they were to fly back to the coast and return to Langebaanweg.

In tight formation the Mercuriuses roared over the showgrounds as ordered, but 10 seconds later than laid down in the schedule. This information was radioed to them and duly acknowledged. Then there was a ghastly thunderclap of sound as the three little aircraft hurled themselves to total destruction against the great stony flank of Devil's Peak where it towers over Cape Town to the left of Table Mountain.

Somehow they had drifted three kilometres west of the precisely-planned course that should have taken them safely past the Mother City's mountain guardians.

Almost a year later a magistrate at the inquest announced his findings; that 'no living person' could be held responsible for the tragedy.

By that time the SAAF had ordered and received three more HS-125s to replace the crashed aircraft. They were delivered in January 1972 and have served without loss ever since.

The newest aircraft in No. 21 Squadron are sleek little Swearingen Merlin IVAs, the latest in a line of small executive transports built since 1966 by the Swearingen Aviation Corporation of the United States.

In the 1960s Swearingen specialized in the conversion and improvement of existing aircraft, notably the Beechcraft 65 Queen Air, which it modified and marketed as the Queen Air 80, and the original Merlin I, created by mating a newly-designed eight-seat pressurized fuselage to the Beechcraft Queen Air wing and Twin Bonanza undercarriage, and powered by piston engines.

The Merlin I did not develop beyond the prototype stage, being succeeded by the Merlin II, in which the wing had been modified to accept Pratt & Whitney PT6A turboprop engines. The Merlin II flew for the first time on April 13, 1965, and was duly certificated, but by the time it went into production its fuselage had been 'stretched' by 762 mm and it was called the Merlin IIA.

The IIA was followed in June 1968 by the IIB, powered by Garret AiResearch turboprop engines, and in due course other versions appeared, in spite of a slight hiatus in 1971 during which Swearingen went into liquidation and was absorbed by the Fairchild Corporation.

One of these was the Merlin IVA, which incorporated a notably 'stretched' fuselage, and an early military customer was the SAAF, which ordered several to replace a number of Dakotas still being used as VIP transports by No. 21 Squadron.

The first SAAF Merlins were delivered to Rand Airport late in June 1975, followed by others in July, August, September and November, with the final Merlin arriving in March 1976.

One of the SAAF Merlins is permanently fitted out as an air ambulance, featuring the most modern medical equipment, and all carry a Swearingen-designed Aerojet-General rocket installation in the tail-cone, designed to assist the aircraft in emergencies – a useful backstop feature, since No. 21 Squadron is based at Swartkop, which is 1 460 m above sea level.

SAAF Merlins also feature a large cargo door in the rear fuselage, while the passengers leave and enter through a front door equipped with an integral air-stair – a particularly handy feature when operating from airstrips which are not equipped with the necessary ground-support facilities. The seats in the cabin are arranged individually on either side of a central aisle, with a bulkhead separating the rear cargo compartment from the cabin.

Historical note on No 21 Squadron SAAF

Now the South African Air Force's prime transporter of Very Important Persons, No. 21 Squadron has a history of hell-raising bombing raids and desperate air battles dating to the days of the North African campaign of World War II.

No. 21 Squadron was formed at Nakuru, Kenya, on May 8, 1941, and two months later moved to Egypt, where it was stationed at Landing-Ground 21 in the Western Desert as a component of No. 261 Wing – later 3 Wing SAAF.

The squadron entered the Western Desert fray at a fairly hectic time. Typical of many of its early operations is one that took place on September 7, 1941, when nine of the squadron's Maryland light bombers were scheduled to bomb Bardia. Twenty-four kilometres south of Buq Buq the formation was jumped by Bf-109s, which shot down one of the Marylands. It was not a totally one-sided fight, however, as a pilot named Major Britz (later commander of the squadron) shot down a 109 with his front guns and his rear-gunner, Sergeant Petterson, hit another 109, which was seen to spin away, trailing heavy smoke.

The pace became even hotter in November-December 1941, with the squadron flying intensive bombing operations, taking over all of No. 12 Squadron SAAF's Marylands on Boxing Day when that unit went over to Bostons. But the era of the Maryland was fast coming to an end, and No. 21 Squadron was the last remaining operational Maryland bomber unit in the Western Desert when it withdrew to the Nile Delta in late January 1942.

The squadron was non-operational at Amiriya until September 1942, re-equipping and working up on the Baltimores it began receiving from August onwards. In June 1942 the commanding

officer was attached to No. 12 Squadron for experience on Baltimores, while parties of ground crew worked as reliefs for their No. 12 Squadron opposite numbers.

Early in October 1942, with the squadron again operational, it joined No. 232 Wing SAAF and began operations on October 8, but did not stay long with its new formation before being moved to No. 3 Wing SAAF.

The squadron fought in the El Alamein battle and went on to many months of intense air activity. Among other things, the squadron bombed the 15th Panzer Division on March 22, 1943, escorted for the first time by United States Army Air Force P-40 Warhawks of the 79th Fighter Group.

May 12, 1943, saw the squadron take part in the final bombing raid of the North African campaign, and later that month its aircraft also hit the Italian-held island of Pantelleria (which was so hammered by Allied bombers between May 29 and June 11 that when British landed, the 11 000-man garrison surrendered almost without firing a shot).

The squadron moved to Malta and began operations over Sicily. Often they met bitter enemy resistance, and after one particularly heavy contact with Bf-109s, Focke-Wulf FW-190s and Macchi MC-202s Captain A. C. 'Tony' Smit belly-landed his Baltimore at the squadron base with 298 holes from bullets and flak.

Captain Smit had handed out some punishment as well; he shot the canopy off one 109 with his front guns and, on its way past, his gunner, Flight-Sergeant D. Wright, poured a long burst into it as well, to send the German aircraft crashing into the sea in flames.

During the invasion of Sicily the squadron flew several night interdiction raids in addition to its normal daylight operations, and this round-the-clock work continued as the squadron moved to Sicily and was plunged into the Italian campaign.

After flying a total of 217 sorties from Sicily the squadron moved to the Italian mainland and settled in at the big Foggia air base on October 16, 1943. From here operations continued at a furious tempo; on one occasion Lieutenant D. G. Wood – severely wounded, two of his crew dead and the third dying – nursed his seriously damaged Baltimore back to Foggia, for which he was awarded an immediate DSO.

Early 1944 found the squadron operating over three different areas, supporting the Anzio beach-head, the Monte Cassino offensive and Tito's partisan operation in Yugoslavia. A respite came in July, however, when the squadron stood down for conversion to Marauders.

By August 1944 No. 21 Squadron was back in action, bombing targets in northern Italy. It was still operating with No. 3 Wing, and on April 16, 1945, the squadron's Major Musgrove led a wing box of only four aircraft on the first SAAF raid made with the new Shoran bombing aid. (Another member of the squadron, Major R. Farrant DFC, was one of only two SAAF airmen to qualify as a Category 'A' bombing leader during the entire war.)

No. 21 Squadron was disbanded in Italy on September 10, 1945, but was re-formed the following year at AFS Swartkop as a bomber squadron flying Venturas. In this guise it did not last long and on January 1, 1951 it was renumbered to No. 25 Squadron but in February 1968 it was re-formed again, this time as a VIP squadron from part of No. 28 Squadron. Equipped initially with a Viscount and three Dakotas, it received the first of a number of HS-125 Mercurius aircraft from 1970, and after them some Swearingen Merlins (see *No. 21 Squadron: 'Quart in a pint pot'*). The Squadron was granted unit colours in 1976 and moved to AFB Waterkloof in 1981.

130. **There is little uniformity of profile in No. 21 Squadron. Each of these three aircraft has a completely distinctive appearance, the most graceful of all being the Merlin with its long, thin fuselage and wings. But the bulkier Mercurius and even heftier Viscount score heavily when it comes to extra elbow-room – and head-room – for passengers.**

THE DE HAVILLAND VAMPIRE
S.A.'s jet pioneer

131

In South Africa the De Havilland Vampire is rapidly becoming a distant legend. Of the scores of Vampires that once operated, only two still fly, and most of the 'daring young men' who hurled the SAAF's first jet fighter around the sky have acquired middle-age spreads and spend their days piloting papers across desks.

But once upon a time . . . Things were different in the immediate post-war era when SAAF pilots still flew Spitfires and yearned for the day when they, too, would join the jet-propelled club.

The Vampire was the second jet fighter to be designed for the Royal Air Force, and today the 'Vamp' – with its oval cockpit and twin tail-booms – looks almost quaint beside fighters like the Mirage F1. But when the prototype first flew on September 20, 1943, it seemed the ultimate in sleek deadliness.

By modern standards, of course, an early Vampire was distinctly primitive. At its fastest it flew well below Mach 1, the speed of sound, and did not even have an ejection seat. The shadow of the pre-war golden age of aviation which had ended with World War II still lay heavy on it; incredible as it may seem to flyers of the space age, the Vampire's fuselage was built of balsa and ply-wood, although the rest was of metal.

It was impressive for its period, however, and though production Vampires started rolling off the assembly line slightly too late to take part in World War II, the post-1945 years saw late variants used widely in the RAF and many other air forces.

One of these was the SAAF which, in 1949, chose the Vampire as a replacement for its ageing and outdated Spitfire Mk 9s. Initially

10 Vampire F.B.Mk.5s were ordered. Shipped to Cape Town in knocked-down form, they arrived on January 21, 1950, were assembled at AFS Brooklyn, now known as Air Force Base Ysterplaat, and then flown to Waterkloof to re-equip No. 1 Squadron SAAF (some No. 1 Squadron Vampires also operated from the then Air Operational School at Langebaanweg in the Cape).

In August 1951 another 10 Vampires arrived, these being FB-6s with the more powerful Goblin 3 engines. Later, six Vampire T Mk 11s, featuring two side-by-side seats, were imported for advanced training at Langebaanweg. When they arrived these Mk 11s had the standard Vampire tail-fin as seen on the F.B.Mk.5s and F.B.Mk.6s, but later, swept fins were fitted to improve their flying characteristics and aerial manoeuvrability.

About this time, Lieut. Fred Clausen of No. 1 Squadron had the melancholy honour of becoming the first SAAF pilot to survive a jet aircraft crash, bringing down his F.B.Mk.6, No. 218, in the Karoo in spectacular fashion. The guardian angels that watch over young pilots were on the alert that day in February 1953, however, and both Lieut. Clausen and his aircraft survived – although No. 218 was never the same again. Subsequently it was used as an instructional airframe before being prematurely retired.

Another 30 Vampires were delivered. These were the export version of the RAF Vampire F.B.Mk.9s, designated F.B.Mk.52 – a special version adapted for ground-attack and featuring a strengthened wing and air-conditioned cockpit. (Subsequently some of the SAAF's early FB-6s were modified to this standard.)

131. Taxiing along Lanseria runway after its last flight, Vampire 277 is now on display at the SAAF Museum.
132. A Vampire of the SAAF's Test Flight and Development Centre – one of the two still serviceable in the Republic – snarls through the Transvaal sky, wearing a distinctly non-standard trim of white, international orange and arctic blue.

132

The final batch of Vampires delivered to the SAAF were 21 T Mk 55s – export versions of the T Mk 11. The T Mk 55s boasted clear-view instead of framed canopies; some of the later models were also fitted with ejection seats, thus improving one of the worst features of the Vampire – the difficulty of making a quick exit if in trouble.

The Vampire was to serve the SAAF long and well, but did not remain a first-line fighter for long. From 1956 the SAAF began to re-equip with Sabres and most of the Vampires were transferred to AOS Langebaanweg where they were based until the late 1960s when they moved with the unit to its new home at Pietersburg in the Transvaal.

Pietersburg, which became a full-fledged air force base in the early 1970s, continued to operate both single-seater and two-seater Vampires, mainly FB Mk 52s and T Mk 55s. By now many of the earlier F.B.Mk.5s had found their way into storage, while others went on display at various military establishments such as the SAAF Gymnasium; the historic No. 218, Lieut. Clausen's partner in that first crash, can be seen outside Air Force Station Voortrekkerhoogte in Pretoria.

The production of the MB-326 Impala spelled the end of the Pietersburg Vampires. The 'Vamps' were replaced piecemeal as Impalas arrived, and by the end of 1972 all but two had been withdrawn.

Only 257 and 276, both T.Mk.55s, are still airworthy, earning their keep at Waterkloof as test aircraft for electronic equipment. But the chances are that before long they, too, will be retired, and the eldritch screech of the Goblin engine will be heard no more over the South African veld.

The last flight of a Vampire in silver and day-glo livery was made during the 1979 Lanseria air show, when Commandant Bob Masson of the SAAF's Test Flight and Development Centre twice flew 277, giving a spirited display for so old an aircraft – 277 remains with the SAAF Museum.

The Vampire has been one of the most widely used of the early jet combat aircraft, and it operates in countries on all the continents of the world. Although not possessing the charisma of the famed Sabre of slightly later vintage, and having a rather less than spectacular performance by comparison, the Vampire was developed into many fighter and trainer variants. It also gave rise to the later Venom, basically a much-improved Vampire, which the Swiss Air Force still uses in large numbers as a front-line aircraft some 30 years after the prototype's first flight. Add to this the six years before the Venom's first flight, and the Vampire family line has a service record of 36 years, so far. Small numbers of Vampires are still used by Chile, Dominica and Zimbabwe, and once again the Swiss Air Force is the largest operator with some 75 T.Mk.55s and F.B.Mk.6s still in service as trainers.

The Vampire was blooded during the government-toppling Suez débâcle of 1956 and the most recent combat deployment has been in Zimbabwe where Vampire F.B.Mk.9s and T.Mk.55s took part in anti-terrorist operations until the recent cease-fire.

A SPITFIRE CALLED EVELYN

133. **The patchwork of fields below belongs to the Transvaal, not embattled 1940 Britain, but there is no mistaking this beautiful sharp shape . . . With Major Alan Lurie at the controls, 'Evelyn' the Spitfire lets rip with her 1 650 Rolls-Royce horses galloping under her engine-cowling. She wears 'period' 1944 vintage No. 40 Squadron colours, and carries a wing-commander's pennant.**

134. **Overleaf: The No. 40 Squadron badge, 1944 style, is accurately depicted on the SAAF Museum's Spitfire. Except for the name 'Evelyn' – honouring the wife of Larry Barnett – the gallant old machine resembles the fighter Lieutenant-General Bob Rogers flew in Italy in 1944.**

It is not often that a man can stand in the afternoon of his life and watch 30 action-packed years being rolled away in one easy movement. But one May day in 1976 this happened to Lieutenant-General R. H. D. Rogers, then chief of the South African Air Force.

Bob Rogers, though now retired, is a living legend. At that time he was the most decorated man in the South African Defence Force. Row upon row of ribbons beneath the pilot's brevet on his tunic attested to a tremendous career that spanned some of the most momentous years of aviation.

During World War II he had flown Spitfires in the final fling of the propellor-driven warplane; in Korea he had piloted first P-51 Mustangs and then Sabre jets; now, as the most senior military aviator in his country, he presided over an air force which operated Mirage F-1s which flew faster than the speed of sound.

It had been a long and action-packed career. And on that May day at Waterkloof air base near Pretoria, the earliest part of this career was suddenly being recalled, as bright and sharp as a bugle-call.

Roaring over Waterkloof was the unforgettable shark shape of a Spitfire Mk IXE. Dressed in the camouflage scheme of the Italian theatre of operations in 1944, it bore the orange-white-and-blue roundels of the SAAF, the WR code of No. 40 Squadron and the personal R-R monogram of the OC No. 40 Squadron . . . a dashing young airman named Lieutenant-Colonel Bob Rogers.

Except that the wingtips were rounded instead of 'clipped', or squared off, the Spitfire was a replica of the one Bob Rogers had flown in those far-off days. The only other difference was the name 'Evelyn' painted on the engine-nacelle. Evelyn is the wife of one Larry Barnett, but that part of the story comes a little later . . .

It was a memorable day for everyone who attended the ceremony, not least of them a Citizen Force SAAF pilot and irrepressible air enthusiast named Larry Barnett, one of the prime movers who had made it possible.

The Spitfire called Evelyn arrived at Waterkloof that day by a circuitous and unlikely route. It was built by Vickers Armstrong Limited in 1943, given the Royal Air Force serial MA793 and in August that year sent to North Africa, where it was diverted to the United States Army Air Force from October 1943 to May 1944, before again being taken on charge by the RAF.

In June 1945 it was sent back to Britain and moth-balled at No. 39 Maintenance Unit at RAF Colerne. It finally reached South Africa after the end of the war, when the SAAF re-equipped itself with 136 Spitfires which were surplus to RAF requirements.

The first batch was flown out to South Africa, and started arriving at Swartkop air base near Pretoria from June 9, 1947. MA793 was not one of these, however. It came with a later batch shipped to South Africa by sea which arrived on August 30, 1948.

The aircraft was given the SAAF serial number 5601, but its service in South African colours was a short and inglorious one. Just over two years later, on October 14, 1949, No. 5601 was struck off charge and put into storage, and it stayed in moth-balls until being sold – the buyer being, of all things, the Meerhof School for handicapped children – for the princely sum of R3.

There the old Spitfire stood for nearly two decades, gradually becoming more and more dilapidated with the passing of the years, and there it might have stayed till the inevitable last sad journey to the scrapyard.

Enter Larry Barnett and his friend, fellow Citizen Force pilot Alan Lurie, both of them men with a mission – to see that South Africa got a flying Spitfire to complement the honoured, but ground-bound, relics displayed here and there. In 1967 Barnett and Lurie discovered No. 5601, started negotiations with the Meerhof School and eventually bought the old fighter for R20 – a sum which, when allowance is made for the ravages of inflation, represents little advance on the original selling price.

The remains of No. 5601 were hauled off to Barnett's garage, where in August 1969 restoration work began. It was a monumentally ambitious task. Aircraft are expensive things to restore, particularly high-technology fighters which have not been made for almost a quarter-century. Apart from the technical expertise required for the reconstruction work, many spares were unobtainable through normal channels.

Since restorers of old aircraft rarely seem to be men of fabulous wealth, they have to make up for it by a single-minded devotion, coupled with large amounts of energy and ingenuity, not to mention a talent for bartering and general wheedling.

Barnett and Lurie had all the necessary requirements. Helped by fellow enthusiasts, some local and others scattered around the world, they began the reconstruction.

It was a desperate struggle. Barnett and his associates kept at it for nearly six years, lavishing 22 000 man-hours on the old aircraft till the Atlas Aircraft Corporation took over the final stages of the project in May 1975.

Soon afterwards the aircraft took off for the maiden flight of its new career at the hands of Wing-Commander Newton Harrison, a veteran Spitfire pilot of World War II, and shortly thereafter made a brief public debut at the 'Air Africa International '75' show at Johannesburg's Lanseria Airport.

In subsequent months the Spitfire became a familiar sight at air displays, piloted on most occasions by Alan Lurie, its co-owner.

The final chapter was yet to be written, however. On May 6, 1976, at a special parade at Waterkloof, 'Evelyn' was handed over to the SAAF on permanent loan, with General Rogers as the guest of honour. Today the Spitfire called Evelyn is housed at the No. 41 Squadron, Lanseria – a living legend, just like the man whose monogram she wears on each flank of her slim fuselage.

And yes, Bob Rogers has flown her himself . . . which is, when all is said and done, entirely appropriate.

Historical note on No. 40 Squadron SAAF

These days No. 40 Squadron flies Harvards out of Dunnottar, and the fairly sedate nature of its post-World War II training role tends to obscure the fact that it emerged from that conflict with one of the most outstanding combat records of any SAAF unit.

Formed at Waterkloof on May 30, 1940, as an army co-operation squadron for tactical reconnaissance, the unit and its Hawker Hart-

beestes started moving off to East Africa soon after the end of the month.

There it flew tactical, photographic and armed reconnaissance missions in support of the First South African Division. In practice this entailed extensive photo-survey work and also much bombing and strafing, and the squadron was intensively engaged in 'ops' until May 1941, often tangling with Italian aircraft.

In August 1941 the squadron returned to South Africa for reorganization prior to being moved to Egypt in November. Once in the desert, pilots were attached to Royal Air Force and Royal Australian Air Force squadrons for familiarization with 'tac R' in these new conditions.

Re-equipment began in February 1942 with the arrival of Hurricane Mk Is and a few Tomahawks, and the squadron became operational the same month.

Tactical reconnaissance was a risky existence. As practised in the desert it involved flying singly or in pairs behind enemy lines, the pilots concentrating on their ground observations, even though it was axiomatic that an aviator's head was supposed never to cease swivelling around.

The slow, outclassed fighters flown by No. 40 Squadron made matters worse and the equipment situation did not improve until August 1942 when the squadron began to receive the slightly better Hurricane Mk IIs.

Inevitably, losses were heavy. Five pilots were lost during the first half of April 1942, and many others returned to base with damage. Nevertheless, No. 40 Squadron did not fail in its duties, either then or later, although its pilots sometimes had to shoot their way out of difficult predicaments, and had some narrow escapes during the retreat to El Alamein. On one occasion the whole unit nearly 'went into the bag' when its airfield was almost overrun by the swiftly-advancing Afrikakorps.

Pulled back for rest and conversion to Hurricane Mk IIs in August 1942, the squadron returned to operations in time for the Battle of El Alamein in October. Now the Axis forces were retreating, and the squadron followed them up in the camera-equipped Spitfire Mk Vs it had received in February 1943.

Then, at dawn on May 12, 1943, its pilots could find no more sign of enemy movement; the North African campaign was over. It had been a long, hard-fought struggle, and No. 40 Squadron was commended for its exceptional work.

There was little rest for the 'tac R' merchants of No. 40 Squadron, however. In June two flights were posted to Malta in preparation for the invasion of Sicily; on July 10, the day of the invasion, the squadron set a unit record for sorties flown that was not surpassed in all the remaining years of war.

On July 13 the squadron began operating an advanced detachment from a landing-ground in Sicily, the first Allied tactical reconnaissance unit to operate from Italian soil. By August the squadron was flying photo-reconnaissance missions for the impending invasion of Italy, and by way of variation also spent a day spotting naval gunfire for two British battleships which were engaging coastal targets.

In September 1943, the invasion having taken place, the squadron sent a flight to operate from Italian soil (the rest of the unit following soon after), flying tactical and armed reconnaissance sorties in support of both the British and United States armies at such major clashes as the battle for Anzio and the fighting along the Gustav and Gothic Lines.

September was also the month in which the squadron received Spitfire Mk IXs – a far cry from the desperate days in the desert when it had had to make do with slow Hurricanes and Tomahawks.

In December 1944 a detachment of the squadron was temporarily diverted to operate against communist ELAS terrorists in Greece,

during the unrest which followed that country's liberation from German forces.

By now the war in Europe was drawing to a close, but there was still a great deal of work for No. 40 Squadron, and during March and April 1945 it recorded its busiest time ever, flying 283 missions (a total of 563 sorties).

Following the German surrender in early 1945, the only unit of the once-formidable Desert Air Force which continued to operate was No. 40 Squadron. It flew 'tac R' missions till all enemy troop movement had ceased, and is thought to be the last Italian-based Allied unit to come under fire.

From Italy the squadron was sent to Austria to patrol the Yugoslav border when the victorious Tito's attitude towards his former Western allies hardened. The squadron also carried out photo-survey duties, and after moving to Klagenfurt in September 1945, played host to four RAF photo-reconnaissance Spitfire PR Mk XIs on temporary secondment.

In October 1945, however, there was no further work for it in Europe, and No. 40 Squadron was sent home to be disbanded.

No more was heard from this gallant fighting squadron until January 1, 1951 when it was re-formed as an ACF squadron, flying Harvards out of AFS Bloemspruit. The squadron moved to Rand Airport and currently operates from Dunnottar still flying Harvards.

136

135   137

135. 'Achtung – Schpitfeuer.' 'Evelyn' from the average Junkers 88 or Heinkel rear gunner's point of view during, say, the Battle of Britain.
136. Photographer Herman Potgieter was in good company when he took this self-portrait during one of his many flights. At the left is 'Evelyn' the Spitfire in all her shark-nosed glory, and to the right is a bull-nosed old Harvard, one of the faithful tutors of innumerable fledgling pilots of the SAAF.
137. 'Evelyn's' shapely elliptical wings – a distinctive Spitfire feature until the introduction of 'clipped' (squared-off) wingtips. 'Evelyn' also boasts the earlier standard canopy.

THE FIESELER STORCH
Rommel's runabout

138. A ghost from a past now growing ever more distant, the SAAF Museum's Fieseler Storch – one of the few still known to be flying in the world – touches down under the expert guidance of Commandant Bob Masson. The historic photograph was made at the end of the Storch's first public appearance after being restored, at AFB Waterkloof's air show on February 2, 1980, to mark the SAAF's 60th anniversary. In the passenger's seat is a former Luftwaffe airman Max Uhde who flew in Storchs during World War II.

Some aircraft become and remain legends. Thanks to some dedicated SAAF restorers, South Africa boasts one such in its ranks, even though it has the straight black crosses of Hitler's Luftwaffe on its wings, instead of the castle and leaping springbok of the South African Air Force. It is the Fieseler Storch and, in its day, it was one of the finest – if not the finest – light military aircraft to serve in any air force in the world.

The SAAF's Storch has had a chequered career since it was built in Occupied France in 1944, but that is in the past, and it lives in pampered splendour at Lanseria Airport, where the SAAF Museum's workshop is sited.

The Storch type resulted from a 1935 *Reichsluftfahrtministerium* specification for a small, single-engined monoplane with short take-off and landing characteristics, suitable for army co-operation, rescue and liaison duties.

Next year the prototype Storch was unveiled. It was altogether a remarkable aircraft, in appearance as well as in performance. As its name implies it was indeed stork-like, thanks to its spindly but

sturdy long-stroke undercarriage, designed to absorb the shocks of the aircraft's high rates of vertical descent.

The cockpit appeared to have been borrowed from a larger aircraft, to judge by the way it bulged over the narrow fuselage; which meant, of course, that it gave the occupants excellent downward vision.

The Storch's flying characteristics were incredible. For slow flying and short take-offs and landings it had no peers. It could stagger along under full control at a mere 50 km/h in still air, and if there was a wind of that velocity a skilled pilot could make it hover like a helicopter.

It could land in just 125 metres (although it is recorded that with a medium head-wind the little aircraft could touch down in just five metres, incredible as that may sound). If necessary it could take off in only 35 metres, provided the pilot kept his foot on the brake till the engine had developed full power.

Small wonder, then, that the Germans made tremendous use of Storchs in all theatres of World War II, from the shivering snowscapes of the Eastern Front to the desert west of Egypt.

Field-Marshall Erwin Rommel, the famed 'Desert Fox', used to fly himself around the battlefront in a Storch (often to the horror of his staff, who would have visions of their leader being shot down by anti-aircraft fire or some roving Allied fighter).

When the hulking Colonel Otto Skorzeny plucked the deposed Benito Mussolini from captivity in an Alpine hotel, he flew him off in a Storch, the only aircraft capable of taking to the air from the cramped space available. For his well-nigh unbelievable exploit, Skorzeny was awarded a Knight's Cross; Hitler should have given one to the long-legged little aircraft as well.

A total of 2 549 Storchs had been built for the Luftwaffe by the end of World War II, mostly in Germany but some by Morane-Saulnier in France and Mraz in Czechoslovakia (both the French and Czech production continuing for a while after the war).

The Allies laid hands on 145 flyable Storchs, many of which were handed to France, Norway and The Netherlands, while the British Army and the RAF used the rest for communications duties in occupied Germany. A few Storchs were also delivered to the Royal Aircraft Establishment at Farnborough for testing, and one of these was the aircraft which eventually arrived in South Africa.

Delivered to the RAE on September 5, 1945, it was a late-model Fil56-C7 built 11 months earlier in Occupied France, and its markings were those of the Russian Front.

After arrival at the RAE the Storch was allocated the Air Ministry serial AM99, and for the next four months, till January 10, 1946, it was put through extensive performance tests. Then it was flown to No. 47 Maintenance Unit RAF, where it was dismantled and crated for transport to South Africa. It arrived in Cape Town on November 6, 1946, and was taken on charge by the SAAF.

The Storch's public career was brief. During March 1947 it was transported to the Central Flying School, Dunnottar, where a few flights were made with it, and late that year it appeared at the Baragwanath Air Display. Soon afterwards, on October 28, 1947, the Storch was grounded with overheating and oil-pressure problems after only 640 flying hours in South Africa.

And that, for nearly three decades, was that. The Storch spent years in storage at Dunnottar. Eventually it was transferred to the South African War Museum in Johannesburg, but because of space problems could not be put on display.

Things did not improve until February 1974, when the Storch was offered on loan to the SAAF and transferred to AFS Snake Valley, near Pretoria. There it was lovingly restored to an inaccurate colour-scheme, with which it went on show as a static exhibit at the Lanseria Air Display of the following year.

Things began to look up for the Storch when it was donated to the SAAF Museum in May 1976. Having been inspected and found to be repairable to flying condition, the Storch was moved to No. 1 Air Depot for restoration.

It was a fearsomely difficult task. A serious lack of technical manuals complicated the work; no spares were available for the Argus engine (the restorers solved that one by rebuilding the engine from scratch). Not surprisingly, it took the men of No. 1 Air Depot three years to get the Storch back into flying condition.

When the work had been completed, the Storch was restored to its authentic World War II colour-scheme under the personal supervision of a Citizen Force SAAF Captain called Ronald Belling, a renowned expert on the subject. Then, on November 28, 1979, the Storch took off on an unofficial and unheralded test flight at Swartkop air base near Pretoria.

Two days later it made its return to the public stage when Commandant J. G. P. Marais of the SAAF's Test Flight and Development Centre put the long-legged little aircraft through its paces for reporters and TV cameramen.

Slightly more than two months later, on February 2, 1980, the Storch took to the air again at Waterkloof air base, where Commandant Bob Masson, a test pilot at the TFDC, showed off all of its many virtues at the SAAF's 60th anniversary air display.

Soon afterwards, on March 29, 1980, the Storch made another public appearance at Lanseria Airport when the chief of the SAAF, Lieutenant-General Mike Muller, officially opened the SAAF Museum's workshop, where it has remained ever since.

THE SAAF MUSEUM

Though it is concerned mainly with the past, and the preservation of by-gone aircraft and records, the SAAF Museum is one of the youngest sections of the Air Force, its creation being authorized only on October 26, 1973. During the early years of the SAAF's existence no attempt was made to preserve examples of its early aircraft, and it was only with the establishment of the South African War Museum (now the S.A. National Museum of Military History) in 1942 that the first efforts were made to preserve them.

During the later years of World War II, as a result of the efforts of Captain W. A. Bellwood, OC of the aircraft section of the museum, a growing collection of aircraft was housed at Milner Park, Johannesburg. It included a Wapiti, Tutor, Hartbees, Fury, D.H.9, SE-5a, Ju-88, Ju-52/3m and two Bf-109s. But a suggestion by Captain Bellwood in August 1944 that a separate SAAF Museum should be established was not taken any further.

In the post-war years the museum acquired a Spitfire Mk VIII, a Hurricane IIC and a Mosquito PR IX, but disposed of its rare Tutor, Wapiti and Fury, and other aircraft standing outside deteriorated, the Ju-88 and the Ju-52/3m eventually being sold for scrap.

The SAAF made no attempt to preserve any of its historic aircraft, disposing of them to various private individuals and commercial undertakings which used them for promotional purposes.

However, SAAF units gradually awakened to the need for preserving historical aircraft and, following the practice of many airforce bases overseas, displayed aircraft at their entrance gates.

By 1971 the War Museum was so pressed for space that its director, Brigadier J. C. Lemmer revived Captain Bellwood's suggestion that a separate SAAF Museum be established. Colonel P. M. J. McGregor, long associated with the history of the SAAF, had been campaigning along similar lines and on May 14, 1973 the proposal was approved in principle by the Chief of the SADF and in October the Minister of Defence gave the project his blessing.

A week after the Museum came into being a Lockheed PV-1 Ventura, which had been used as a ground trainer for loading casualties, was offered by the SA Medical Corps Training School, making storage space an urgent requirement. On November 23 authority was given for the use of half of No. 13 Hangar at AFS Snake Valley, near Pretoria, and soon after this the Museum acquired the Ventura – its first aircraft.

In the years that have followed, enthusiasts throughout the country have aided the Museum's small staff in recovering and restoring as many as possible of the past aircraft of the SAAF. Search and recovery operations have been carried out not only for aircraft and their parts, but for other historical items. But though the Museum preserves items ranging from photographs and models, to uniforms and medals, the aircraft remain its central interest.

By August 1980 the Museum possessed 31 basically complete airframes, and large components from another 35 incomplete aircraft. In storage or awaiting collection were parts from at least 28 different Avro Ansons, from which it is hoped to build two.

From this large stock several restoration projects are currently under way or completed. Being restored at present are two Spitfire Mk IXs and a Tiger Moth (at Lanseria), a Miles Gemini and two Bell 47G helicopters (in Johannesburg), a Vampire FB Mk 6 (at Olifantsfontein), a Sikorsky S-51 (at AFB Ysterplaat) and a Chipmunk and Dornier Do-27 (at D. F. Malan Cape Town).

Completed projects include a Fieseler Storch, Sabre Mk 6, Vampire T Mk 55 and PV-1 Ventura (at Lanseria) and a Percival Prentice (stored at Snake Valley).

The SAAF Museum's workshop is open to the public at Lanseria at weekends and is run from its headquarters at AFB Swartkop, where it is intended eventually to open the museum.

Historical note on No. 6 Squadron SAAF

Thanks to a wartime organizational quirk, this part-time SAAF squadron can claim to be an 'ancestor' of No. 1 Squadron, the oldest unit in the air force and its senior by many years.

No. 6 Squadron was formed as a 'shadow' fighter unit but was equipped with Westland Wapiti IIIs at Cape Town in April 1939, becoming operational in September of that year. Its first duties after the outbreak of war consisted of flying anti-submarine coastal patrols from the city's Youngsfield airfield but the aircraft soon became unserviceable.

In February 1940 the unit ceasd to exist as such when it was moved to Waterkloof air base and renumbered to No. 1 Squadron, but on February 26, 1942, a new No. 6 Squadron was formed at Swartkop air base and equipped with Curtiss Mohawk IVs.

Within two months, however, the new squadron was hurriedly moved to Groutville, near Stanger, because of a Japanese invasion scare. The threat did not materialize, and in August the squadron was moved to Eerste River in the Cape Province, where a variety of obsolete aircraft – Wapitis, Fairey Battles and Hawker Furies – were taken on strength.

On July 31, 1943, the Japanese invasion scare having finally subsided, No. 6 Squadron was disbanded, and was not heard of again until it was re-formed as a part-time Active Citizen Force unit on July 5, 1952, based in Port Elizabeth and flying Harvards.

It lasted till 1959 before being disbanded as an economy measure, but in May 1961 it was re-formed, still flying Harvards. From 1973 to 1976 the squadron also operated a lone Cessna 185, but since March 1975 it has been flying Impala Mk Is.

Historical note on No. 7 Squadron SAAF

No. 7 Squadron can boast of being the first South African unit to serve outside Africa in World War II, albeit only briefly and, strictly speaking, illegally. It has seen hard times and known bitter losses in its career, which stretches back (with some interruptions) to January 12, 1942, when it was formed at Swartkop air station as a fighter unit and equipped with Harvards and Mohawks.

On April 2, 1942, it passed the Mohawks on to No. 6 Squadron before embarkation for Egypt, where it arrived in May and converted to Hurricane Mk Is which, events were soon to show, were no improvement.

By June 1942 the bulk of the squadron was at Haifa in Palestine for patrol duties. This excursion did not last long, since at this time South African forces were limited to service in Africa only and before the month was out it had been quietly pulled back to Egypt.

On July 2, 1942, it joined No. 243 Wing at Landing-Ground 154 in the Western Desert, but the limitations of its aged Hurricane Mk Is confined its pilots to meteorological and local-defence flights.

Soon, however, the squadron entered a more active phase when it became the only SAAF squadron in the new No. 7 Wing SAAF, based at LG 89, and the Squadron's first patrol was flown by four Hurricanes on July 4.

The following day one flight of No. 7 Squadron was re-equipped with Hurricane Mk IIBs and asked to act as top cover for the Mk Is in the fighter-bomber operations. The squadron's first brush with Bf-109s took place soon afterwards, on July 11, but its activities until September 1942 have grown shadowy because part of its records have been lost.

By that month, however, No. 7 Squadron was taking part in fighter-bomber operations and also providing top cover for RAF Hurricanes, including the tank-busters of No. 6 Squadron.

Now it fell on hard times. On September 3 its pilots went through its first recorded major combat incident when Bf-109s 'bounced' them. Thanks to the pilot's inexperience and poor equipment, it was a savage defeat, the Germans shooting down four Hurricanes without suffering any losses. Three days later the Germans again pounced, shooting down five of six aircraft that the squadron had sent on a mission and killing the squadron commander.

On September 9 the remnants of No. 7 Squadron were withdrawn to Shandur Air Station for a badly-needed rest and re-equipment, and by the end of the month had begun converting to the Hurricane Mk IID 'tank-buster' and receiving specialized training in the use of the IID's two 40mm cannon.

In October it was paired with No. 6 Squadron RAF as the Desert Air Force's 'Flying Can-openers' of No. 211 Group, and on the night of the great El Alamein barrage (October 23 and 24, 1942) the South Africans flew interdiction sorties behind enemy lines. These were continued after dawn, and several vehicles were knocked out by the potent 40mm cannon.

Now Rommel's Afrikakorps was on the retreat, and the squadron harried the withdrawing Germans on the long road that ended in final capitulation in Tunisia, suffering losses from flak and fighters.

In January 1943 the squadron moved to Benina, flying Hurricane Mk IICs and a few Spitfire Mk Vs on shipping and coastal reconnaissance patrols for several months before returning to the front lines with new Hurricanes.

The war in Africa ended, the squadron was attached to No. 212 Group, (Air Defence Eastern Mediterranean), and in July 1943 received new Spitfire Mk Vs, with which it flew convoy escorts and fighter-interception sorties.

But great and terrible things awaited No. 7 Squadron.

On September 10 that year six of its pilots and a Dakota with ground staff were suddenly ordered to Cyprus to set up an advanced base. From there, it transpired, they and their six Spitfire Mk Vs were to supply the total air cover at the start of the ill-fated British move into the Dodecanese Islands.

On September 13 they landed on the island of Kos, where they were joined next day by two more of the squadron's Spitfires. Dawn-standing patrols began on September 15, while more of the squadron's men and equipment moved to Cyprus.

A few days later the Kos detachment made its first interception, and soon afterwards the squadron found itself involved in ever more furious fighting, scoring several victories but also suffering losses; soon the OC No. 7 Squadron, Major Corrie van Vliet, found himself becoming Senior Air Officer on Kos after the previous incumbent, and RAF group-captain, was injured.

Late in September, Spitfires of No. 74 Squadron RAF (the legendary A. G. 'Sailor' Malan's old unit) arrived as reinforcement. But the Luftwaffe onslaughts on Kos had begun to tell; the primitive airfields had been badly bombed and by October 1 there was only one serviceable Spitfire in all of No. 7 Squadron.

On October 3 German landing operations started and the grounded SAAF personnel had to make their escape by whatever means could be found. Lieutenant Cecil Golding – formerly of No. 1 Squadron SAAF – crossed to Turkey in a tiny native coracle).

The squadron reassembled in North Africa and counted the cost of its brief but bloody excursion. Six officers had been killed and 15 other ranks were missing; on the other hand 12 enemy aircraft had been shot down.

The squadron remained in Egypt for a few months, and then in April 1944, equipped with Spitfire Mk IXs, rejoined No. 7 Wing in Italy. Here it took part in fighter-bomber operations and also flew armed reconnaissance (with 30-gallon drop tanks) and bomber escorts (with 90-gallon drop tanks).

By the end of 1944 the squadron had flown 808 missions – a total of 4 000 sorties – for the loss of 17 pilots (some of whom, however, managed to make their way back). Among the latter was the commanding officer, Major Bob Kershaw, the hero of the Diredawa rescue while a pilot in No. 3 Squadron in Abyssinia.

At the end of the war in Europe the squadron embarked for the Far East, where the Japanese were still resisting, but the fighting there ended before it arrived and it was turned back at Ceylon.

No. 7 Squadron arrived in South Africa on September 10, 1945, and was promptly disbanded. In August 1951 it was re-formed at Cape Town's Ysterplaat air station, flying Harvards, but was disbanded again in 1959. On August 1, 1961, it was re-formed for the second time at Youngsfield, on Cape Town's outskirts, and again equipped with Harvards.

On October 31, 1969 it moved to Ysterplaat (which was an air force base by now), receiving its squadron colours on October 30, 1967. It is classed as a Citizen Force squadron, its commanding officer and some of its pilots being regulars and the others part-time. In 1977 the squadron received Impala Mk Is, and moved to D. F. Malan Airport in 1978.

Historical note on No. 8 Squadron SAAF

Formed in February 1942 using Furies of No. 43 Squadron, and disbanded on August 24 of the same year, No. 8 Squadron never became operational and was one of the shortest-lived SAAF units of World War II. Its 100 airmen were transferred to No. 27 Squadron and it was not heard of again until January 1, 1951.

The Squadron was then reinstated from the Active Citizen Force element of No. 24 Squadron, based at AFS Bloemspruit and flying Harvards.

In the mid-1970s the unit became the fourth SAAF squadron to re-equip with Impala Mk Is. It operated some Impala Mk IIs late in 1975, and now operates both Mk Is and Mk IIs at Bloemspruit.

Historical note on the The Central Flying School

Using a motley collection of aircraft, which included DH-9s, Avro Avian IVMs and Westland Wapiti IIIs, the Central Flying School was established at Zwartkop Air Station in 1932, to train both pupil pilots and instructors. And though it has moved several times since then, its purpose remains the same – to create pilots of the highest possible calibre.

The outbreak of World War II saw an immediate need, even more for instructors than for pilots and, accordingly, at the end of November 1939 the CFS was changed to a school for instructors only, in which new role it was transferred from its original base to Kimberley. But even this stay was short-lived and on May 27, 1940 the unit moved again – this time to Tempe airfield, Bloemfontein.

Here it was renamed No. 62 Air School on November 11, 1940, but it was nevertheless referred to unofficially as 'CFS' throughout the years of World War II. With the training of instructors still its primary concern, during February 1943 – the year when its wartime activities were at a peak and as many as 100 pilots were on course at any given time – it had 119 aircraft on strength, representing 11 different types which ranged from 47 Tiger Moths to a solitary Lockheed Ventura.

On February 24, 1945, 62 AS was disbanded, but was re-formed at AFS Nigel in 1946, where Harvards, Oxfords and Tiger Moths were the backbone of its training fleet. On June 6, 1949, by which time pupil pilots were being trained as well as instructors, the Nigel base was renamed Dunnottar.

Though this was a new move as far as Central Flying School was concerned, Dunnottar already had its own history as a wartime training centre, and had been officially opened on July 29, 1941, as part of the wartime British Commonwealth Air Training Plan (formerly the Empire Air Training Scheme). The unit operating there was No. 24 Air School, an element of Air Force Station Nigel; at that time pupil pilots were given about 90 hours of *ab initio* training on

Tiger Moths and similar aircraft before being posted to No. 24 AS to continue their flying training.

Training at Dunnottar continued throughout World War II – between July 1941 and August 1945, when No. 24 AS was disbanded, some 35 war courses of pupil pilots qualified there. Since an average of 40 pupils attended each course, No. 24 Air School alone contributed at least 1 400 qualified pilots to the Allied cause.

No. 24 AS became inactive in 1945, and the Central Flying School moved in from its home base of Bloemfontein, operating Harvards and, initially, a few Dakotas.

The CFS has been at AFS Dunnottar ever since, although not always under the same name – on February 2, 1968, its designation was changed to Flying Training School Dunnottar.

January 3, 1977, saw a reversion to the old title, and today the CFS and No. 40 Squadron are both based at Dunnottar, operating all the Harvards still flying in the SAAF.

Today Dunnottar is where the long, hard grind of pilot training starts, with pupils receiving about 120 hours' *ab initio* training on Harvards before moving on to FTS Langebaanweg for another 120 hours or so of more advanced training before receiving their 'wings', the much-coveted pilots' brevet.

A large number of 'pupes' do not make it; jealous of its traditionally high standards, the SAAF is ferociously strict during training. The pupils who finally step up to the Chief of the SAAF to receive their wings are undoubtedly the most rigorously trained in Africa – and many other parts of the world.

And the arduous road that leads them finally to the saluting base where the Chief of the SAAF is waiting to pin the brevets on their chests starts at the Central Flying School, Dunnottar.

Historical note on The Flying Training School, Langebaanweg

The SAAF installation at Langebaanweg, which is today the Flying Training School, dates back to 1942/43, when Air Force Station Congella (Langebaan Section) was built.

Langebaan Lagoon was in constant use by airmen around this time. No. 262 Squadron Royal Air Force, based at Durban and flying Catalina flying boats, made use of Langebaan, and for some time in 1943 a detachment of Royal Netherlands Navy Catalinas from No. 31 (Dutch) Squadron, RAF, was also active in the area.

On November 14, 1945, AFS Congella (Langebaan Section) was renamed No. 3 Air Depot Section, only to become AFS Saldanha on December 12.

The first aircraft to land at the new air force station was an Avro Anson, which arrived in February 1946, but the airfield was not officially proclaimed until April 5 of that year. Four months later Langebaan became the home of the new Bombing, Gunnery and Air Navigation School (BGANS). The following month, September, 10 Ansons were received and advanced training began.

On April 14, 1947, The BGANS was renamed AFS Langebaanweg, and received its first Harvards and Venturas. The following year it received its first Spitfires for advanced fighter training, and in fact the pilots who went to Korea with No. 2 Squadron trained at Langebaanweg before they left.

In October 1952 Langebaanweg received its first Vampire fighters, and the 'Vamps' remained as advanced trainers till October 1967, when they were transferred to Pietersburg air base along with the Air Operational School (later No. 85 Advanced Flying School). By 1966 the first Impala Mk I – an aircraft destined to become famous at the hands of the FTS's aerobatics team, the 'Silver Falcons' – had arrived.

On February 1, 1968 AFS Langebaanweg was given its present name, and most of the SAAF's Impala Mk Is are stationed here, where pupil pilots' training – started at the Central Flying School – is rounded off.

AIRCRAFT SPECIFICATIONS

DASSAULT-BREGUET MIRAGE F.1

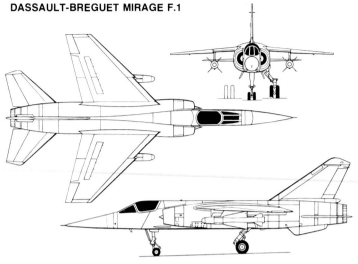

Country of origin and manufacture: France.

First flights: Prototype: 23.12.1966
First production Mirage F.1: 15.2.1973

Power plant: One SNECMA-Atar 09K-50 turbojet rated at 11 090 lb st
(5 035 kg) or 15 800 lb st (7 166 kg) with afterburner

Principal dimensions: (F 1CZ): Length: 49 ft 2½ in (15,00 m)
Height: 14 ft 9 in (4,50 m)
Wingspan: (without missiles): 27 ft 6¾ in (8,40 m)

Maximum gross mass: (F 1CZ): 32 850 lb (14 900 kg)

Basic performance figures: Maximum speed (at 40 000 ft/12 000 m):
Mach 2,2 (at low altitude Mach 1,2 may be reached)
Service ceiling: 65 600 ft (20 000 m)
Endurance: 3 hours 45 minutes.
Time to climb to Mach 2 at 40 000 ft (12 192 m): 7 min 30 sec.

Armament: Two 30 mm DEFA cannon in forward fuselage beneath engine
intakes. All other armament is carried externally, with two strong points
under each wing, a ventral strong point, and provision for a single missile
on the wing-tip for interception missions. In the interceptor rôle (F 1C)
typical armament could comprise two MATRA R550 air-to-air missiles
(one on each wing-tip), plus two MATRA R530 air-to-air missiles (one
under each wing – see drawing above) plus a drop-tank under the
fuselage. For air-to-ground missions (F 1A) the two underwing strong
points may be fitted with multiple tube rocket launchers plus a belly drop
tank (see photograph on the front cover).

Supplied to: France, Ecuador, Iraq, South Africa, Spain, Greece, Kuwait,
Libya, Morocco and currently in service with the Air Forces of these
nations.

Production status: In production, with production reaching 600 at the time of
publication.

First delivery to SAAF: First F 1CZ delivered April 4, 1975 with the first F 1AZ
arriving late in 1975.

Variants operated by SAAF: Mirage F 1CZ and Mirage F 1AZ.

Squadron status in SAAF: Mirage F 1CZs are operated by 3 Squadron and
Mirage F 1AZs by 1 Squadron.

Basic current SAAF colour scheme: Camouflaged upper surfaces of Olive
Drab (BSC298) and Deep Buff (BSC360) and Light Admiralty Grey
(BSC697) fuselage undersides

Three view drawing: Mirage F 1CZ.

DASSAULT-BREGUET MIRAGE III

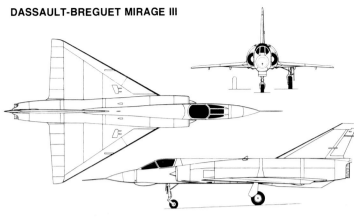

Mirage 111EZ

Mirage 111CZ

Country of origin and manufacture: France

First flights: Mirage III-001 (Prototype): 17.11.1956
Mirage IIIA (Pre-production version): 12.5.1958
Mirage IIIB (Two-seat version of IIIA): 20.10.1959
Mirage IIIC (Production version of IIIA): 9.10.1960
Mirage IIID (Two-seat version of IIIE): November 1966
Mirage IIIE (Fighter-Bomber version of IIIC): 5.4.1961
Mirage IIIR (Reconnaissance version of IIIE): 11.1961.

Power plant: Mirage IIICZ: One SNECMA-Atar 09B turbojet rated at 9 370 lb
(4 250 kg) static thrust, or 13 230 lb (6 001 kg) with afterburner.
Mirage IIIBZ: Similar to Mirage IIICZ
Mirage IIIEZ: One SNECMA-Atar 09C turbojet rated at 9 436 lb (4 280 kg)
static thrust, or 13 670 lb (6 200 kg) with afterburner
Mirage IIIDZ and Mirage IIIRZ: Similar to Mirage IIIEZ
Mirage IIID2Z and Mirage IIIR2Z: One SNECMA-Atar 09K-50 turbojet
rated at 11 090 lb (5 035 kg) static thrust, or 15 800 lb (7 166 kg) with
afterburner.

Principal dimensions: Length: Mirage IIIB: 50 ft 6¼ in (15,40 m)
Mirage IIIC: 45 ft 5¼ in (13,84 m)
Mirage IIIE: 49 ft 3½ in (15,03 m)
Mirage IIIR: 50 ft 10¼ in (15,50 m)
Height: (IIIB/IIIC/IIID/IIIE/IIIR): 13 ft 11½ in (4,25 m)
Wingspan: (IIIB/IIIC/IIID/IIIE/IIIR): 27 ft 0 in (8,22 m)

Maximum gross mass: Mirage IIIB: 26 455 lb (12 000 kg)
Mirage IIIC: 26 015 lb (11 800 kg)
Mirage IIIE and Mirage IIIR: 29 760 lb (13 500 kg)

Basic performance figures: Maximum speed:
Mirage IIIC: Mach 2,1 at 40 000 ft (12 000 m)
Mirage IIIE: Mach 2,2 at 40 000 ft (12 000 m)
Service ceiling (Mirage IIIC/IIIE): 55 000 ft (16 764 m)
Combat range: Mirage IIIC: 745 miles (1 198 km) Mirage IIIE: 750 miles
(1 206 km)

Armament: Standard fixed armament for all Mirage III versions are two internal 30 mm DEFA cannon in forward fuselage beneath engine intakes. All other armament is carried externally on pylons under the wings (two under each wing) and a single pylon under the fuselage belly. Inboard pylons under wings are stressed for heavier loads than outer ones.

In the interceptor rôle (IIIC) typical external load may comprise two missiles on outboard pylons together with a 1 700 litre drop tank on each inboard wing pylon. Alternatively fuel tanks may be fitted on the inboard wing pylons and a single MATRA R530 air-to-air missile placed under the fuselage.

In the ground attack rôle (IIIE) the external pylons may be utilized to carry various combinations of ground attack stores such as a combined multiple tube rocket pod/fuel tank (18 rockets in the front portion and 250 litres fuel in the rear portion), one under each wing. Alternatively a NORD AS30 air-to-surface missile may be carried on the centre (belly) pylon together with fuel tanks on inboard wing pylons. In place of the AS30 missile the centre pylon may be fitted with two large bombs in tandem, or smaller bombs in pairs. The Mirage IIIE is equally suitable as an interceptor and as such may utilize the MATRA R.530 air-to-air missile attached to the strong point under the fuselage.

All the Mirage III variants have the same external weapons attachment points. The Mirage IIIR has five OMERA 31 cameras in the nose in place of radar.

Supplied to: Mirage III: France, Argentinia, Australia, South Africa, Brazil, Spain, Israel, Lebanon, Pakistan, Switzerland, Venezuela
Mirage 5 (simplified ground attack version of IIIE): France, Abu Dhabi, Belgium, Colombia, Egypt, Gabon, Libya, Pakistan, Peru, Venezuela and Zaïre
Mirage 50: (Atar 09K-50 powered version of Mirage 5): Sudan.
Production status: Production of the Mirage III/5/50 family continues slowly and by May 1, 1979 some 1 480 examples had been ordered
First delivery to SAAF: Mirage IIICZ: April 1963
Mirage IIIBZ: November 1964
Mirage IIIEZ: July 1965
Mirage IIIRZ: 1967
Mirage IIID2Z and IIIR2Z: 1974
Squadron status in SAAF: Mirage IIICZ/BZ/RZ/R2Z: 2 Squadron.
Mirage IIIEZ/DZ/D2Z: 85 Advanced Flying School.
Basic current SAAF colour scheme: All versions are camouflaged utilizing the standard French Air Force pattern. Colours for upper surfaces are Olive Drab (BSC298) and Deep Buff (BSC360) and for under surfaces Light Admiralty Grey (BSC697)
Three view drawings: Mirage IIICZ, Mirage IIIEZ.

HAWKER SIDDELEY BUCCANEER

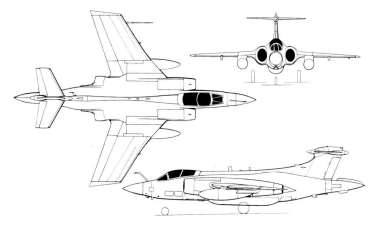

Country of origin and manufacture: United Kingdom
First flights: First pre-production aircraft: 30.4.1958
First Buccaneer S.Mk 2: 17.5.1963
Power plants (Model S.Mk 50): Two Rolls Royce RB.168-1A Spey Mk 101 turbofans of 11 100 lb (5 035 kg) thrust AND one Bristol BS. 605 twin chamber rocket engine of 8 000 lb (3 630 kg) thrust housed in retractable panels in lower part of rear fuselage just forward of air-brakes.

Principal dimensions (S.Mk 50): Wingspan: 44 ft (13,41 m)
Height: 16 ft 3 in (4,95 m)
Length: 63 ft 5 in (19,33 m)
Maximum take-off mass (S.Mk 50): 62 000 lbs (28 123 kg)
Basic performance figures (S.Mk 50): Maximum low-level (200 feet or 61 m above sea-level) design speed in level flight: 645 mph (560 knots or 1 038 km/h) (Mach 0,85) Range: (basic) 2 000 nautical miles (3 700 km). Range can be extended by means of air-to-air refuelling from another Buccaneer. Underwing air-to-air refuelling tank for supply aircraft holds 140 Imp gall. (636 litres) but may be fed from main fuel system. An extra fuel tank, 440 Imp gallons or 2 000 litres, may be installed in the bomb-bay (see drawing above) in addition to the normal bombs carried therein. Underwing slipper tanks (either 250 or 430 Imp. gallons) may also be fitted to extend range. (see drawing above – 250 Imp gall. tank)
Armament: (S.Mk 50): Internal weapons bay may accommodate four 1 000 lb (454 kg) bombs or camera pack; Four underwing attachment points may each be fitted with multiple-tube MATRA rocket pod or a Nord AS 30 air-to-surface missile.
Crew: One pilot and one navigator, seated in tandem.
Supplied to: Royal Navy/Fleet Air Arm
Royal Air Force;
South African Air Force.
Service status: In service with Royal Air Force and South African Air Force.
Production status: Production completed late 1975
Total production just over 200.
First delivery to SAAF: May 26, 1965 at RNAS Lossiemouth, Scotland
Variant operated by SAAF: Buccaneer S.Mk 50
Squadron status in SAAF: No 24 Squadron.
Basic current SAAF colour scheme: Dark Sea Grey (BSC638) upper surfaces PRU-Blue undersurfaces (BSC636).

CANADAIR CL13B SABRE Mk 6

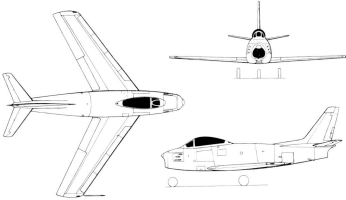

Country of origin: United States of America
Country of manufacture: Canada
First flights: Prototype (designated North American XP-86): 1.10.1947.
Canadair CL13B Sabre Mk 6: 2.11.1954
Power plant ((Sabre Mk 6): one Orenda 14 turbojet of 7 275 lb st (3 300 kg)
Principal dimensions (Sabre Mk 6): Length: 37 ft 6 in (11,72 m)
Wingspan: 37 ft 1 in (11,27 m)
Height: 15 ft 0 in (4,57 m)
Maximum gross mass (Sabre Mk 6): 17 611 lb (7 988kg)
Basic performance figures (Sabre Mk 6): Maximum speed at sea level: 710 mph. (Mach 0,93) (1 142 km/h)
Ferry range (with 333 imperial gallon underwing ferry tank): 1 495 miles (2 405 km)
Combat radius without underwing fuel tanks: 363 miles (584 km)
Armament: Six 0,5 in Colt-Browning machine guns in nose, plus four underwing strong points permitting two missiles and two 1 000 lb bombs to be carried. Outboard strong points may be fitted with ferry fuel tanks of various capacities.
Service status: In early 1980 the principal operator of the Sabre (F-86F) was Japan but these are due for retirement soon. Other operators of Sabres early in 1980 were Bolivia (F-86F); Indonesia (Australian built Sabre

Mk 32); S. Korea (F-86F); Philippines (F-86F); Portugal (F86F/Canadair CL13B); Tunisia (F-86F) and South Africa (Canadair CL13B); The SAAF Sabres have been placed in storage after retirement on June 4, 1980

Production status: Final F-86F Sabre was completed on February 25, 1961, being the last of 300 examples assembled in Japan by Mitsubishi. Final Canadair Sabre Mk 6 was completed on October 9, 1958.

Delivery to SAAF: First CL13B Sabre delivered to South Africa by sea in August 1956 and assembled at No 1 Air Depot.

Variants operated by SAAF: American produced F-86F Sabres were used by No. 2 Squadron in Korea, but last example returned to US Air Force on October 12, 1953. (none of the F86Fs ever came to SA). Canadian Sabre Mk 6 is the principal variant operated in South Africa, 34 being ordered from Canadair.

Squadron status in SAAF: Operated by No. 1 and 2 Squadrons at Waterkloof initially. In late 1963 No. 2 Squadron's Sabres were transferred to 1 Squadron, this squadron moving to Pietersburg in January 1967. In October 1975 the remaining Sabres joined No 85 Advanced Flying School at Pietersburg.

Basic current SAAF colour scheme: Camouflage of Olive Drab (BSC298) and Deep Buff (BSC360) with Light Admiralty Grey (BSC697) fuselage undersides

ENGLISH ELECTRIC CANBERRA

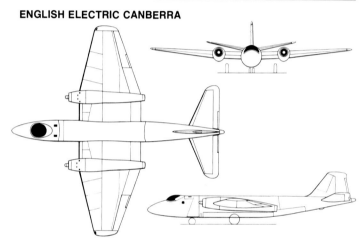

Country of origin and manufacture: United Kingdom
First flights: Prototype (designated A.1): 13.5.1949
First T.4: June 1952
First B(I)8: June 1955
Power plants: (Canberra T.4): Two Rolls Royce Avon 101 turbojets of 6 500 lbs st (2 954 kg)
(Canberra B(I)12): Two Rolls Royce Avon 109 turbojets of 7 400 lbs st (3 357 kg)
Principal dimensions: Wingspan (T.4/B(I)12): 63 ft 11½ in (19,51 m)
Length (T.4/B(I)12): 65 ft 6 in (19,96 m)
Height: (T.4/B(I)12): 15 ft 8 in (4,77 m)
Maximum gross mass: Canberra T.4: 38 000 lb (1 724 kg)
Canberra B(I)12: 55 000 lb (24 945 kg)
Basic performance figures: Maximum speed: (T.4): 570 mph (at 40 000 ft/12 192 m) B(I)12: 580 mph (at 30 000 ft/9 144 m)
Maximum operational altitude (B(I)12 and T.4): 38 000 ft (11 582 m)
Range: (T.4): 3 100 miles (4 988 km) (B(I)12): 3 790 miles (6 100 km)
Crew: Canberra T.4: Pilot and instructor side-by-side with a navigator's position behind cockpit.
Canberra B(I)12: Pilot with second crew member seated forward of cockpit. The latter may move forward in a lying position as bomb aimer.
Armament: Canberra B(I)12: 6 000 lb (2 720 kg) of ordnance may be carried internally. A 1 000 lb ordnance (bombs, rocket pods etc) may be attached to a hard point under each wing. Rear half of bomb-bay adapted to carry a detachable pack of four 20 mm cannons with sufficient ammunition for 60 sec. continued firing. In the latter configuration three 1 000 lb bombs may still be accommodated in the forward bomb-bay, (The Canberra T.4 is also equipped with a bomb-bay.
Service status: Canberras ordered by: Venezuela, Australia (many licence built), Ecuador, France, India, Peru, New Zealand, South Africa, United

Kingdom, Zimbabwe, West Germany, Sweden, Ethiopia, Argentina. (Sweden, Australia and New Zealand have retired their Canberras.) (A considerable number of Canberra variants and developments were produced in the USA, by Glenn L Martin Co, the initial versions being known as Martin B57As)

Production status: Final Canberras built new were six B(I)12s, constructed in 1963 for the South African Air Force.

First delivery to SAAF: First Canberra flown out to SA and delivered at Waterkloof on 30.9.1963.

Squadron status in SAAF: Both the T.4 and B(I)12 are operated by No 12 Squadron.

Basic current SAAF colour scheme: Both versions in SAAF service are overall PRU-blue (BSC636).

Three view drawing: Canberra T.4.

AERMACCHI/ATLAS MB326M IMPALA Mk 1 and

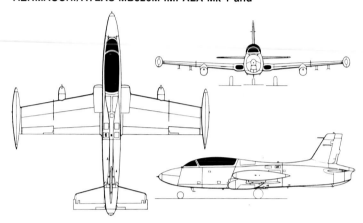

MB326KC IMPALA Mk 2

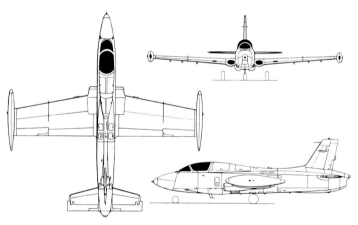

Country of origin: Italy
Country of manufacture: South Africa (Initial examples were made in Italy)
First flights: Prototype MB326 dual trainer: 10.12.1957
Prototype single seat MB326K: 22.8.1970.
Power plant (MB326M and MB326KC): One Rolls-Royce Viper Mk 540 turbojet of 3 410 lb static thrust (1 547 kg)
Principal dimensions: Length: (MB326M): 34 ft 11¼ in (10,65 m)
(MB326K): 35 ft ¼ in (10,67 m)
Height: (MB326M and MB326K): 12 ft 2 in (3,72 m)
Wingspan: (MB326M): 34 ft 8 in (10,56 m)
(MB326K): 35 ft 7 in (10,85 m)
Maximum gross mass: (MB326M): 8 300 lb (13 765 kg)
Basic performance figures: (MB326M): Maximum level speed (at sea level and AUW of 7 500 lb/3 400 kg): 478 mph (770 km/h)
Service ceiling: 41 000 ft (12 500 m)
Range 1 035 miles (1 665 km)
Armament: MB326M: The underwing attachment points may be utilized to carry the following loads alternatively:

Two gun pods with cannon (illustrated in three view);
Two multiple tube rocket packs each containing six 80 mm rockets;
Two 500 lb (240 kg) bombs;
Tactical photo recce pods (each with four 70 mm cameras); or towed targets may also be carried.

MB326K: Two 30 mm DEFA cannon in lower front fuselage. This version has six underwing attachment points to which up to 4 000 lb (1 814 kg) of ordinance may be carried. (In addition to the items listed above, the MB326KC in SAAF service is also often seen with underwing fuel tanks) (The MB326K also has the capability to carry air-to-air missiles such as the MATRA R550)

Supplied to: (single seat and dual versions): Argentine Navy, Australia, (licence built in Australia), Bolivia, (Xavante) Brazil (licence built as the Xavante), Dubai, Ghana, Italy, South Africa (licence built as Impala Mk 1 and Mk 2), Togo (Xavante), Tunisia, Zaïre, Zambia. These remain in service with the Air Forces of these nations.

Production status: Both the two seat version (as the MB326GB and MB326L) and the single seat MB326K remain in production, the former versions being two-seaters with uprated motors and similar attack/close support capabilities as the K version.

First delivery to the SAAF: MB326M: May 1966
MB326KC: April 1974

Variants operated by SAAF: Dual version: Atlas MB326M Impala Mk 1 single seat version: Atlas MB326KC Impala Mk 2.

Squadron status in SAAF: The Impala Mk 1 is flown by 4 Squadron, 5 Squadron, 6 Squadron, 7 Squadron, 8 Squadron, Flying Training School and 85 Advanced Flying School; Impala Mk 2s are flown by 4 Squadron, 8 Squadron and 85 Advanced Flying School.

Basic current SAAF colour scheme: Impala Mk 1s are all over silver painted but some examples now are finished in Olive Drab/Dark Earth camouflage with Light Admiralty Grey undersurfaces. Although the first Impala Mk 2s are finished in a wide variety of different camouflage schemes, the standard camouflage scheme for these aircraft now is Olive Drab (BSC298) and Dark Earth (BSC450) upper surfaces with Light Admiralty Grey (BSC697) fuselage undersides.

DOUGLAS C47 DAKOTA

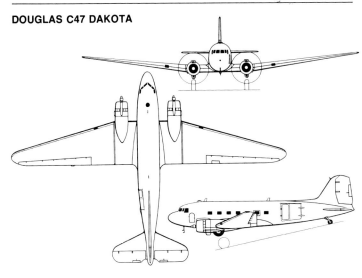

Country of origin and manufacture: United States of America
First flights: Prototype: 17.12.1935 (Commercial DC-3)
Power plants: Two Pratt & Whitney R-1830-92 (Dakota Mk III) or R-1830-90B (Dakota MK IV) nine-cylinder radial piston engines of 1 200 hp (882 kW)
Principal dimensions: Length: 64 ft 6 in (19,66 m)
Height: 16 ft 11½ in (5,16 m)
Wingspan: 95 ft (28,96 m)
Maximum gross mass: 31 000 lb. (14 061 kg)
Basic performance figures: Maximum speed: 215 mph (346 km/h)
Normal cruising speed: 185 mph (298 km/h)
Service ceiling: 19 000 ft (6 300 m)
Range with maximum payload: 1 510 miles (2 430 km)
Crew: Pilot and co-pilot

Accommodation in cabin: Normal configuration: 27 passengers
Service status: Since World War II the C47 (and its variants) have seen extensive service with many air arms and are today still operated, mostly with civil operators on a world-wide basis. Many are still in service with the smaller air forces. The South African Air Force with some 40 Dakotas on strength is today one of the largest single operators of Dakotas in the world.
Production status: A total of 10 655 DC-3/C47 (and variants) were produced when the last example rolled off the assembly line on 6.5.1946
First delivery to SAAF: 21.6.1943 at Accra, Gold Coast (Ghana)
Variants operated by SAAF: Douglas C47A Dakota Mk III
Douglas C47B Dakota Mk IV
Squadron status in SAAF: 44 Squadron, 25 Squadron, and 86 Advanced Flying School.
Basic current SAAF colour scheme: Upper fuselage camouflage of Olive Drab (BSC298) and Dark Earth (BSC450) with PRU-blue (BSC636) fuselage undersides.
A single example is finished all over yellow with black stripes for target towing duties.

DOUGLAS DC-4

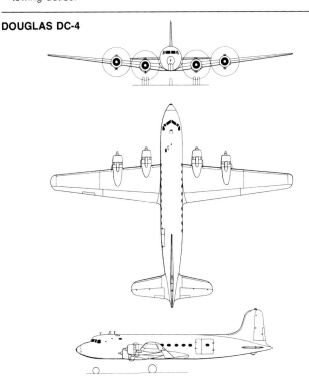

Country of origin and manufacture: United States of America
First flight (Military version – C54 Prototype): 14.2.1942
Power plants: Four Pratt & Whitney R-2000-2SD-13G Twin Wasp piston engines of 1 450 hp (1 066 kW) each
Principal dimensions: Length: 93 ft 11 in (28,79 m)
Height: 27 ft 7 in (8,41 m)
Wingspan: 117 ft 6 in (35, 82 m)
Maximum gross mass: 73 000 lb (33 112 kg)
Basic performance figures: Maximum speed: 265 mph (426 km/h)
Normal cruising speed: 207 mph (333 km/h)
Service ceiling: 19 000 ft (5 791 m)
Accommodation: Pilot and co-pilot plus 54-66 passengers.
Service status: Only a few of the military C54 variant remain in military service. The SAAF is now thought to be the sole military operator of the civil DC-4-1009 variant.
Production status: Production of the C54 came to just over 1 000 by the time WW2 ended. Many were civilianized post war, but 79 new examples were built post war as Civil DC-4-1009s. Production ceased in August 1947, and the last DC-4 built was in fact delivered to South African Airways on August 9, 1947 and to the SAAF in January 1966.
First delivery to SAAF: January 1966
Variant operated by SAAF: Douglas DC-4-1009

Squadron status in SAAF: 44 Squadron.
Basic current SAAF colour scheme: Upper fuselage camouflage of Olive Drab (BSC 298) and Dark Earth (BSC 450) with PRU-Blue (BSC 636) fuselage undersides.

LOCKHEED C130 HERCULES

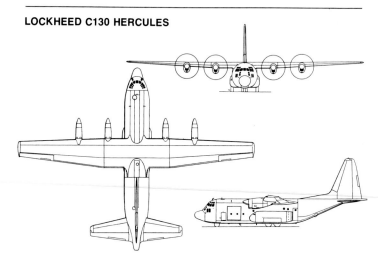

Country of origin and manufacture: United States of America
First flights: Prototype (YC130): 23.8.1954
C-130B: 10.12.1958
Power plants: (C130B) Four Allison T56-A-7A Turboprops of 4 050 shp (2 978 kW) each.
Principal dimensions: (C130B): Wingspan: 132 ft 7 in (40,41 m)
Length: 97 ft 9 in (29,78 m)
Cabin volume: 4 300 cu ft (121,7 m²)
Height: 38 ft 4 in (11,58 m)
Basic performance figures: (C130B) Maximum speed (at gross weight): 368 mph (618 km/h)
Range: (with max payload): 2 200 miles (3 539 km) (with max. fuel): 4 850 miles (7 803 km)
Accommodation: Four crew (pilot, co-pilot, navigator and flight engineer/loadmaster. The hold may accommodate a maximum of 90 troops or 64 fully equipped paratroops or 74 stretchers (and 2 attendants) in the mass CASEVAC rôle
Service status: Late in 1979 the C130 was in service with some 45 Air Arms, besides the US Military Forces.
Production status: Current production version is in the C130H and L100-30
First delivery to SAAF: January 1963
Squadron status in SAAF: Operated by 28 Squadron since delivery.
Basic current SAAF colour scheme: Overall camouflage on fuselage and both sides of wings in Olive Drab (BSC298) and Dark Earth (BSC450). Underside of fuselage is Dark Sea Grey (BSC638).

TRANSALL C-160

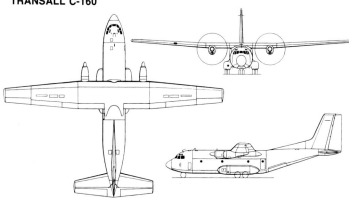

Country of origin: France and Germany
Country of manufacture (C160Z): France

First flights: Prototype: 25.2.1963
C-160Z: 28.2.1969.
Power plants: Two Rolls Royce Tyne R.Ty.20 Mk 22 Turboprops of 6 100 shp (4 550 kW) each
Principal dimensions: Wingspan: 131 ft 3 in (40 m)
Length: 106 ft 3½ in (32,4 m)
Cabin volume: 4 072 cu ft (115,3 m²)
Height: 40 ft 7 in (12,36 m)
Basic performance figures: Maximum speed at 14 760 ft (4 498 m): 333 mph (536 km/h)
Service ceiling (at 99 225 lbs AUW): 27 900 ft (8 503 m)
Range (with 8 ton payload (800 kg, 17 640 lbs) and 30 min reserves): 2 832 miles (4 558 km)
Accommodation: Four crew (pilot, co-pilot, navigator and loadmaster/flight engineer) plus 90 troops as typical payload. Alternatively up to 64 fully equipped paratroops OR 62 stretchers (and 4 attendants) in the mass CASEVAC rôle
Service status: Transalls were ordered new by the Air Forces of France, West Germany and South Africa. The Turkish Air Force operates a number of ex-West German Air Force machines while four ex-French Air Force machines are operated by Air France as C160Ps for the night postal service.
Production status: Production ceased in October 1972, with 179 Transalls built, but production line was re-opened in 1977 to meet a French Air Force requirement for additional aircraft.
First delivery to SAAF: July 1969
Variant operated by SAAF: Transall C-160Z
Squadron status in SAAF: Operated by 28 Squadron.
Basic current SAAF colour scheme: Overall camouflage on fuselage and both sides of wing in Olive Drab (BSC298) and Dark Earth (BSC450) underside of fuselage is Dark Sea Grey (BSC638).

AVRO SHACKLETON

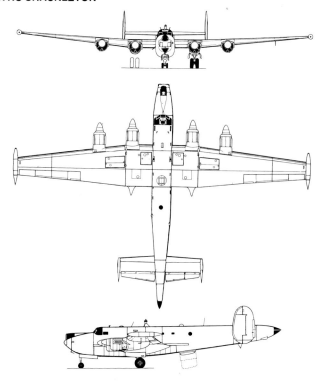

Country of origin and manufacture: United Kingdom.
First flights: Prototype (Shackleton GR.1): 9.3.1949 Shackleton MR.3: 2.9.1955
Power plants: (Shackleton MR.3): Four Rolls Royce Griffon 57A piston engines of 2 455 h.p. (1 831 kW) each
Principal dimensions: (Shackleton MR. 3): Length: 92ft 6 in (28,19 m)
Height: 23 ft 4 in (7,11 m) Wingspan: 119 ft 10 in (36,52 m)
Maximum gross mass (Shackleton MR.3 SAAF version) 100 000 lbs (45 360 kg)

Basic performance figures (Shackleton MR.3): Maximum speed (at 12 000 ft./3 657 m): 302 mph (486 km/h) Typical operating altitude: 1 500 ft (460 m) above sea level; Service ceiling: 19 200 ft (5 852 m); Range (at 1 500 ft/460 m ASL, 200 mph/322 km/h): 4 215 miles (6 782 km).

Crew: (SAAF version): Pilot and co-pilot plus 11

Armament: (Shackleton MR.3): Two 20mm Hispano cannons in nose which are removable. Bomb bay may be fitted with a variety of items on an *ad hoc* basis, including three Mk 30 or Mk 44 torpedoes or depth charges, or nine Sonobouy or nine 250 lb (113 kg) bombs, etc. In the search and rescue configuration Lindholme-gear (a set of five rope-connected cylindrical containers with supplies, including a dinghy in the middle one) or other items on an *ad hoc* basis may be carried. (The use of the SARO Mk 3 airborne life boats, one of which could be fitted on the outside of the closed bomb bay doors, has been discontinued by the SAAF.)

Supplied to: Royal Air Force and South African Air Force.

Service status: The RAF continues to operate 12 Shackleton AEW.2s but these are due to be replaced by Nimrod AEW.3s early in 1982. The SAAF continues to operate seven Shackleton MR.3s.

Production status: A total of 180 Shackletons of all variants were built when production ceased in June 1959.

First delivery to SAAF: May 21, 1957 at Woodford, England.

Variant operated by SAAF: Avro 696 Shackleton MR.3 (Phase 3)

Squadron status: 35 Squadron.

Basic current SAAF colour scheme: White fuselage top; Extra Dark Sea Grey (BSC 640) on top of wings and engine nacelles. Remainder of fuselage is finished in PRU-blue (BSC 636) propeller spinners are Post Office Red (BSC 538)

PIAGGIO P166

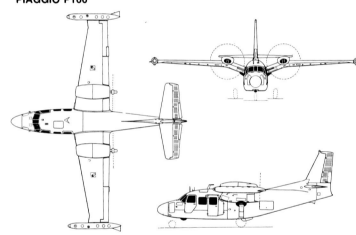

Country of origin and manufacture: Italy

First flights: Prototype: 26.11.1957
Piaggio P166S: October 1968

Power plants: (P166S) Two Piaggio-Lycoming GSO-480-B1C6 six cylinder horizontally opposed piston engine of 340 hp (254 kW)

Principal dimensions: (P166S) Length: 39 ft 0 in (11,90 m)
Height: 16 ft 5 in (5, 00 m)
Wingspan 48 ft 2 in (14,69 m)

Maximum gross mass: (P166S): 8 115 lbs (3 680 kg)

Basic performance figures: (P166S): Maximum speed: 222 mph (357 km/h)
Range: 1 200 miles (1 930 km)

Accommodation: Pilot and co-pilot. Cabin is fitted with two seats in addition to photographic equipment.

Supplied to: (military) Italy and South Africa.

Production status: Current production version is the turbo-prop powered P166-DL3, but at time of publication no orders for this version had been reported. More than 100 of all piston engined variants were built when production of piston engined versions ceased in 1973 when the SAAF order for 20 P166Ss was fulfilled

First delivery to SAAF: early 1969

Variant operated by SAAF: Piaggio P166-BL1 (or P166S) Albatross

Squadron status in SAAF: 27 Squadron.

Basic current SAAF colour scheme: White fuselage top, with PRU-blue (BSC 636) fuselage sides and wing undersides. Upper surfaces of wings and tailplane are Dark Sea Grey (BSC638)

WESTLAND WASP HAS. MK 1

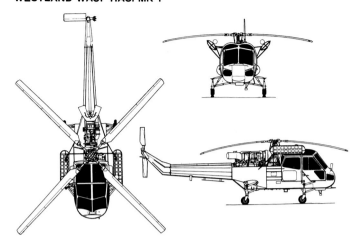

Country of origin and manufacture: United Kingdom

First flights: Prototype: 20.7.1958
First production example: 28.10.1962.

Power plant: One 710 shp (530 kW) Rolls Royce-Bristol Nimbus 503 turboshaft.

Principal dimensions: Length: (fuselage)· 30 ft 4 in (9,24 m)
Main Rotor diameter: 32 ft 3 in (9,83 m)

Maximum gross mass: 5 500 lb (2 495 kg)

Basic performance figures: Maximum level speed at sea level: 104 knots (120 mph, 193 km/h)
Maximum range (standard fuel): 263 nautical miles (303 statute miles, 488 km)

Accommodation: Two crew (pilot and flight engineer) plus three passengers in rear portion of cabin. A stretcher may be carried across rear of cabin. Dual controls are fitted for training purposes.

Armament: Two ventral attachment points may be fitted with two Mk 44 homing torpedoes or depth charges.

Service status: Ordered by: South Africa (17); New Zealand (3); Netherlands (12); Brazil (three, plus six ex Royal Navy machines); Great Britain (Royal Navy) (98). All aircraft designated Wasp HAS Mk 1

Production status: Production completed. Final Wasps built were for SAAF in 1972/73 making the SAAF the largest export customer for the type.

Delivery to SAAF: First of initial order of six delivered late 1963.
Repeat order for further four delivered from early 1966
Final order for seven (six delivered) placed in February 1972

Squadron status in SAAF: All operated by No 22 Squadron.

Basic current SAAF colour scheme: Overall Dark Sea Grey (BSC638)

SUD AVIATION (AEROSPATIALE) ALOUETTE III

Country of origin and manufacture: France

First flights: Prototype: 28.2.1959
SA316B: 27.6.1968

Power plant: One 570 shp (425 kW) Turboméca Artouste IIIB turboshaft.

Principal dimensions: Length: (fuselage): 32 ft 10¾ in (10,03 m)
Main Rotor Diameter: 36 ft 1¾ in (11,02 m)

Maximum gross mass: (SA316B): 4 850 lbs (2 200 kg)

Basic performance figures: (SA316B)
Maximum level speed at sea level at maximum gross mass: 130 mph (210 km/h)
Service ceiling: 10 500 ft (3 200 m)
Range: 335 miles (540 km)

Accommodation: Pilot, flight engineer plus five passengers
Two stretchers may be fitted.

Service Status: (military): Over 40 Air Arms operate the type at the time of publication.

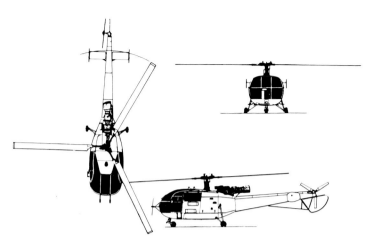

Production status: Currently in production with over 1 400 sold at time of publication. SE3160 (or SA316A) and SA316B versions no longer in production.

First delivery to SAAF: 1962

Variants operated by SAAF: Sud Aviation SE3160 Alouette III and Aérospatiale SA316B Alouette III. The latter version is similar in configuration and power plant to the original SE3160, but features strengthened main- and tail rotor transmissions permitting heavier loads to be carried.

Squadron status in SAAF: 16 Squadron, 17 Squadron, 22 Squadron and 87 Advanced Flying School.

Basic current SAAF colour scheme: Camouflaged all over in Olive Drab (BSC298) and Dark Earth (BSC450)

AEROSPATIALE SA330 PUMA

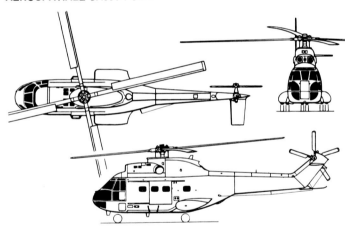

Country of origin and manufacture (SAAF examples): France

First flights: Prototype SA330: 15.4.1965
SA330C (initial export version): September 1968.

Power plants: SA330C: Two Turboméca Turmo IIIC-4 turbo shaft engines, each rated at 1 328 shp (991 kW) for take-off and 1 185 shp (884 kW) for continuous operation
SA330H/L: Two Turboméca Turmo IVC turbo shaft engines of 1 575 shp (1 175 kW) each.

Principal dimensions: Length (fuselage): 46 ft 1½ in (14,06 m)
Main Rotor Diameter: 49 ft 2½ in (15,00 m)

Maximum gross mass: SA330C: 14 770 lb (6 246 kg)
SA330L: 16 315 lb (7 400 kg)

Basic performance figures: (SA330L)
Maximum speed (AUW of 6 000 kg): 182 mph (294 km/h)
Service ceiling (AUW of 6 000 kg): 19 680 ft (6 000 m)
Range at normal cruising speed, 6 000 kg AUW and no reserves: 355 miles (572 km)

Accommodation: Pilot, co-pilot and flight engineer plus 16 passengers.

Service status: In service with Abu Dhabi, Algeria, Cameroun, Chile, France, United Kingdom, Indonesia, Ivory Coast, Kuwait, Mexico, Nigeria, Pakistan, Portugal, Rumania, South Africa, Zaïre and others.

Production status: Current version in production is the SA330L and its civilian counterpart, the SA330J. The SA332 is a development of the SA330 with uprated Turboméca Makila motors and other improvements and is also now on offer. More than 600 SA330s of all versions have been sold at time of publication.

Variants operated by SAAF: SA330C, SA330H and SA330L

First delivery to SAAF: December 1969.

Squadron status in SAAF: 19 Squadron.

Basic current SAAF colour scheme: All over camouflage in Olive Drab (BSC298) and Dark Earth (BSC450)

Three view drawing: SA330C

SUD AVIATION (AEROSPATIALE) SUPER FRELON

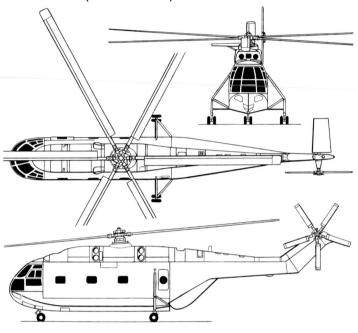

Country of origin and manufacture: France

First flights: Prototype 7.12.1962
First production Super Frelon: 30.11.1965

Power plants: Three Turboméca Turmo IIIC-6 turbo shaft engines rated at 1 320 shp (985 kW) each.

Principal dimensions: Length (fuselage): 63 ft 7¾ in (19,40 m)
Main Rotor Diameter: 62 ft 0 in (18,90 m)

Maximum gross mass: 28 660 lb (13 000 kg)

Basic performance figures: Maximum speed (at sea level) 171 mph (275 km/h)
Range (at sea level): 509 miles (820 km)
Service ceiling: 10 325 ft (3 150 m)

Accommodation: Pilot, co-pilot and flight engineer plus 27 passengers.

Service status: Military versions were ordered by France, South Africa, Israel, Iraq, Iran, Libya, China and Zaïre.

Production status: Slow production rate of four per year brought sales to around 100 at the time of publication.

First delivery to SAAF: June 1967

Variant operated by SAAF: SA321L Super Frelon.

Squadron status in SAAF: 15 Squadron.

Basic current SAAF colour scheme: All over camouflage in Olive Drab (BSC 298) and Dark Earth (BSC 450)

NORTH AMERICAN HARVARD

Country of origin and manufacture: United States of America

First flight: (BC-1A) 1937

Power plant: One 550 hp (409 kW) Pratt & Whitney R-1340-AN-1 radial piston engine.

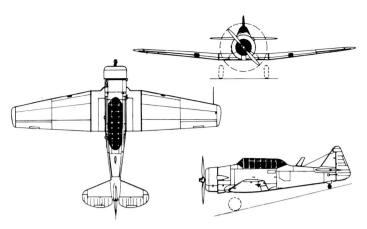

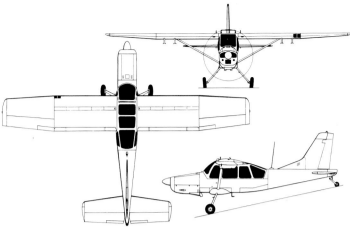

Principal dimensions: Length: 29 ft 6 in (9,0 m)
  Height: 11 ft 8½ in (3,50 m)
  Wingspan: 42 ft 0 in (12,90 m)
Maximum gross mass: (T6G) 5 617 lb (2 550 kg)
Basic performance figures: (T-6G) Maximum speed: 212 mph (341 km/h)
  Service ceiling: 21 500 ft (6 560 m)
  Range: 870 miles (1 400 km)
Armament: Some Harvards are fitted with two 7,62 mm machine guns in wings, with an underwing attachment point under each wing where a variety of light stores may be attached, ie flour bombs for training or multiple tube rocket pods (see illustration on page 134)
Service status: The T-6 (and its various versions) saw extensive service world-wide as an *ab initio* trainer especially in the early post WW2 period. The type continues in service with some two dozen of the world's smaller air forces, but now appears on civilian registers in increasing numbers as the aircraft are retired from military service. More than a dozen ex-SAAF Harvards among others were offered for sale by the Portuguese Air Force in 1978/79 and several of these are now on the British Civil Aircraft Register.
Production status: Production continued until 1954 by which time more than 10 000 of all variants had been built.
First delivery to SAAF: First batch delivered late 1942 and continued throughout the remainder of WW2 with further examples delivered post-war as detailed above. (A small batch of Harvard Mk Is, believed to total 9, was delivered between February 1940 and November 1942) During WW 2, a total of 633 Harvard Mk IIa and Harvard Mk IIIs were delivered to the SAAF but, on settlement of the Lend-Lease arrangement between the USA and SA, 300 of the survivors were returned although an estimated 120 of these were acquired for post-war SAAF use. In 1952/53 a further 65 Harvards, all ex-USAF AT-6As and AT-6Cs and US Navy SNJ-3s and SNJ-4s (modified to AT-6C standard) were delivered and in 1953/4 a further 30 T-6Gs were delivered. Final delivery of Harvards to the SAAF was in 1961 and consisted of four Harvards (two Mk IIa's and two Mk IIIs) formerly of the Belgian Air Force.
Variants operated by SAAF: Harvard Mk IIa (similar US versions were designated AT-6C);
  Harvard Mk III (similar US versions were designated AT-6D or SJN-4);
  AT-6C (similar to Harvard Mk IIa although delivered post-war directly from the USA);
  T-6G (remanufactured version of former WW 2 machines).
Squadron status in SAAF: Central Flying School and 40 Squadron.
Basic current SAAF colour scheme: All over silver painted with fire orange day-glo bands and patches. Top of wings are painted Dark Sea Grey (BSC638).

AERITALIA/AERMACCHI AM.3C BOSBOK

Country of origin and manufacture: Italy
First flight (prototype): 12.5.1967
Power plant: One Piaggio/Lycoming GSO-480-B1B6 six-cylinder horizontally opposed piston engine of 340 hp (254 kW)
Principal dimensions: Length: 28 ft 8 in (8,73 m)
  Height: 32 ft 1¾ in (9,80 m)
  Wingspan: 38 ft 6 in (11,73 m)

Maximum take-off mass: (with two crew only): 3 306 lb (1 500 kg)
  (with full underwing weapons): 3 750 lb (1 700 kg)
Basic performance figures: Maximum speed: (at sea level): 161 mph (260 km/h); (at 8 000 ft/2 438 m): 173 mph (278 km/h)
  Service ceiling: 27 550 ft (8 400 m)
  Maximum range (at 5 000 ft/1 524 m with 30 minutes reserves): 615 miles (990 km)
  Take-off run: 280 ft (85 m)
  Landing run: 217 ft (66 m)
Crew: Pilot and observer/co-pilot seated in tandem, with provision for a passenger to be seated behind the observer. Observer/co-pilot's seat and his control column may be removed to accommodate a stretcher.
Armament: Four under-wing hard points. Inner points stressed for 375 lb (170 kg) and outer points stressed for a 200 lb (91 kg) load. A variety of weaponry may be fitted to these points, i.e. 7,62 mm machine gun pods, multiple-tube rocket pods, single air-to-surface missiles, etc. A camera may be installed on the cabin floor beneath the co-pilot's seat.
Supplied to: Italian Army (for evaluation)
  Rwanda Air Force (3)
  South African Air Force
Service status: In service with the Rwanda Air Force and the South African Air Force.
Production status: Production completed.
First delivery to SAAF: March 1973
Variant operated by SAAF: AM.3CM
Squadron status: 41 Squadron and 42 Squadron.
Basic current SAAF colour scheme: Two-tone all over camouflage:
  Olive Drab (BSC298) Dark Earth (BSC450)

ATLAS C.4M KUDU

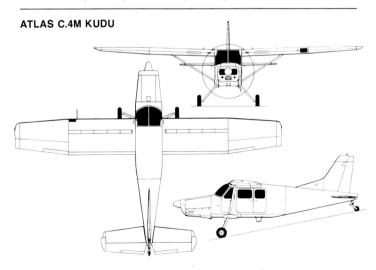

Country of origin and manufacture: South Africa
First flight: 16.2.1974 (then designated AL60-C4M)
Power plant: One Piaggio/Lycoming GSO-480-B1B3 six-cylinder horizontally opposed piston engine of 340 hp (250 kW)

Principal dimensions: Length: 29 ft 8 in (9,04 m)
  Wingspan: 42 ft 7⁴/₅ in (13,00 m)
  Height: 12 ft 0 in (3,66 m)
Basic performance figures: Maximum speed (at 8 000 ft/ 2 440 m): 161 mph (260 km/h). Maximum range with no reserves: 806 miles (1 297 km). Take-off run: 705 ft (215 m). Landing run: (from 50 ft/15 m): 853 ft (260 m)
Accommodation: Pilot and seven passengers.
Supplied to: South African Air Force.
Service status: In service with the South African Air Force 41 Squadron and 42 Squadron.
Production status: In production for the SAAF.
First delivery to SAAF: August 1974.
Variant operated by SAAF: C.4M (sole production version)
Basic current SAAF colour scheme: Two-tone camouflage: Olive Drab (BSC298) Dark Earth (BSC450) (A single example is all-over white with red crosses, operating in the CASEVAC role)

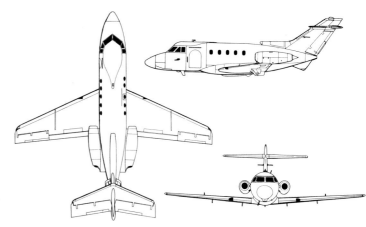

CESSNA 185

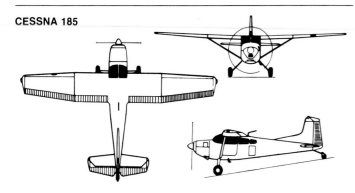

Country of origin and manufacture: United States of America
First flight: July 1960
Power Plant: (Cessna 185A): One Continental IO-470-F six-cylinder horizontally opposed piston engine of 260 hp (194 kW)
Principal dimensions: Length: 25 ft 6 in (7,77 m)
  Height: 7 ft 6 in (2,29 m)
  Wingspan: 36 ft 2 in (11,92 m)
Maximum gross mass: 3 200 lb (1 451 kg)
Basic performance figures: (260 hp motor):
  Maximum speed (at sea level): 176 mph (283 km/h)
  Service ceiling: 17 300 ft (5 273 m)
  Maximum range: 1 235 miles (1 987 km)
Accommodation: Pilot and 5 passengers.
Service status: Apart from the SAAF, other military operators of Cessna 185s (as Cessna U-17s) include Bolivia, Costa Rica, Vietnam, Jamaica and Peru.
Production status: Still in production for civil operators.
First delivery to SAAF: May 1962
Variants operated by SAAF: Cessna 185A, Cessna 185D and Cessna 185E.
Squadron status in SAAF: 11 Squadron.
Basic current SAAF colour scheme: All over camouflage of Olive Drab (BSC298) and Dark Earth (BSC450)

HAWKER SIDDELEY 125 (MERCURIUS)

Country of origin and manufacture: United Kingdom
First flights: Prototype (DH 125): 13.8.1962
  HS125 Series 400: 1968
Power plants: (Series 400B): Two Rolls Royce-Bristol Viper 522 turbojets of 3 360 lbs s. thrust (1 525 kg).
Principal dimensions (Series 400B): Length: 47 ft 5 in (14,45 m)
  Wingspan: 47 ft 0 in (14,33 m)
  Height: 16 ft 6 in (5,03 m)
Maximum take-off mass (series 400 B): 23 300 lbs (10 568 kg)
Basic performance figures (series 400B): Maximum cruising speed: (at 31 000 ft/9 450 m) 411 knots (508 mph; 818 km/h): Economic cruising speed: (above 37 000 ft; 11 300 m): 391 knots (450 mph; 724 km/h)
  Service ceiling: 41 000 ft (12 500 m)

Range: (60% payload and 45 minutes reserves): 1 750 statute miles (2 817 km)
Crew (Series 400B in SAAF service): Pilot and co-pilot and one female cabin attendant.
Cabin accommodation (Series 400B in SAAF service): 3 Crew (pilot, co-pilot and cabin attendant) plus 5 passengers.
Supplied to: (military only): Royal Air Force; Brazil Air Force; Royal Aircraft Establishment; Ghana (since replaced); Royal Malaysian Air Force; South African Air Force; Argentine Navy and Irish Air Corps.
Service status: In service worldwide as executive jets with civilian and military operators; some used as airport navigation-aid calibration aircraft (including a series 400B with the South African Department of Transport)
Production status: Series 700 only remaining production version.
First delivery to SAAF: March 1970 (Three replacements for the ones destroyed, delivered in January 1972)
Variant operated by SAAF: HS125-400B; type designation in SAAF service: Mercurius.
Squadron status in SAAF: 21 Squadron.
Basic current SAAF colour scheme: White fuselage top, tailplane and engine nacelles, and painted silver undersides divided by an Aircraft-blue (BSC108) cheat-line. Cockpit anti-glare panel also Aircraft blue.

SWEARINGEN (FAIRCHILD) MERLIN IVA

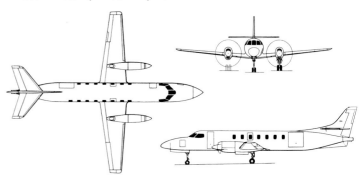

Country of origin and manufacture: USA
First flights: Merlin II: 13.4.1965
  Metro: 26.8.1969
Certification: Merlin IV: 22.9.1970
Power plants: (Merlin IVA) Two Garrett AiResearch TPE 331-3UW-303G turboprops of 940 shp (691 kW)
  One Aerojet-General solid fuel rocket unit of 350 lb st (159 kg)
Basic dimensions: (Merlin IVA) Wingspan: 46 ft 3 in (14,10 m)
  Height: 16 ft 10 in (5,13 m)
  Length: 59 ft 4 ¼ in (18,09 m)
Basic performance figures: (Merlin IVA) Maximum cruising speed: 310 mph (499 km/h)
  Range at maximum cruising speed: 1 575 miles (2 534 km)
  Service ceiling: 27 000 ft (8 230 m)
Accommodation: 3 crew (pilot, co-pilot and cabin attendant) as well as 7 passengers

Military operators: Chile Police Force (Metro) (12)
Royal Oman Police (Metro) (2)
South African Air Force (Merlin IVA) (7)
Argentine Air Force (Merlin IVA) (3), (Merlin IIIA) (4)
Belgian Air Force (Merlin IIIA) (6)
Royal Thai Air Force (Merlin IVA) (2)
Production status: In production as Merlin IIIA and Merlin IVA/Metro II
First delivery to SAAF: June 20, 1975
Variant operated by the SAAF: Swearingen SA226-AT Merlin IVA
Squadron status in SAAF: No 21 Squadron.
Basic current SAAF colour scheme: All top surfaces white, all undersurfaces painted silver. Divided by Aircraft Blue cheat line (BSC108).

VICKERS VISCOUNT

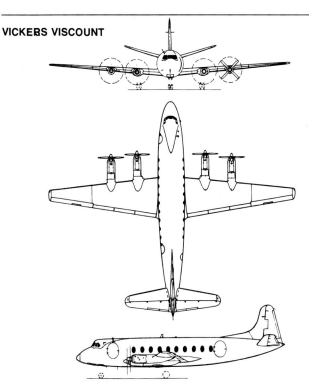

Country of origin and manufacture: United Kingdom
First flights: Prototype: 16.7.1948
Viscount 700: 19.4.1950
(Certification of improved Viscount 700D obtained late in 1955)
Power plants (Viscount 700D): Four Rolls-Royce R.Da.6 Dart Mk. 510 turboprop motors of 1 780 hp (1 308 kW) each
Principal dimensions (Viscount 700D): Length: 81 ft 10 in (24, 93 m)
Height: 26 ft 6 in (8,07 m)
Wingspan: 93 ft 8½ in (28, 54 m)
Maximum take-off mass (Viscount 700D): 64 500 lb (29 257 kg)
Basic performance figures (Viscount 700D):
Maximum cruising speed: 334 mph (537 km/h)
Service ceiling: 27 500 ft (8 382 m)
Range (with maximum payload with allowance for normal airline reserves): 1 330 miles (2 140 km)
Crew (Viscount 781D): Pilot and co-pilot with a senior NCO as technician; cabin-crew as required.
Cabin accommodation (Viscount 781D): 20 passengers in VIP seating arrangement.
Supplied to (military only): Royal Australian Air Force (2) (disposed of in 1969)
Brazilian Air Force (2) (One still active 1979)
United Kingdom (6 received military serial numbers, none are current)
Indian Air Force (2) (disposed of)
Sultan of Oman Air Force (disposed of)
Pakistan Air Force (1) (disposed of)
South African Air Force (1) (current)
Turkish Air Force (3) (current)

Production status: A total of 436 Viscounts of all variants had been built when production ceased in 1964.
Service status: Many Viscounts of all variants remain in airline service worldwide, although only three military operators remain as detailed above.
First delivery to SAAF: June 16, 1958
Variant operated by SAAF: Vickers Viscount 781D (named 'Casteel')
Squadron status: 21 Squadron.
Basic current SAAF colour scheme: White fuselage top and tail; highly polished natural metal fuselage sides with Aircraft Blue (BSC108) cheat line and cockpit anti-glare panel.

DE HAVILLAND VAMPIRE

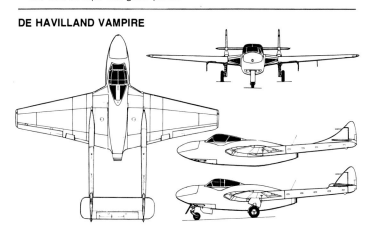

Country of origin and manufacture: United Kingdom
First flights: Prototype: 20.9.1943
Vampire T.11: 15.11.1950
Power plant: (Vampire T.11): One de Havilland Goblin 35 turbojet of 3 500 lb st (1 587 kg)
Principal dimensions: (Vampire T.11): Length: 34 ft 5 in (10,5 m)
Wingspan: 38 ft (11, 58 m)
Height: 6 ft 2 in (1,87 m)
Maximum gross mass: (Vampire T.11): 12 920 lb (5 860 kg)
Basic performance figures: (Vampire T.11): maximum speed (at sea level): 538 mph (866 km/h)
Range: 853 miles (1 372 km)
Service ceiling: 40 000 ft (12 192 m)
Crew: Vampire FB.5/6/9: pilot; or Vampire T.11: pilot and student (side-by-side)
Armament: ((Vampire FB.5/6/9/T.55): Four 20 mm Hispano 404 cannon in nose. Underwing strong points inboard and outboard of each tail boom permitted various combinations of external stores to be carried, i.e. eight 60 lb (27 kg) rockets and two 500 lb (227 kg) bombs, or two 1 000 lb (454 kg) bombs. In place of external ordnance, two 200 Imp. gallon (909 litre) drop tanks could be fitted.
Service status: Few single-seaters remain in service, although Zimbabwe was known to still operate FB.9s as recently as early 1980. Other current operators include the Dominican Republic and Switzerland. Likewise very few two-seaters remain active, principal operators being Zimbabwe and Switzerland, with two T.55s still active in South Africa.
Production status: Production completed
Delivery to SAAF: Vampire FB.5: Initial batch of 10 delivered by sea to Cape Town on January 21, 1950
Vampire FB Mk 6: Further batch of 10 delivered by sea in 1951
Vampire FB Mk 52: 30 delivered in 1953
Vampire T.55: Initial batch of six T.11s delivered in 1953.
Follow-up batch of 21 new T.55s delivered 1954 to 1956
Variants operated by SAAF: see above under Delivery section.
Current status in SAAF: Only two T.55s remain active and are used in test and evaluation avionics by TFDC (Test, Flight and Development Centre).
Basic current SAAF colour scheme: White upper fuselage and top of wings, with Arctic Blue (BSC112) undersurfaces and under wings. Two colours on fuselage are separated by an International orange (BSC592) line along centre of fuselage.
Three view drawing: Early version of Vampire T-11. Additional side view shows a Vampire T-55 with revised cockpit glazing and swept tail.

SUPERMARINE SPITFIRE

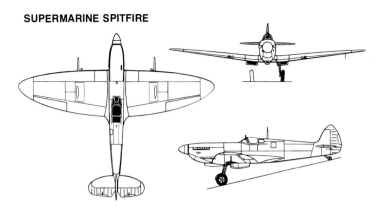

Country of origin: United Kingdom

First flights: Prototype (Supermarine Type 300): 5.3.1936
Spitfire IX (converted Mk. V): early 1942

Power plant: One 1 475 hp (1 084 kW) Rolls-Royce Merlin 70 twelve-cylinder liquid cooled piston engine

Principal dimensions: Length: 31 ft 4½ in (9,65 m) Height (with airscrew vertical and tail down): 12 ft 7¾ in (4,02 m) Wingspan: 36 ft 10 in (11,25 m)

Maximum gross mass: 7 500 lbs (3 402 kg)

Basic performance figures: Maximum speed (at 27 000 ft/8 229 m): 416 mph (669 km/h) Service ceiling: 45 000 ft (13 716 m) Range (with internal fuel): 434 miles (698 km)

Armament: (not applicable to the restored Spitfire PT672 described elsewhere in this book) Two 20 mm Hispano cannon. Two 0,5 in Browning machine guns. One 500 lb (227 kg) bomb. Two 250 lb (113 kg) bombs.

Production status: A total of 20 334 Spitfires (excluding 2 408 Seafires) was built. Total production of Spitfire Mk IX was 5 665.

Basic current colour scheme: Details of Spitfire IXE PT672: This Spitfire (described and illustrated on pages 156/157) was painted to represent a specific Spitfire F.R. IX (PT672) flown in 1944/45 by 40 Squadron/SAAF. The colours are non-standard for that period and are Dark Green and Dark Earth camouflage with Azure undersides. These colours are the temperate land scheme for a tactical reconnaissance aircraft.

FIESELER Fi 156 STORCH

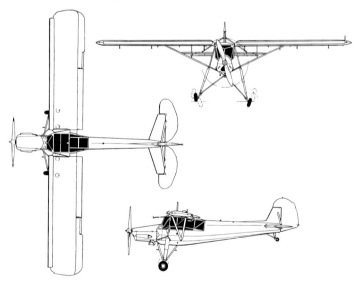

Country of origin and manufacture: Germany

First flight: Prototype: 1936

Power plant: (Fi 156-C): One Argus AS 10-C eight-cylinder air-cooled piston engine of 240 hp (176 kW)

Principal dimensions: Wingspan: 46 ft 9 in (14,22 m)
Length: 32 ft 5¾ in (10 m)
Height: 9 ft 10 in (3 m)

Maximum gross mass: 2 910 lb (1 320 kg)

Basic performance figures: Maximum speed: 109 mph (175 km/h)
Cruising speed: 93 mph (150 km/h)
Landing run (at maximum gross mass from a height of 15 m until standstill): 125 metres
Take-off run (at maximum gross mass with release of brakes at full throttle): 35 metres.

Principal variants: Fi 156VL to Fi 156V5: First five prototypes
Fi 156A: Initial production version
Fi 156B: Projected civil version (abandoned)
Fi 156C: Principal production version appearing in 1939
Fi 156D: Special CASEVAC version with larger cabin.
Fi 156E: Experimental version for extreme rough field operation
Versions produced in France by Morane-Saulnier were designated MS.500 (Argus 10-C motor); MS 501 (Renault 6Q motor) and MS.502 (Salmson 9ABC motor)
Versions produced in Czechoslovakia were designated Mraz K-65 Cap

Production status: Production for Luftwaffe by the end of WW 2 came to 2 549 machines, but production continued post-war in France and Czechoslovakia as detailed above. No longer in production.

First delivery to SAAF: 6.11.1946

Variant operated by SAAF: Fieseler Fi 156C-7

Basic current colour scheme: Repainted in authentic Luftwaffe Scheme used in Eastern Europe towards the end of WW 2.
Fuselage and wings were camouflaged in 70 *Schwarzgrün* and 80 *Olivgrün* with 65 *Hellblau* fuselage undersides. An identification colour 27 *Gelb* was sprayed on the wing tip and nose undersides. Cockpit interior finished in 66 *Schwarzgrau*.

INDEX

Numbers given in bold refer to photographs, and numbers printed in italic refer to specifications.

AOS Langebaanweg 157
Aboukir filter 30
Abyssinia (Ethiopia) 24, 39
Advanced Flying Schools
  Bloemspruit (No 87) 119, 163
  Brooklyn 156
  Langebaanweg 167
  Pietersburg (No 85) 36, 45, **49, 50, 59,** 60, 71
  Ysterplaat (No 88) 111
  (**see also** Air Schools)
Aerial Observation Post (AOP) 150
Aeritalia 145
Aeritalia/Aermacchi AM-3C Bosbok
  see Bosbok
Aermacchi/Atlas Impala
  see Impala
Aeronautica Macchi 144, 145
Aérospatiale Alouette
  see Alouette
Aérospatiale Puma
  see Puma
Aérospatiale Super-Puma
  see Super-Puma
African Aviation Syndicate Ltd 16
Afrikakorps 166
Air ambulance 153
Air Force Development Programme 21
Airmail Service 20
Air-sea rescues 97, 102, 103, 113, 124, 125
Air Schools
  Bloemfontein (No 62) 167
  Pietersburg (No 26) **29**
  Standerton (No 25) **29**
  (**see also** Advanced Flying Schools and Central Flying School, Dunnottar)
Air-to-air missile 47
Air-to-air refuelling **54**
Albatross, Piaggio P-166S 103, 108-111, **108, 110,** *173*
Allen, Lt. 37
Allison T56-A-7 turboprop 90, 91
Alouette, Aérospatiale III 118-123, **118, 120, 122, 123,** *173-174*
Angolan Campaign 35
Anson, Avro 22, 23, 29, 34, 68, 81, 84, 85, 87, 97, 104, 113
Anti-submarine warfare 113
Armstrong Siddeley Panther engine 21
Atar 9C turbojet 45
Atar 9K-50 turbojet 45
Atlas Aircraft Corporation 71, 145, 159
Atlas Kudu, **see** Kudu
Auster 148, 150
Audax 21
Avian IVM, Avro **20**
Avro 504K 18
Avro.Anson **see** Anson
Avro Avian **see** Avian
Avro Shackleton Mk 3 **see** Shackleton
Avro Tutor 20, 21
Azcarate, General Luis 144

Baltimore light bombers 25, 27, 29, 33, 133, 153, 155
Baragwanath Air Field 21
Barnett, Larry 158, 159
Bazzochi, Dr I.E. 71
Beaumont, Wing-Commander Roland 64
Beauchamp-Proctor, Capt. Andrew Weatherby 18
Beaufighter **31,** 125, 133
Beaufort bomber 23, 119, 133
Beechcraft Queen Air **see** Queen Air
Beech Expediter 97
Bell X-1 58
Belling, Capt. Ronald 165
Bellwood, Capt. W.A. 165
Beyers, Brig.-Gen. Christiaan 16

Bisley **see** Blenheim MkV
Blenheim 21 Mk V (Bisley) 27, 119, 133
Bleriot 16
Boeing B-29 Superfortress **see** Superfortress
Bombing, Gunnery and Air Navigation School 167
Bonaero Beleggings (Pty) Ltd 71
Bonaero Park 71
Bonuskor 71
Bosbok AM-3CM 144-145, **144,** 148, **149,** *175*
Boston bombers 25, 53, 56, 66, 68
Boston, Douglas **28**
Boston Squadron 26, 27
Botha, Gen. 17
Brand, Maj. Quintin 18
Britz, Maj. 153
Buccaneer, Hawker-Siddeley 52-53, **52, 54, 56,** *169*

Cameras, reconnaissance 45, 65
Canadair Sabre Mk 6 **see** Sabre
Canberra, English Electric 64-65, **64, 66, 68, 69,** *170*
Carpenter, airman 17
Casilaghi, Prof. Giovanni 108
Catalina Flying boat 23, **31,** 85, 103
Central Flying School,
  Dunnottar 138-139
  Historical note: 167
Cessna 185, 150-151, **150, 151,** *176*
Chapman, Lt. W.J.B. 151
Church, Capt. J. 125
Clausen, Lt. Fred 156
Coastal Reconnaissance Flights 22
Coningham, Air Vice-Marshal Sir Arthur 26
Constellation 87
Council for Scientific and Industrial Research 70
Creed, G.S. 17
Crocodile rescue 133
Curtiss Mohawk **see** Mohawk
Curtiss seaplane 17
Curtiss Tomahawk **see** Tomahawk
Cutler, H.D. 17
Cyrano I bis navigation and fire control radar system 44, 45
Cyrano IIB multi-function radar system 45

D.H.4 18
D.H.9 18, **19,** 20
Dakota, Douglas C-47 33, 34, 80-84, **80, 82, 84, 85, 88,** 97, 111, 155, *171*
Daphne, Capt. Peter 29
Decorations and Medals 33, 34
De Havilland DH-9 18, 36
De Havilland Vampire **see** Vampire
De Havilland Venom **see** Venom
Double Eagle 25
Douglas C-47 Dakota **see** Dakota
Douglas DC-4 Skymaster **see** Skymaster
Douglas Boston **see** Boston
Driver, Evelyn 16
Drug raids 119
Dunnottar Airforce Station 159
  (**see also** Central Flying School)
Du Toit, Maj. Danie 24, 65

EMD AIDA 2 radar unit 36
East Africa 37
El Alamein, Battle of 27, 66, 155, 159
Emmett, E.C. 17
English Electric Canberra **see** Canberra
Entebbe raid 90
Eritrea 27
Ethiopia **see** Abyssinia
'Evelyn' (Spitfire) 158-159, **158, 160, 162, 163,** *178*

Fairchild Corporation 153
Fairey Battle light bombers 21, 25, 28, 119, 133, 151, 166
Farabioschi, Alberto 108
Farrant, Maj. R. DFC 155
Fieseler Storch **see** Storch
Fire-fighting, Dept. of Forestry 119

Flying Cheetahs, No. 2 Squadron **see** Squadron No. 2
Flying Training Schools
  Dunnottar 167
  Langebaanweg 167
Focke-Wulf Fw 190 27
Foggia air base 155
Francke, Col. 17
Frost, Maj. Jack E. 27, 37, 72
Fury, Hawker **20,** 24, 36, 37, 45, 58, 71

Garret AiResearch turboprop engine 153
Gauntlet, Gloster 45
Gazelle 124
German South West Africa 17
Gerneke, Cmdt. 34
Gibraltar 33
Gladiator, Gloster **23,** 37, 45
Gloster AS 31 **23**
Gloster Gauntlet **see** Gauntlet
Gloster Gladiator **see** Gladiator
Goblin 3 engine 156
Golding, Lt. Cecil 166
'Gooney bird' **see** Douglas Dakota
Graf Spee pocket battleship 133
Griffon engine 102

Harrison, Wing-Commander Newton 159
Hartbees, Hawker **20, 21, 24,** 36, 37, 45, 71, 145, 151, 159
Harvard, North American 22, 29, 37, 39, 47, 56, 73, 75, 104, 138-139, **138, 140, 142, 143,** 159, 163, 166, 167, *174-175*
Hawk, Miles M2H **23**
Hawker Fury **see** Fury
Hawker Hartbees **see** Hartbees
Hawker Hind **see** Hind
Hawker Hurricane **see** Hurricane
Hawker-Siddeley Buccaneer **see** Buccaneer
Hawker-Siddeley Mercurius **see** Mercurius
Helicopters **see** Alouette, Puma, Sikorsky, Super Frelon, Super Puma, Wasp
Henning, Cmdt. L.F. 153
Henri Farman F27 **17**
Hercules, Lockheed C-130B 53, 90-91, **90, 92, 94, 95, 96,** 97, 100, *172*
Hercules, DH66 transports 21
Hind, Hawker 21
Hispano 20mm Cannon 65
Hobart Starter **47**
Howitson, Lt. 39
Hurricane, Hawker 24, **26,** 71
  Mk 1 21, **24, 26,** 36, 37, 45, 145, 159, 166
  Mk II 37, 145, 159

Impala, Aermacchi/Atlas
  Mk I 37, 56, 60, 70-71, **70, 72, 74, 75, 78, 79,** 166, 167, *170-171*
  Mk II 60, 70-71, 72, **76, 77, 78, 79,** 167, *170-171*
Impala Park 71
'Imperial Gift' 18,36
Induna, search for 91
Italian Dodecanese 30
Italian East Africa 24, 25

Joint Air Training Scheme 22, 33
Jungmanns 21
Junkers
  Ju-52 21, **22,** 34, 81, 119, 125
  Ju-86 21, **22, 23,** 65, 119, 133
  Ju-87 26
Jupiter 1XF engine 21

Kearey, Lt. Charles 25
Kershaw, Maj. R.H.C. (Bob) 37, 167
Kesselring, Field Marshal 33
Khartoum 20
Kimberley 16
Kinkhead, Capt. S.. 18
Kittyhawk 27, 28, 31, 75
  IA 45

III 45, 72
IV **33,** 72
Koningsberg 17
Korean War 34, 58, 158
Kos, island of 30, 31, 166
Kudu, Atlas C-4M 144-145, **146,** 148, **149,** *175-176*

Lancaster 33
Lanseria
  Airfield 157, 159, 164
  Air show 157
Lindholme rescue gear 91, 102
Le Mesurier, Maj. C.J. 26
Lemmer, Brig. J.C. 165
Leros, island of 30
Liberator B, Mk VI **30,** 31, 33
Liberator B, Mk VI 30, 31, 33
Lockheed Hercules C-130B **see** Hercules
Lockheed Lodestar **see** Lodestar
Lockheed B-34 Ventura **see** Ventura
Lodestar, Lockheed 81
Loftus, Lt.-Col. Douglas 27
Luftwaffe 27, 164
Lurie, Maj. Alan 158, 159
Lycoming engine 108
Lynx, Westland WG-13 113, 124

Magisters 21, 23
Malta 29, 155, 159
Marais, Cmdt. J.G. P. 165
Marauder 31, 33, 85, 155
  Mk III 56, 68
  Mk III **32,** 56, 68
Martin, Col. Harry 'Kalfie' 26
Maryland light bomber 23, 25, **26,** 66, 119, 133
Masson, Cmdt. Bob 157, **164,** 165
Master, Miles II **29**
MATRA R.530 36
McGregor, Col. P.M.J. 165
Menzies, Sir Robert 64
Mercurius, Hawker-Siddeley HS-125 executive jet 152-153, **152, 154,** *176*
Merlin, Swearingen 152-153, **152, 154,** 176-177
MiG-15 58, 59
Miles M2H Hawk **see** Hawk
Miller , Lt. A.M. 'Shorty' 29
Miller, Maj. Allister 18
Mirage III, Dassault 44-45, **44, 46, 48, 50, 51,** *168-169*
  IIIA 44
  IIIB 45
  IIIC 44, 45
  IIICZ 44, 45, **46, 50,** 60
  IIIDZ 45, 60
  IIID2Z 45, **47, 50, 51**
  IIIE 45
  IIIEZ 45, **49,** 60
  IIIRZ 45
  IIIR2Z **44,** 45
Mirage F1, Dassault-Breguet 36-37, **37, 38, 40, 42, 43,** *168*
  F1AZ 36, 37, **43**
  F1CZ 36-37, **37, 38, 40,** 42
  F2 36
  F3 36
  FG 36
Mirage G 36
Mohawk, Curtiss 23, **26,** 71, 72, 166
Mombasa 17
Montgomery, Gen. Sir Bernard 27
Moon, Capt. W.L.O. 'Bushy' 28
Morris, Hendrik 20
Mosquitoes 29, 34
Moth Major 21
Muller, Lieut. Gen. A.M. (Mike) 53, 60, 165
Musgrove, Maj. 155
Mussolini, Benito 24, 164
Mustang, North American
  III 75
  IV 75
  F-51D **34,** 59
  P-51 58
Mystère 20 36

Neptune Sapphire, air-sea rescue 124
Nettleton, Squadron Leader J.D. 33
Nord AS20 53
  AS30 53
North American
  FJ-1 Fury 58
  F-86 Sabre 58
  F-86F Sabre 59
North American Harvard see Harvard
North American P-51 Mustang see
  Mustang
North American XP-86 86

Oakes, Lt. 32
Operation Sibasa 133
Orenda 14 turbojet 59
Oxford (aircraft) 22, 29, 104

Pantellaria, island-fortress of 27, 155
Paterson Aviation Syndicate Ltd 16
Paterson, Cecil Compton 16
  Bi-plane 16, 17
Pep Ice, air-sea rescue 97, 125
Petterson, Sgt. 153
Photo reconnaissance (No. 60
  Squadron) 25
Piaggio P-166S Albatross see Albatross
Pidsley, Maj. D.W. 27
Pietersburg Air Force Base 36, 37, 157
  (see also Advanced Flying Schools)
Ploesti oil fields, Rumania 29
Poole, Maj.-Gen. 81
Pratt & Whitney
  PT 6 A turboprop engine 153
  Wasp radial engine 80
Preller, Maj. R.H. 151
Prins, Cmdt. Chris 71
Pro Patria Medal 35
Proserpina 27, 133
Puma, Aérospatiale 97, 124-125, 124,
  126-131, 174

Queen Air 80, Beechcraft 153

Radar, Cyrano I bis navigation and fire
  control system 44, 45
Radar, Cyrano IIB multi-function
  system 45
Radar, EMD AIDA 2 Unit 36
Rautenbach, 'Pikkie' 66
Refuelling, air-to-air 54, 55
Rhodes, island of 30
Roberts Heights 18, 20
Rogan, Lt. Douglas 'Shorty' 28
Rogers, Lt. Gen. R.H.D. 52, 53, 158, 159
Rolls-Royce
  Griffon Engine 106, 107
  Tyne turboprop engine 97
Rommel, Field-Marshal Erwin 26, 164
Roux, Prof. L.J. 70
Ryan S.T. 21

SAAF Museum 156, 157, 159, 164, 165
SA Agulhas 125
SA Pioneer 53
SA National Museum of Military
  History 165
SA Seafarer air-sea rescue 120
SAS Jan van Riebeeck 112, 113
SAS President Kruger 113
SAS President Pretorius 113
SAS President Steyn 113
SAS Protea 113
SAS Simon van der Stel 112, 113
Sabre F-86F North American 34, 58-60,
  169-170
Sabre Mk 6, Canadair 34, 47, 58-60,
  58-63, 169-170
Safair 93
Saro Mk 3 airborne lifeboat 102
Saunders, Air Chief Marshal Hugh 18
Saville, Maj. E.C. 'Shorty' 28
Sclanders, Maj. James 124
Scout, S.E. 5a 18
Shackleton air-sea rescues 102, 103
Shackleton Mk 3, Avro 53, 102-103,
  102, 104, 106, 107, 109, 172-173
Shir Yib air-sea rescue 113
Shoran bombing aid 155

Sicily 29, 155, 159
Sikorsky helicopter
  S-51 34, 35, 68, 118, 120
  S-55 118, 120
Silver Castle, collision of 53
'Silver Falcons' 70, 71, 73, 78, 79, 167
Simonstown Agreement 52, 53
Skorzeny, Col. Otto 164
Skymaster, Douglas DC-4 86-87, 86,
  88, 171-172
Slabbert, Capt. Johannes
Smuts, Jan Christiaan 16, 18, 19, 20
Snyman, Lt. 151
Somaliland 24, 39
South African Aviation Corps 17
Spitfire, Supermarine 31, 34, 47, 71, 73,
  104, 158-159, 158, 160, 162, 163, 178
  Mk V 30, 37, 159
  Mk VIII 37
  Mk IX 37, 47, 145, 156, 158, 159,
  160-163
  VC 47
Squadron No. 1 24, 25, 26, 27, 29, 31,
  34, 36, 45
  Historical note: 36
Squadron No. 1, Citizen Force 37
Squadron No. 2 (Flying cheetahs) 25,
  26, 27, 28, 34, 44, 46, 47, 60
  Historical note: 45, 47
Squadron No. 3 25, 27, 36, 37, 45
  Historical note: 37, 39
Squadron No. 4 25, 26,27
  Historical note: 71, 72
Squadron No. 5 (Chaka) 26, 27, 31, 33,
  70, 74, 78, 79
  Historical note: 72, 75
Squadron No. 6 23
  Historical note: 166
Squadron No. 7 30, 31, 167
  Historical note: 166
Squadron No. 8
  Historical note: 167
Squadron No. 10 23
Squadron No. 11 24, 150, 151
  Historical note: 151
Squadron No. 12 26, 45, 74
  Historical note: 65, 66, 68
Squadron No. 15 27, 31, 132
  Historical note: 133
Squadron No. 16 27, 31, 118, 119, 120,
  123
  Historical note: 119
Squadron No. 17 32, 118, 119, 120
  Historical note: 119
Squadron No. 19 (Puma) 31, 118, 119,
  124
  Historical note: 125
Squadron No. 21 27, 28, 29, 34,
  152-153, 152, 154, 155
  Historical note: 153, 155
Squadron No. 22 33, 112, 113, 114, 115
  Historical note: 113
Squadron No. 24 25, 26, 28, 32, 34, 52,
  53, 54, 55, 66
  Historical note: 53, 56
Squadron No. 25 81
  Historical note: 84, 85, 87
Squadron No. 26 17, 27, 32, 33
Squadron No. 27 103, 108-111
  Historical Note: 109-111
Squadron No. 28 31, 34, 81, 87, 90, 96,
  98, 99
  Historical note: 97, 100
Squadron No. 30 31, 32
Squadron No. 31 30, 31
Squadron No. 32 30, 31
Squadron No. 35 31, 34, 102-105, 109,
  111
  Historical note: 103-104
Squadron No. 40 24, 25, 26, 29, 30, 31,
  139, 143
  Historical note: 159-163
Squadron No. 41 24, 25, 28, 150
  Historical note: 148
Squadron No. 42 150
  Historical note: 148
Squadron No. 43 81
Squadron No. 44 31, 80, 81, 85, 87, 88
  Historical note: 87

Squadron No. 60 25, 27, 29, 34, 81
Storch, Fieseler Fi 156 164-165, 164,
  178
Sud Aviation Super Frelon see Super
  Frelon
Suez 156
Sunderland GR5 Flying boat 33, 35, 104
Super Frelon, Sud Aviation
  SA-321L 132-133, 132, 134-136, 174
Super-Puma, Aérospatiale 125
Superfortress B-29, Boeing 90
Supermarine Spitfire see Spitfire
Swakopmund 17
Swales, Capt. Edwin, V.C. 33
Swartkop Air Force Station 36, 37, 153,
  155, 159, 166
  see also Zwartkops
Swearingen Merlin see Merlin

Tasker, Col. W.T.B. 22
Tedder, Air Chief Marshal Sir Arthur 28
Texan see Harvard
Thomas, Capt. W.W. Carey 19
Thomson – CSF Cyrano 1V multi-function
  radar system 36
Tiger Moth 21, 22
Tomahawk, Curtiss 27, 45, 72, 159
Transall C-160Z 96-97, 96, 98, 100, 101,
  172
Turbomeca Turmo IIIC engine 132
Turner, B.H. 17

Valentia, Vickers 25, 81
Vampire, De Havilland 37, 156-157,
  156, 157, 177
  FB-MK 52 35, 47, 59
  T Mk 55 44
Van Breda Theron, Capt. Servaas 37
Van der Spuy, K.R. Maj. Gen. 17, 19
Van Ryneveld, Lt.-Col. Helperus Andrias
  (Sir Pierre) 18, 19, 21, 31, 34
Van Vliet, Maj. Corrie 30, 166
Venom, De Havilland 157
Venter, Maj. Gen. C.J. 'Boetie' 18
Ventura G.R.V. light bomber 33, 120
Ventura, Lockheed B-34 22, 23, 34, 56,
  84, 97, 104, 113
Vickers Armstrong Ltd 158
Vickers Valentia see Valentia
Vickers Vimy see Vimy
Vickers Viscount see Viscount
Vickers Wellington see Wellington
Vimy, Vickers 'Silver Queen' 18
Viscount, Vickers 97, 152-153, 152, 154,
  155, 177
Von Lettow-Vorbeck, Col. 17

Wafra, skinking of 53, 103
Wallace, G.P. 17
Walvis Bay 17
Wavell, Sir Archibald 25
Wapiti, Westland 20, 21, 71, 84, 166
Warwick, Vickers Armstrong G.R.V. 32,
  120
Wasp, Westland 112, 113, 112, 114, 116,
  117, 173
Waterkloof Air Force Base 34, 36, 37,
  38, 39, 156, 158, 159, 164
Watussi 22, 133
Wellington, Vickers 32, 33, 81, 97, 120
Westland WG-13 Lynx see Lynx
Westland Wapiti see Wapiti
Westland Wasp see Wasp
White, Capt. Denzil 34
Williams, M.S. 17
Wood, Lt. D.G. 155
Women's Auxiliary Air Force 22
Wright, Air-Sergeant 151

Yugoslavia 155, 163
Ysterplaat Air Force Base 36, 156, 167
(see also Advanced Flying Schools)

Zimbabwe 157
Zwartkop Air Station 19, 20, 21, 23, 167
(see also Swartkop)

180

24 Squadron

PER NOCTEM PER DIEM

Through night, through day

25 Squadron

ADIUVAMUS

We help

27 Squadron

PROTEGIMUS

We protect

28 Squadron

PORTAMUS

We carry

40 Squadron

EXERCITUI OCULUS

The eye of the army

41 Squadron

DETEGIMUS HOSTES

We find the enemy

The Silver Falcons (Afrikaans name: *Die Silwer Valke)* aerobatic team comprises some of the finest pilots in the SAAF; all are instructors at the Flying Training School at Langebaanweg. At the time of writing, the Silver Falcons fly standard Impala trainers which bear consecutive numbers on their tailfins.

44 Squadron

PROSUMUS

We are useful

FTS

TENAX PROPOSITI VINCO

Holding fast to my purpose,
I conquer

AFS 85

DETRIMENTO SUMUS

Our purpose is damage

AFS 86

DOCEMUS VOLATUM

We teach flying

AFS 87

We teach